WOMEN AND DRAMATIC PRODUCTION
1550–1700

LONGMAN MEDIEVAL AND RENAISSANCE LIBRARY

General editors:

Charlotte Brewer, Hertford College, Oxford and *N. H. Keeble*, University of Stirling

WOMEN AND DRAMATIC PRODUCTION 1550–1700

ALISON FINDLAY AND
STEPHANIE HODGSON-WRIGHT,
WITH GWENO WILLIAMS

Longman

An imprint of **Pearson Education**

Harlow, England · London · New York · Reading, Massachusetts · San Francisco
Toronto · Don Mills, Ontario · Sydney · Tokyo · Singapore · Hong Kong · Seoul
Taipei · Cape Town · Madrid · Mexico City · Amsterdam · Munich · Paris · Milan

Pearson Education Limited
Edinburgh Gate
Harlow
Essex CM20 2JE
England

and Associated Companies throughout the World.

Visit us on the World Wide Web at:
www.pearsoneduc.com

First published 2000
© Pearson Education Limited 2000

The right of Alison Findlay, Stephanie Hodgson-Wright and
Gweno Williams to be identified as authors of this Work has
been asserted by them in accordance with the Copyright,
Designs and Patents Act 1988.

ISBN 0-582-31983-8 LIMP
      0-582-31982-X CASED

British Library Cataloguing-in-Publication Data
A catalogue record for this book can be obtained from the British Library.

Library of Congress Cataloging-in-Publication Data
Findlay, Alison, 1963–
    Women and dramatic production, 1550–1900 / Alison Findlay and Stephanie
Hodgson-Wright, with Gweno Williams.
        p. cm. — (Longman medieval and Renaissance library)
    Includes bibliographical references and index.
    ISBN 0–582–31983–8 (alk. paper) — ISBN 0–582–31982–X (alk. paper)
        1. Women in the theater—England—History—17th century. 2. Women in the
theater—England—History—16th century. 3. English drama—Early modern and
Elizabethan, 1500–1600—History and criticism. 4. English drama—17th century—
History and criticism. 5. English drama—Women authors. I. Hodgson-Wright,
Stephanie. II. Williams, Gweno. III. Title. IV. Series.

PN1590.W64   F56   2000
792′.082′094109032—dc21   00–063361

10 9 8 7 6 5 4 3 2 1
05 04 03 02 01 00

Typeset by 35 in 11/13pt Baskerville
Produced by Pearson Education Asia Pte Ltd.
Printed in Singapore

To
Eleanor Findlay,
Barbara Wright
and
Rose Gordon

CONTENTS

ACKNOWLEDGEMENTS

We wish to thank the talented and open-minded performers and production staff who have contributed to all our productions. We also thank staff at Lancaster University Library, the Brotherton Library, Leeds, Sunderland University Library, the University College of Ripon and York St John Library, the British Library, the Bodleian Library, Oxford, and the Folger Shakespeare Library for their help while we have been researching materials for the book. Our special thanks are due to Marion Wynne-Davies, Jacqueline Pearson, Betty Travitsky and S. P. Cerasano for their pioneering work in the field and their unwavering support and enthusiasm for our project in all its various manifestations. We have benefited much from presenting our research at the 'Attending to Early Modern Women: Crossing Boundaries Conference' (University of Maryland, 1997) and 'Forms of Persuasion: Fourth International Conference Literature and History' (University of Reading, 1998) and express our gratitude to the participants who helped to sharpen our ideas with positive feedback. We are especially indebted to Neil Keeble, the General Editor of the Series, for his expert help in producing the book, and to Gill Hayton for painting the excellent picture for the cover.

In addition, Alison Findlay thanks Tess Cosslett, Alison Easton and Lynne Pearce for their generous sharing of ideas in the English Department at Lancaster. She offers heartfelt thanks to her husband David who has given his love and support throughout. Her children, Robert and Eleanor, have been like a light at the end of the tunnel and she thanks them too.

Stephanie Hodgson-Wright would like to thank the British Academy for a Small Research Grant, the Newberry Library, Chicago for a Lester J. Cappon Fellowship and, at the University of Sunderland, the School of Humanities and Social Sciences for research leave, the Graduate Research School, especially Andrew Slade, for moral and financial support and the English Department for its highly conducive collegial atmosphere. Particular thanks are due to Maureen Meikle, a valued colleague whose knowledge of Anna of Denmark has been a source of inspiration. The enlightening conversations with and encouraging remarks from Isobel Grundy, Lynne Magnusson, Diane Purkiss, Shari Zimmerman and Alex Bennett have been much appreciated, as has the patient love and support from Anthony Bentley, Jo Evans, Danielle Fuller, Alison Younger and Barbara Wright.

Gweno Williams offers thanks to staff at York Minster Library. She also wishes to thank the colleagues, friends and family who have helped and supported her in this project: Lesley Clark, Roger Clark, Sally Curtis, Cliff Curtis, Andrew Gordon, Isobel Gordon, Rose Gordon, Toby Gordon, Julie Hirst, John Marland, Liz Savage, Ruth Stevenson.

Note on texts

For all plays, we have used a modern, accessible edition where possible. In the absence of any modern edition, we have used the original printed text or manuscript. References to these texts are given in full the first time they are used in each chapter; thereafter, by page numbers or page signatures as appropriate. All references to Shakespeare's plays are to Stephen Greenblatt, Walter Cohen, Jean E. Howard and Katherine Eisaman Maus, (eds) (1997) *The Norton Shakespeare*, New York and London: W. W. Norton. All biblical references are to the King James Bible (1611).

Introduction

ALISON FINDLAY AND
STEPHANIE HODGSON-WRIGHT

In arguing for the emergence of feminist theatre post 1968, Loren Kruger states:

> There is a saying that women have always made spectacles of themselves. However, it has only been recently, and intermittently, that women have made spectacles themselves. On this difference turns the ambiguous identity of feminist theatre.
>
> (1996: 27)

While accepting the importance of 1968 as a turning point in feminist consciousness, this book takes issue with the thesis that, in earlier periods, women's involvement in dramatic production simply took the form of 'making spectacles of themselves' as though this were a self-compromising project. We argue that a select number of women took an active part in directing and controlling dramatic self-representations: that they made the spectacle themselves. In the chapters that follow, we show how women in the late sixteenth and the seventeenth centuries shaped dramatic productions as scriptwriters, and as directors and performers. According to Kruger's definition, this makes their theatre 'feminist' before its time. Such a label seems anomalous, anachronistic even, in a period governed by an ideology of female subservience, and the term 'feminist' is used with some caution in the pages that follow. Nevertheless, we firmly believe that the texts we discuss, despite their huge differences, share a common strand in the promotion of a female-centred aesthetic. They show women taking the stage in order to foreground interests particular to their sex.

Of course it is important to acknowledge differences: the women who made dramatic spectacles are drawn from across a huge social and cultural spectrum. For example, Queen Henrietta Maria, the main performer in her extravagant court masques, and the Quaker woman who went naked for a sign at a Whitehall church in 1652, were practitioners with very different individual needs and interests. These must be taken into account alongside the different venues in which their entertainments were staged. Therefore, this account of women's dramatic production does not present a homogenous, developing female aesthetic, but rather a discontinuous, multi-faceted tradition. By virtue of its discontinuity, it escapes the dangers Teresa de Lauretis outlines for a feminist theatre, which seeks to define itself according to a monological female aesthetic, namely 'to remain caught within the master's house and there . . . to legitimate the hidden agendas of a culture we badly need to change' (1987: 131). While some of the texts we discuss do display signs of being confined within a male-dominated tradition, others explicitly seek to redefine that tradition by taking the stage in alternative ways.

'Taking the stage' is almost as vexed a term as the collective 'women', since it groups together texts that were definitely performed and those for which we have no performance history. In our discussions, we have provided production details, such as performance dates, based on the evidence currently available to us. Since women did not participate in the major professional theatre companies as either dramatists or actors until 1660, their dramatic activities are not recorded in the usual sources, such as the records of the Master of the Revels. Performances written or staged by women in the household could still have been public events, as the example of Lady Elizabeth Delavel's production of *Il Pastor Fido* shows (*see* Chapter 5), but since spectators did not pay to watch, these productions were not automatically included in financial or official documents. Domestic performances which relied on the resources already available in the household may not even have been noted in the household accounts. The evidence we do have is probably incomplete and has come down to us, almost by chance, from personal writings like Lady Elizabeth Delavel's spiritual mediations. We therefore believe that lack of evidence does not preclude the possibility that plays by women were produced at the time of their composition, or were intended for performance.

We have worked from the assumption that, in composing a play, a woman made an active and informed choice of genre. Her script was written with a theatrical arena in mind, whether or not evidence of a production has survived in documentary form. It is therefore only proper to accord to these texts the same kind of critical attention as any other piece of drama, rather than automatically classifying them as 'closet' plays intended for reading rather than performance. In any case, the categories 'reading' and 'performance' were not mutually exclusive for early modern writers and readers. People steeped in a culture of display, costume and ritual would automatically bring a theatrical sensibility and imagination to the scripts in the processes of composition and reading. It is mistaken to assume that plays for which we have no production history are unperformable and not even intended for performance. Our own experiments in staging work by early modern women has proved that, in the words of Margaret Cavendish, 'the Play is ready to be Acted' (Findlay, Hodgson-Wright and Williams 1999a).

The discussion of women's drama in the following chapters has grown out of an inter-disciplinary research project dedicated to exploring the interface between women's writing and dramatic practice. Alison Findlay directed a full-length production of *The Concealed Fancies* with Jane Milling in 1994. Stephanie Hodgson-Wright directed full-length productions of *The Tragedy of Mariam* in 1994 and *Iphigeneia at Aulis* in 1997. Gweno Williams devised a production of central scenes of *The Convent of Pleasure*, directed by Bill Pinner in 1995.[1] Practical work continues with a 'household' reading of *The Tragedie of Antonie*, directed by Marion Wynne-Davies and Alison Findlay (1999) and a production of *Love's Victory*, directed by Stephanie Hodgson-Wright (1999). These have been followed, as the book goes to press, with television productions of scenes from Cavendish and Brackley's *A Pastorall*, directed by Alison Findlay, and from Margaret Cavendish's *Lady Contemplation*, and *The Female Academy*, directed by Gweno Williams. The experience of moving these plays from the page to the stage (or screen) has allowed us to approach the scripts we discuss from the perspective of theatre practitioners. Although we have not addressed the texts from the director's viewpoint in this book, we have endeavoured to maintain a theatrical sensibility, a heightened sensitivity to their multi-dimensional nature.

More than any other literary form, drama relies on material presences: visual spectacle, sound and the presence of actors and audience within specific physical spaces. Women of the sixteenth and seventeenth centuries were adept in manipulating these dimensions of dramatic production for their own purposes. Lynda Hart has noted women's skill in exploiting theatrical space 'to disclose and critique women's confinement while suggesting liberating strategies from the patriarchal order' (1989: 8–9). Our book pays attention to the spatial dimension of plays: elements such as Aphra Behn's astute stagings of the 'discovery' scene in Restoration theatre

---

1. *See* Alison Findlay, Stephanie Hodgson-Wright and Gweno Williams (1999b) *Women Dramatists 1550–1670: Plays in Performance*, Lancaster: Lancaster University Television Unit, a teaching video, which includes extracts of these productions and discussion of the plays in performance.

to disorientate the conventional fetishisation of woman as the object of a male gaze, for example, or Margaret Cavendish's creation of a liberated space in which women can direct their own lives behind walls in *The Convent of Pleasure*. The importance of sound, music and dance in some of the texts are also highlighted in our discussions. Chapters 2 and 3, for example, include consideration of spectacle and song as presented in noblewomen's masques and pastorals and Chapter 5 examines the role of the female singer in *Rare en Tout*.

The appearance of a female character on stage is potentially a means of objectifying women or confining them to stereotypical roles that reinforce the cultural prescriptions designed to govern female behaviour in the sixteenth and seventeenth centuries. Women dramatists seize on female presence as an opportunity to 'create a theatrical discourse that highlights the politicization of feminine appearance, foregrounding the categorization, containment and misrecognition of women's diversity' (Hart 1989: 8). Our study of texts from across the period reveals a continued interest in redefining some significant feminine types, such as the woman as sacrificial victim, as goddess, villainess, virgin or whore. From the eponymous heroine of Jane Lumley's *Iphigeneia at Aulis*, or the self-staging Catholic martyr Margaret Clitherow, to the outspoken Camilla in Katherine Philips's *Horace*, we see women embracing the role of tragic sacrifice as an autonomous act, rather than passively accepting it as victims. Similarly, the Petrarchan stereotype of woman as goddess is shown as ridiculously confining in plays like Mary Wroth's *Love's Victory* and Mary Pix's *Ibrahim*. It is rearticulated as a powerful shaping presence in masque performances by Queens Anna of Denmark and Henrietta Maria. Chaste virginity, the bedrock of the homosocial traffic in women, is transformed from an appearance of female passivity into active sisterly choice in Elizabeth Polwhele's *The Faithfull Virgins*.

Negative stereotypes are also rewritten in many women's dramatic productions. Anna Trapnel's appearance in the courtroom to answer charges of witchcraft allowed her to redefine her spiritual testimonies as the public proclamations of a dutiful, sober, daughter of Christ. Plays such as Cary's *Tragedy of Mariam* represent female villainy as a form of victimisation, showing how the actions of 'wicked' women are often the result of their confinement within male-dominated ideologies. Sexual stereotyping of women and the pejorative associations engendered thereby are rigorously interrogated in the plays of Aphra Behn. Later plays, like Catherine Trotter's *Agnes de Castro* and Delariviere Manley's *The Royal Mischief*, deliberately re-structure the common pairings of chaste virgin and villainess, played by actresses famed for representing those types, in order to critique such categorisation. Another technique common to several female-authored texts is the physical dramatisation of the ideologies used to 'frame' women, often using concrete

4

props. Thus, in Cavendish and Brackley's *The Concealed Fancies*, the heroine Luceny considers the prescriptions placed on wifely behaviour by contemplating her image, dressed as a bride, in a mirror. In Pix's *Ibrahim*, the villainess's imprisonment within the dominant patriarchal ideology is shown when she exclaims 'Break all the flattering Mirrors! / Let me ne'er behold this rejected Face again' (13).

In spite of the importance of non-verbal elements, 'language remains a primary tool for the dramatists' (Hart 1989: 11), especially since the texts we have of dramatic productions from 300 or 400 years ago can necessarily only give occasional hints of elements which combined with the verbal script. In this book, we have concentrated primarily, although not exclusively, on scripted drama. Despite Juliet Mitchell's view (*Times Literary Supplement* 23 August 1996) that attempts to construct a female-authored canon of Renaissance drama would necessarily mean 'scraping the bottom of the barrel' in terms of quality, we have been impressed by the richness and complexity of much of the writing we have studied. It deserves attention, first, as a territory that still needs to be charted. Pioneering books like Jacqueline Pearson's *The Prostituted Muse* (1989) and Nancy Cotton's *Women Playwrights in England 1363–1750* (1980) present valuable collocations of information about female dramatists, to which we are indebted. Since these studies are readily accessible, we have not attempted to give detailed biographical sketches of the writers whose scripts we examine, but refer readers to Cotton and Pearson's work. As Mitchell's comment demonstrates all too clearly, however, the importance of that territory – those female contributions to the canon – needs reiterating. Plays by Lady Mary Wroth or Margaret Cavendish or Anne Wharton are not established within the dramatic canon; their value as scripts which engage with the dynamics of performance has not been widely appreciated. One goal of our book has been to redress this imbalance.

Besides their importance in the wider literary field, the plays are worthy of study in their own right. We have found an amazing depth of writing in scripts that engage provocatively with the cultural moments in which they were composed and with the theatre forms for which they were written. Lady Jane Lumley's covert exploration of the religious politics surrounding Lady Jane Grey's execution in *Iphigeneia at Aulis*, and Elizabeth Polwhele's examination of the power of the actress on the Restoration stage in *The Frolicks* are just two contrasting examples. It is important to point out, however, that new criteria are necessary to assess much of this early work by female theatre practitioners. Previous studies of masques, progresses, plays written for the Renaissance public stage or the private theatres, carry inbuilt expectations that are themselves implicitly gendered by theatrical traditions centred on male authors and performers. While paying attention to the mainstream theatrical contexts in which women's dramatic productions took place then, we have concentrated mainly on the texts themselves as sources of meaning.

Lizbeth Goodman points out that women's intervention as producers of drama 'both "usurps" the power of creation, and assumes the right to restructure the values and expectations according to which creative work tends to be judged' (1996: 39). This is exactly what we see in much women's drama of the sixteenth and seventeenth centuries. Since they did not participate in the major professional theatre companies as either dramatists or actors until 1660, women's dramatic productions necessarily challenge the values and expectations according to which drama was, and still is, judged. Taking account of alternative types of drama staged in the royal court or the country house or in non-official venues like the street, obliges us to rethink our definitions of theatre. This is especially obvious in the case of more marginal forms of 'experimental' theatre such as courtroom appearances, scaffold speeches and spiritual testimonies. A major regret we share is that we have been unable to cover more of these alternative forms of theatre within the book. The reason for this is, however, encouraging. In order to do justice to the complexity of women's scripted drama, we have found it necessary, within our word limit, to leave out lots of potentially interesting material. Another book is needed to look in more detail at the complex dynamics involved when women seized the opportunity to stage themselves in alternative public spaces, or in political or religious demonstrations. The archives of regional record offices and the evidence already made available in the *Records of Early English Drama* series suggests there is material which needs to be explored specifically as theatre. Indeed, the process of editing our work has made it abundantly clear that the subject matter of each of the chapters warrants lengthier study.

Chapter 1 covers the most varied manifestations of women's dramatic production, as we consider the impact of a range of women appearing as speaking subjects in different public spaces. The overriding need to appropriate and mediate arenas and discourses previously characterised as masculine is apparent in the material dealt with in this chapter. The four queens regnant, Jane Grey, Mary I, Elizabeth I and Mary, Queen of Scots, who were in power during the Tudor period, all occupied a position which, by the law of primogeniture, properly belonged to a man. Their accessions all relied on the lack of a masculine heir. The effects of the Reformation, most keenly felt in the changing religious affiliations of the monarchs throughout the period, and resultant prosecution of dissenters, both allowed and required women to speak for themselves in the courtroom and the scaffold, spaces presided over by men. The full dramatic texts of the period, Jane Lumley's *Iphigeneia at Aulis* and Mary Sidney's *Tragedy of Antonie* are both translations of texts authored by men and written by women who lived within a literary culture populated by male relations and clients. Yet these apparent constraints offered the opportunity for feminised re-workings. The power of the queen to direct the production as autonomous subject in alternative forms of theatre appears in the queens' coronations, progresses and entertainments. The courtroom and scaffold afforded women speakers legitimate attention – the male authority figures who demanded testimony were also obliged to listen to it – and gave them the opportunity for ultimate self-fashioning as they embraced a martyr's death rather than a silent and obedient life. In Jane Lumley's play, Iphigeneia effects a similar transformation. The absent Iphigeneia, initially constructed as sacrificial victim to her father's political ambition, becomes the present and vocal saviour of her country as she offers to die for it just at the moment when her life could be saved. Mary Sidney's play concerns itself with the tension between the private passion and public duty of Antonie and Cleopatra. The sympathetic treatment of Cleopatra particularly legitimates the passion of the individual woman, in contrast to her public role as queen, as fit subject matter for the self-fashioned feminine speaking subject. The chapter also considers both of these plays in the context of the emergent culture of self-staging women to argue strongly for the presence of a performance dimension within each play.

Chapter 2 deals with the ways in which women as producers of drama began to present, argue for, and assert an iconic feminine theatrical presence by appropriating and re-defining the ideologically feminine qualities of beauty and chastity. The two early Stuart queens, Anna and Henrietta Maria, had grown up in a cultural milieu where the elite woman as producer and performer of dramatic entertainments had an important role. In bringing this sensibility with them, they appropriated and transformed the court stage into a playing arena that is, topographically speaking, the true ancestor of the modern proscenium arch theatre. While all the masques in which Anna and Henrietta Maria participated were ostensibly written by men, namely Samuel Daniel, Ben Jonson, and William Davenant, for the purposes of this study, the issue of authorship is necessarily problematic. As Jerzy Limon has argued, 'it seems clear that the masque-in-performance and the printed literary masque not only belong to different systems, but also that their authorship is not the same' (1990: 28). Masques were a form of cultural production whose 'true' existence was in the performance, the printed text merely being a journalistic record of the event. In many senses the creators of the masques were those people who commissioned and performed them. While Anna and Henrietta Maria might not have had their names on the title pages, in the spectacle of the masque in performance, there can have been little doubt who was the presiding 'authority' in that cultural moment.

Cupid's Banishment, written by Robert White for the ladies of Deptford Hall to perform for Anna, and Walter Montagu's *The Shepherd's Paradise*, have also been included as legitimate examples of women and dramatic production in this period. They each mark crucial moments in which women acted with both body and voice; they also underscore the extent to which the particular agendas of Anna and Henrietta Maria informed apparently male-authored texts. In tandem with such developments at court, the chapter also demonstrates the dramatic activity of women in the country house setting, where the striking emergence of the female performer in a dramatic rather than purely emblematic context keeps pace with the developments at court. Moreover, the country house entertainment was a genre in which women wrote as well as commissioned and performed. The household entertainments of Lady Rachel Fane are considered in detail, paying particular attention to the ways in which she addresses her immediate geographical and familial context and creates opportunities for her younger siblings of both sexes to perform for the senior members of the household. Significantly, alongside such entertainments, a fragment of a play by Fane survives, offering the possibility that the household stage and actors she used for her entertainments might also have been involved in lengthier dramatic productions. The chapter then turns to the two surviving full play texts of the period, Lady Elizabeth Cary's *The Tragedy of Mariam* and Lady Mary Wroth's *Love's Victory*. Rather than considering these plays as excluded from the masculine context of the public stage, the chapter evaluates the ways in which they address themselves to the aesthetic and ideological values of the contemporary feminine dramatic context. The dynamics of household entertainment, the spectacle and plotting of masque and the exposure of patriarchal ideology's inadequacy to articulate the female subject, are utilised to tragic effect in *Mariam* and to ultimate comic effect in *Love's Victory*. Both of the plays hint at the essential instability of patriarchal authority, whether as exhibited by a self-deluding tyrant, or a mildly treacherous classical deity.

The special circumstances created by the English Civil War and Interregnum are considered in Chapter 3. The closure of the public theatres from 1642 to1660 had the advantage, for women dramatists, of creating a newly-levelled playing field on which to work. The crisis in government was accompanied by a turbulent social environment, in which conventional gender roles and forms of authority were open to question and to change. Drama was used strategically and self-consciously by women during these years as a means of renegotiating their places within the microcosm of the family and the wider Commonwealth. The play and pastoral written collaboratively by Jane Cavendish and Elizabeth Brackley are discussed as dramatic explorations of the position held by many aristocratic noblewomen

8

in the English Civil War: often imprisoned within their houses, but simultaneously empowered and liberated as managers, in the absence of their husbands or fathers. While Cavendish and Brackley display nostalgia for royal entertainments like the masque and the pastoral in these pieces, the chapter shows how they also manipulate the literary forms for more controversial feminist purposes.

Moving on from these household entertainments, Chapter 3 examines religious and political demonstrations and personal testimonies staged in public arenas. The very theatrical modes in which female preachers expressed their message are explored with reference to male condemnations of female performance. The vexed problem of whose voice is speaking in the case of visionaries is discussed using the model of acting, in which the female performer can be defined as a creative interpreter of God's holy word. Her position as enactor of the indwelling spirit creates a space for intensely powerful self-representation as well as a celebration of divine authority. Women's participation in political demonstrations is also briefly considered as another form of public enactment. The spaces women used for dramatic productions during these years were necessarily outside the arenas officially designated for performance. Their location in the household, the street, the inn, allies them in form with feminist theatre practice which, as Loren Kruger (1996) points out, deliberately locates itself 'outside', in order to challenge patriarchal institutions.

The physical location of alternative theatre has resulted in unfair discrimination. Theatre criticism has 'historically excluded as illegitimate those groups whose performances in diverse and multi-purpose spaces are held to demonstrate their 'instability' and thus their unreliability in rising to the proper occasion of theatre' (Kruger 1996: 52). By concentrating on some examples of women's alternative theatrical practices during the English Civil War years, the chapter aims to relegitimise them as drama. Kruger points out that 'the place and occasion of a performance (in a national theatre or a makeshift hall, for aesthetic contemplation or for immediate recreational or educational use) contribute as much to its legitimation (addition to the repertoire or one of the subsidized theatres and publication) as its apparently autonomous literary value' (1996: 52). Given the discrimination against non-official theatre venues, women's admission to the King's and the Duke's theatre companies in 1660 would seem to be an important step forward. Michel Adam goes so far as to argue that, after this point, to go on writing scripts for an alternative 'private' arena would be nothing less than masochism on the part of a woman dramatist (Adam 1993: 106).

Nevertheless, in 1662 and 1668, Margaret Cavendish proudly published 19 plays, which were not written for either of the professional theatre companies. Chapter 4 examines aspects of her dramatic corpus in some detail, starting with a consideration of the emphasis she placed on publication and the ways she used it to style herself after the giants of the male dramatic tradition: Jonson, Shakespeare, and Beaumont and Fletcher. The importance of her husband William as a literary mentor and collaborator in some of her work is examined. Cavendish's contradictory attitudes to performance, as revealed in the numerous prefaces to her first collection, are explored with reference to her own experience of different types of theatre, as part of Henrietta Maria's court and through her husband's close connections with the profession as both writer and patron. The chapter considers Cavendish's paradoxical attitude to public exposure: actively seeking fame (and performing an extravagant version of herself as one way of achieving it), while simultaneously defining herself as bashful. Perhaps this goes some way to explaining why she did not, apparently, present her own plays for performance on the public stage, reserving them instead for the fantasy theatre of her imagination or possibly domestic performance.

Discussion of a selection of Cavendish's plays reveals a staging of issues central to female experience, undertaken with an informed dramatic imagination. Chapter 4 considers Cavendish's presentation of autonomous, often strongly empowered, female characters who are able to renegotiate courtship and marriage on their own terms, or pursue alternative life patterns. Special focus is given to the way her plays explore gender construction, and how she dramatises idealised and more realistic versions of the English Civil War. Margaret's position within the Cavendish household, where her scripts might have been played, is discussed with reference to *Love's Adventures*, in which it is possible to trace an antagonistic response to her step-daughters' earlier play *The Concealed Fancies*. By considering her scripts in a theatrical rather than literary context, the chapter reveals a dramatist who was adept at entertaining, while promoting ideas about gender which were often subversive.

The appearance of female actors on the professional stage in 1660 marked a significant change in women's relationship to the institution of theatre. Chapter 5 traces how women dramatists responded to the challenge presented by this new arena, which seemed to offer great opportunities and yet also carried its own forms of prescription. The earliest plays, Katherine Philips's translations of Corneille's *Pompey* and *Horace*, are examined as resonant with national and sexual politics, speaking directly to the new order after the Restoration of Charles II, as well as to the role of woman within the family and state. The actress was a novel spectacle on the public stage. The first original plays for the professional theatre, *Marcelia* by Francis Boothby and Elizabeth Polwhele's *The Frolicks* and *The Faithfull Virgins*, seem to exploit the convention of women's positioning as the object of an erotically-charged male gaze. Elements of Laura Mulvey's argument that woman's 'to-be-looked-at-ness' is built 'into the spectacle' of cinema can also be applied to the position of the actress in the theatre (Mulvey 1975: 11). The chapter argues that in self-consciously staging the female body, however, these plays simultaneously critique the objectification of woman. In addition, they draw attention to the actress's power to control the scene by returning the gaze of the audience and reconfiguring herself as a desiring subject whose skills in performance allow her to play constructively with the sexual energies within the theatre.

The close relationship between the theatres and the world of the court allows these first professional women dramatists to offer criticisms of royal behaviour. Charles II's extramarital affairs with actresses and noblewomen are anatomised in the plays of Elizabeth Polwhele. Chapter 5 explores how her tragedy adopts a high moral tone to criticise royal lust and sympathise with the isolation of Charles's slighted queen, Catherine of Braganza. Analysis of the court entertainment *Rare en Tout* directed by Madame Le Roche-Guilhen, reveals that this too is a highly politicised commentary on royal favours. The play is designed to illustrate the power of the court mistress and the actress to sway national politics via the king. Women's continued use of non-professional theatre forms is also explored in a discussion of Lady Elizabeth Delavel's production of *Il Pastor Fido* at her aunt's country house. The evidence which has come down to us about such entertainments reveals that women's admittance to the commercial theatre did not represent the only avenue open to female practitioners, although its importance is obvious.

The success of Aphra Behn as a playwright in the public theatre is crucial to any work on women's drama of the period. Due to the sheer size of Behn's dramatic oeuvre, it has been impossible to deal with each play in detail, so the chapter is organised thematically. A chronological and biographical delineation of Behn's theatrical career has already been effected, in work such as Maureen Duffy's *The Passionate Shepherdess* (1977, rev. 1989) and Angeline Goreau's *Reconstructing Aphra: A Social Biography of Aphra Behn* (1980). As with the general works of Cotton and Pearson, we would direct the reader towards these studies for an overview of Behn's life and career. Aphra Behn has a somewhat heroic status in women's history as the first woman to earn her living by writing (though Germaine Greer has recently questioned the accuracy of this view 1995: 173–96). Behn's audacity and success led Virginia Woolf to call for 'all women together ought to let fall flowers upon the tomb of Aphra Behn' (Woolf, 1977: 63). Yet her 'firstness' and 'uniqueness' in the theatre is perhaps dangerously redolent of the 'token woman', rendering her vulnerable to the scenario proposed by Kruger: 'the theatre institution can absorb individual female successes without in any way threatening the legitimacy of the masculinist and capitalist definition of that success' (1996: 50).

Possibly the problematic status of Behn *vis-à-vis* the public stage has engendered reluctance among feminist scholars to consider her as a playwright, rather than as a novelist or poet. The relatively small amount of critical material on her plays (with the notable exception of *The Rover*) compared to that on her prose or poetry is striking, especially when one considers that, of Janet Todd's seven-volume edition of the *Works of Aphra Behn* (1996), the plays occupy three. This reluctance to acknowledge fully Behn's credibility as a playwright is perhaps epitomised by the list of plays chosen for Royal Shakespeare Company's 1999 season. While *The Widow Ranter* received a single rehearsed reading, one of Behn's prose works, *Oroonoko*, featured as a full production in a modern adaptation, which totally erases the voice and character of the narrator. Moreover, apart from Elin Diamond's incisive chapter in *Unmaking Mimesis: Essays on feminism and theater* (1997: 56–82), Behn's stagecraft is a largely unexplored territory. The aims of Chapter 6 are therefore twofold, incorporating consideration of both textual and theatrical strategies in Behn's plays. Rather than exploring plays individually, the chapter investigates the ways in which Behn selected and manipulated generic features, feminine character types, and the presence of the actress, to create heroines of psychological substance who offer images of female empowerment. In counterpoint to this, the chapter also examines the ways in which Behn's plays expose the perverse limitations placed upon women by the socio-economic conditions, ideological milieu and generic conventions operating in late seventeenth-century England.

The material dealt with in Chapter 7 is an apposite mixture of drama written for private consumption and that written for the public stage. It provides a fit conclusion to the book, encouraging the reader to acknowledge the different auspices utilised by the seventeenth-century women playwrights who came after Behn, but also to recognise their common gender-political agenda, which sought to question and transcend the material and ideological limitations imposed on women as writers and as speaking subjects. Here again we challenge Michel Adam's comment (*see* above), by refusing to see the pioneering work of Aphra Behn as the point at which women eventually 'made it' in the theatre. To do so would privilege the professional over the amateur, the public over the private, and the commercial over the non-profit making. Such privileging is the result of an historical application of specifically twentieth-century values. It also makes the assumption that the necessarily masculinist values of 'professionalism' are the only ones by which dramatic texts were and are judged, implying that those who wrote for sites other than the public theatre were demonstrably lesser writers and that they accepted their inferior status. In fact, the women writers who chose to withhold their plays from the public stage, namely Ephelia, Anne Wharton and Anne Finch, were well-known and prolific writers who use drama to engage in a debate about the literary and theatrical representation of female characters, women performers and women playwrights. The semi-permeable nature of the divide between private and public theatres is demonstrated in Delariviere Manley's Prologue to *The Lost Lover*, in which she gives her reason for writing the play as 'only to pass some tedious Country Hours' (A2v). She explains that her friends persuaded her to put it on the public stage where 'the bare Name of being a woman's play damn'd it beyond its own want of Merit' (A3r). Thus, the women who wrote for the public stage in this period shared the debate with their sister writers who kept their scripts out of the playhouse.

While the novelty of the woman playwright appears to have been used as a marketing tool in the case of Ariadne's *She Ventures and He Wins*, the problematic status of the woman playwright in the public theatre is consistently raised by Catherine Trotter, Delariviere Manley and Mary Pix. These women were doubly vulnerable at the moment of their plays' public realisation on stage by being absent from the occasion of performance (a liminality also suffered by male playwrights), and yet exposed to public view *as women*. They sought to reconfigure the woman playwright as a positive presence. Although they came together as a distinct feminine force in the theatre, their playwriting strategies were highly individual. We consider the very different ways in which each playwright addresses both the dramatic tradition in which she is writing and the material conditions in which the play will be realised. For example, in *The Lost Lover* Manley explores the inadequacies of comedy to represent the cast-mistress. Trotter stages love between women in *Agnes de Castro*, effecting de Lauretis' point that 'in the very act of assuming and speaking from the position of subject, a woman could concurrently recognize women as subjects *and* as objects of female desire' (1990: 17). We reconsider Mary Pix in terms of her pragmatism and lengthy career to give a reading that departs from previous critical assessments of her as less obviously feminist than her sister playwrights.

We began this project with the intent of taking individual responsibility for discrete chapters, and of writing the introduction and final chapters collaboratively. As with dramatic productions, however, changes in schedule, crises, and the pressing deadline, have obliged us to reassign material in order to complete the book for the 'opening night'. While we all take responsibility for the 'final production', we have chosen to make explicit our various contributions to the project by attributing each chapter to its proper authors, thus giving a 'local habitation and a name' (*A Midsummer Night's Dream* 5.1.17) to our different approaches and writing styles. As a theatre programme breaks down a performance into its constituent actors and backstage practitioners, we hope that this will enable readers to take up our arguments, take issue with our findings, and cite our work on individual texts more easily. Working collaboratively, the basis of any dramatic production, has been characterised by both benefits and frustrations. As we have read each other's work, the thrill of making connections across periods and between very different female-authored texts, has been one of the real pleasures of the composition process. We invite the reader to join us in the process of comparison and connection, in order to construct a tradition of women and dramatic production 1550–1700.

CHAPTER 1

Translating the Text, Performing the Self

GWENO WILLIAMS[1]

In Act 4 of Thomas Kyd's *The Spanish Tragedy* (1592), the aristocratic Bel-imperia transcends gender constraints by publicly enacting her revenge in a court performance of 'Soliman and Perseda', authored and directed by Hieronimo. The tragedy, performed in several languages, is dramatic cover for his audacious revenge plot in which he and Bel-imperia stab Lorenzo and Balthasar respectively, before a court audience which includes the King and Balthasar's father, the Viceroy. Bel-imperia ends her performance by telling Balthasar:

> Yet by thy power thou thinkest to command
> And to thy power Perseda doth obey:
> But were she able, thus she would revenge
> Thy treacheries on thee, ignoble prince: [*Stab him*]
> And on herself, she would be thus revenged.   [*Stab herself*]
>   (4.4.64)

The marked plot similarities between 'Soliman and Perseda' and Bel-imperia's own experiences make it clear that she is acting in two senses, simultaneously playing out a symbolic fiction, and performing her own real life tragedy. The metatheatrical dimensions to the scene provide multiple perspectives on this female performance. The audience of the Spanish court see an aristocratic woman play a fantastic murder, which turns out to be real; the audience of *The Spanish Tragedy* in the public theatre see a boy actor

---

1. I wish to thank Alison Findlay and Stephanie Hodgson-Wright for their revision and additions to this chapter.

counterfeiting what a woman would do 'were she able' (Findlay 1999a: 60). From either viewpoint, women's entry to the theatre, at court or on the public stage, is defined as a dangerous, threatening force. What is more, Bel-imperia becomes author as well as actor when she revises Hieronimo's script to conclude with her own suicide. His masculine reading of her re-scripting is dismissive: 'Poor Bel-imperia missed her part in this' (4.4.140), yet arguably this is an example of a woman authoring and performing her own noble death when every other avenue for self-empowerment is closed to her. She has the last word and dies claiming centre stage, costumed as a goddess: a visibly gendered statement of resistance and independence.

The Tudor period offers examples of dramatic production by women who, like Bel-imperia, move between theatrical and self-presentation. Women were culturally debarred from writing for or performing on the public or the university stages, yet they undoubtedly seized a variety of opportunities to engage with dramatic production. Like Kyd's heroine, they often worked through the interstices of the male-authored dramatic texts available to them, including translation, court entertainments and public ceremonials. Women were principally confined to the private sphere, yet their self-staging evolved from the personal to the public. They are shown acting out indi-vidual dilemmas, but also staging themselves to access or highlight the ways in which performance represents empowerment. Women in public roles were already actively staging themselves. Queens and religious martyrs found a public space in which to perform a version of themselves, which transcended the personal and became a dramatic signifier. Elizabeth I's splendid costumes, and the visible 'joy' of martyrs at their executions are both manifestations of women's capacity to transgress gender categories and perform in a public arena. This chapter also explores the possible meanings and status that drama in translations by women might have held for early modern authors and audiences and considers the texts in relation to these public self-staging activities.

The earliest dramatic texts produced in English by women were transla-tions; this chapter argues that women translators found ways to interpolate their own dramatic voices within these texts. The first known dramatic work by an Englishwoman is a version of Euripides' play *Iphigeneia at Aulis* (*c.* 1553) by Lady Jane Lumley (1537–76), which survives in a unique holo-graph manuscript (MS Royal 15. A. IX). A fragment of a translation from Seneca's *Hercules Oetaeus* by Elizabeth I[2] (1533–1603) is extant in manu-script, though her translation of an unidentified play by Euripides is lost. Mary Sidney (1561–1621) published two editions of *The Tragedie of Antonie*

---

2. *See* Cerasano and Wynne-Davies (1996: 7–9) for a discussion of the attribution of this text.

(1590), her translation of Robert Garnier's *Marc Antoine* (1578), a French play based on the familiar story of Antony and Cleopatra, recorded by Plutarch. At least one further unidentified translation by Mary Sidney is lost, possibly in the substantial fire at her Wilton home in 1647 (Hannay 1990: 198). Translations of classical texts, or texts originating in classical narratives, produced by highly-educated aristocratic women, function simultaneously to acknowledge indebtedness to a series of male sources and to assert the possibility of gendered revision of such narratives. Margaret Hannay suggests that 'subversion of existing texts was a necessary strategy for women because silence was considered one of the primary feminine virtues throughout the Tudor period' (1985: 4). These plays have been critically neglected because translation is generally viewed as a subsidiary, derivative or transparent literary form. Yet in the early modern period, translation was one relatively uncontroversial way for a woman writer to borrow or acquire male authority and gain an audience. Educated aristocratic women studied the classics extensively and, like Bel-imperia, were often fluent in several ancient and modern languages. Translation exercises were a standard early modern educational tool and a starting point for some women to define themselves as writers.

One of the most significant and interesting points about Jane Lumley's prose drama 'The Tragedie of Euripides called Iphigeneia translated out of Greake into Englisshe' (Lumley *c.* 1554: fol. 63) is that it is an adaptation, rather than a precise translation of Euripides' play. It is a radically shortened version, with a number of speeches significantly transposed between characters subtly to alter emphasis, characterisation and interpretation; Lumley also adds a number of new lines. Lumley's tragedy retains its dramatic impact and pathos, despite the reduction in length. She demonstrates considerable dramatic skill in creating a distinctive performance version of Euripides' play, which is also open to local Catholic and dynastic readings. The date of Lumley's play is uncertain, though an earliest likely date of 1553 is suggested by the fact that the only Lumley library copy of a Greek Euripides text, a companion to Erasmus, was first acquired in that year (Hodgson-Wright 1998: 130). Jane Lumley, daughter of Henry Fitzalan, the Catholic Earl of Arundel, was highly educated in the humanist tradition: it seems to have been a family tradition for Arundel to receive texts in translation as gifts from his children (Purkiss 1998: 169). For example, two accompanying undated translations from Isocrates in the same manuscript are dedicated to Arundel by Jane Lumley in Latin: 'which I offer as a gift to you as an example of my studies' (Lumley *c.* 1554: fol. 4r).[3] Translation

---

3. I wish to thank Marie Loughlin for this text and Peter Lock for the translation.

from Greek displayed Jane Lumley's classical education to the full; drawing on Erasmus in addition indicated discrimination and appropriate humanist values (Devereux 1983: 18). Elaine Beilin has also suggested that the Christian echoes in Lumley's version are drawn from Erasmus (1987: 156–7). While Lumley's translation may have originated as an academic exercise (Child 1909: vi), to view it principally as such is seriously to understate the play's creative originality and dramatic potential.

In translating *The Tragedie of Iphigeneia*, Lumley selected one of Euripides' most family-orientated tragedies, centering on the relationship between Agamemnon and his favourite daughter, Iphigeneia. Agamemnon, captain of the Grecian army setting out for Troy to avenge the abduction of Helen (wife to his brother Menelaus), learns that only the sacrifice of Iphigeneia to the goddess Diana will bring the Greeks a fair wind to Troy, and 'a glorious victorie' (Lumley 1998: 895). Agamemnon vacillates between political necessity and family love, eventually summoning Iphigeneia and his wife Clytemnestra to Aulis under the fictitious cover of Iphigeneia's impending marriage to the hero Achilles. Clytemnestra, Achilles and Iphigeneia are horrified to discover the truth, but in an extreme dramatic reversal Iphigeneia eventually resolves to die 'for the wellthe of my countrie' (927–80). At the moment of sacrifice, a white deer sent by Diana appears on the altar, and Iphigeneia vanishes. As Stephanie Hodgson-Wright has argued (1998: 133–7), the play's subject matter, the sacrifice of a daughter for political reasons, may contain resonances of the political career of Jane Lumley's Protestant first cousin, Lady Jane Grey (1537–54), the 'nine days queen' arrested in 1553 and executed under Mary I in 1554. Arundel was responsible for exposing the plot to put Jane Grey on the throne of England, having initially pretended sympathy with the conspirators. Lumley's choice of text may well have been motivated by her recognition of Euripides' dramatic exploitation of political changes and uncertainties.

Lumley reduces Euripides' text by more than half by cutting large sections of the Chorus, and omitting numerous extended classical references, particularly those detailing the ancestry of individual characters. She adapts and amends her version to highlight certain parallels and relationships. One of the most distinctive features of Lumley's play is her new emphasis on the mutuality and directness of the father–daughter relationship. J. Michael Walton's discussion of Euripides's play suggests that 'there is more physical contact between characters than in perhaps any other tragedy' (1984: 130). Lumley intensifies the immediate quality of Iphigeneia's affection for her father by omitting Clytemnestra's instruction to Iphigeneia to embrace Agamemnon on her first appearance. Iphigeneia's action thus becomes spontaneous: 'I praye you mother be not offended with me, thoughe I do embrace my father' (376–7). Lumley characterises Agamemnon as a devoted father by emphasising his 'lamentinge, and wepinge' (37) at the start of the play, and by transposing some of Clytemnestra's speeches into his mouth, notably the one identifying Iphigeneia as her father's favourite: 'Neither am I sorie of your companye daughter, for of all my children I love you best' (382–3). Lumley adds a speech to emphasise Agamemnon's pride in his daughter's intelligence: 'suerly I am constrained to praise greatly your wit for I do delight much in it' (402–3). Lumley also redirects Agamemnon's speech about his grief at parting and his investment in his daughter towards Iphigeneia, 'yet truly it dothe greve me to bestowe you so farre of, whom with suche care I have brought up' (434–6), whereas in Euripides, Agamemnon speaks these words to Clytemnestra. Lumley characterises Iphigeneia as an increasingly assertive giver of good advice, with political acumen. In a remarkable reversal of early modern parent–child relationships, she repeatedly requests her parents to 'folowe my councell' (848, 882). Both Agamemnon (392) and Clytemnestra (856) respond to her identically: 'I will folowe your councell daughter'. Achilles, too, is an appreciative audience, impressed by her insight: 'for you have spoken very well' (829). Iphigeneia's most detailed, extensive and confident guidance is given at the end of her life to her mother (845–58, 880–92); she even offers advice on marital negotiation: 'Herken O mother I praye you unto my wordes, for I perceive you are angrie with your husband, which you may not do. For you cannot obtain your purpose by that meanes' (794–6). The concluding line, Lumley's addition, opens up an intriguing vista of female domestic political strategy.

The Tragedie of Iphigeneia focuses on individual decision making. Jane Cahill has emphasised 'Greek writers' fascination with placing their characters in situations so refined that every choice of action is catastrophic' (1995: 14). Agamemnon's solution to a political and personal dilemma is to sacrifice his daughter. Her decision is to resist, until it becomes apparent that more is at stake than obedience to her father. Iphigeneia's evolving self-determination is central to the play. As long as Agamemnon is present, her dutiful filial attitude remains exemplary, even when Agamemnon's decision to sacrifice her is revealed. Euripides' text is reshaped by Lumley so that Iphigeneia's response to his 'secrete councell' (648) begins with an internal stage direction visually exemplifying obedience: 'Nowe O father I knelinge upon my knees and makinge most humble sute, do mooste ernestely desier you to have pitie upon me your daughter, and not to sleye me so cruelly' (696–8). This resembles the idealised image of a dutiful daughter on a Renaissance family tomb. Lumley scripts Iphigeneia's words and her action in dynamic counterpoint; she enacts submission while pleading and arguing against his decision. The argument of this long speech (696–717) is highly personalised, with an emotive focus on immediate family relationships, underscored by Iphigeneia's tactic of invoking her baby brother Orestes as unwilling audience to her death. Iphigeneia's oblique question 'for what have I to do with Helena?' (709) overtly rejects any personal or political relationship with her aunt by both blood and marriage and contrasts with her rhetorical evocation of the bonds of loyalty within the immediate nuclear family.

The final parting between father and daughter is full of pathos. Lumley's Agamemnon exits on a transitional note, articulating the tension between his paternal affection and his own powerlessness in the face of political and military necessity: 'I love my children as it becommethe a father, for I do not this of my selfe . . . but rather by compulsion of the hooste . . . I am not able to make any resistance againste them. I am therefore compelled daughter to deliver you to them' (726). Agamemnon's departure is the catalyst for the beginning of a remarkable dramatic transformation towards self-sovereignty in Iphigeneia, as she finds herself doubly bereft of her father: 'Alas mother in what an unluckye time was I born, that myne own father which hathe concented unto my deathe, doth now forsake me in this miserie' (735). She is initially distracted from lamentation into expressions of modesty when Achilles arrives to defend her. Despite Clytemnestra's urgings: 'Daughter you must laie awaie all shamefastenes nowe, for you may use no nicenes; but rather prove by what meanes you maye beste save your life' (746–8), Iphigeneia responds with a resonant silence which lasts for nearly 50 lines, while Clytemnestra and Achilles try ineffectually to plan a strategy to save her. As they await the arrival of Ulysses and the Greek army, Iphigeneia suddenly asserts herself in her longest and most forceful speech of the play (794–823). She adopts a rhetorical declamatory tone to articulate a new politicised independence, which mixes heroism, martyrdom, patriotism and citizenship. She has acquired dramatic agency, resolving to embrace her death, rather than attempt to save her life:

> I muste nedes die, and will suffer it willingelye. Consider I praie you mother for what a lawful cause I shalbe slaine. Do not bothe the destruction of Troie, and also the welthe of grece, which is the most frutefull countrie of the worlde hang upon my deathe? . . . And I shall not onlie remedie all these thinges with my deathe: but also get a glorious renowne to the grecians for ever. Againe remember how I was not borne for your sake onlie, but rather for the commoditie of my countrie.
>
> (800–10)

Paradoxically, Iphigeneia's choice of non-being will immortalise her name creating a public, symbolic and permanent identity for herself. Young women were legally invisible in both Tudor England and classical Greece. Lumley, a highly educated woman lacking an independent political, legal or economic identity, dramatises the evolution of Iphigeneia from an intelligent unmarried daughter without a voice to an articulate citizen taking the initiative to internalise and solve a political dilemma. Iphigeneia will also win a political and military victory on behalf of an entire nation 'for by this meanes I shall not only leave a perpetuall memorie of my deathe, but I shall cause also the grecians to rule over the barbarians' (819–21).

Yet Lumley's play ends on an ambiguous note. The Nuncius reports the off-stage translation of Iphigeneia in detail, an event with affirmative echoes of the Virgin Mary's assumption, concluding with the Christian paradox: 'for this daie your daughter hath bene bothe alive and deade' (955). Yet Clytemnestra's doubting response undercuts any mood of celebration, as do the ironies of the Chorus's choice of adjectives in their final invocation 'O happie Agamemnon, the goddes graunte the a fortunate journie unto Troye, and a most prosperous returne againe' (969–70). Renaissance audiences would immediately recollect the disasters of the Trojan campaign and Agamemnon's murder on his return at the hands of Clytemnestra.

Suggestive internal evidence links *The Tragedie of Iphigeneia* with Nonsuch Palace, the highly decorated and architecturally fantastic building in Franco–Italian style, built by Henry VIII, which became the Arundel household's principal residence from 1557. Lumley's mixing of a Greek name, Iphigeneia, with a Latin one, Diana, rather than the Greek Artemis, has usually been related to her use of both Greek and Latin source texts (Purkiss 1998: 168). However, it is also possible that the deliberate Latin nomenclature of Diana signals the play's close relationship with Nonsuch, the palace described by Paul Hentzner in 1598 as abundantly decorated with classical imagery: 'so many casts that rival even the perfection of Roman antiquity' (Dent 1970: 62). Visitors to Nonsuch also remarked admiringly upon 'the Grove of Diana', 'the fountayne of Diana' representing Actaeon, 'a statelye bower for Diana' decorated with Latin mottos, all apparently constructed by John Lumley, Jane's husband, well within her lifetime (Dent 1970: 60–4, 121–3). The 'fountain of Diana' at Nonsuch seems to have been an illusory device, appearing to some observers as a natural spring from a rock, though surviving repair bills reveal its artificial nature; there may also have been a separate trick water hazard. John Lumley's use of the symbolism of Diana and his interest in illusory effects intersect with the miraculous transformation resulting from the sacrifice of Iphigeneia in Jane Lumley's play, where 'sodenly there chaunced a grete wonder, for although all the people harde the voice of the stroke, yet she vanisshed sodenlye awaye. And whan all they mervelinge at it, began to give a great skritche, then ther appeared unto them a white harte lienge before the aultor, strudgelinge for life' (938–43). There may also be a coded reference here to Nonsuch's setting in an extensive and well-stocked deer park. The fountain sculpture of Actaeon turned into a stag by Diana is a direct mythological contrast with the fate of Iphigeneia. She is saved by the 'harte', he is killed as a stag.

The Arundel household had strong links with drama. Arundel had been the patron of a theatre company (Hodgson-Wright 1998: 138), and records of a number of performances at Nonsuch exist (Dent 1970: 153, 159, 189). Indeed, Nonsuch itself was built to an almost theatrically extravagant design. In 1554 John Lumley and his friend Henry Maltravers wrote to Thomas Cawarden, a previous Keeper of Nonsuch who served as Master of the Revels from 1545, requesting him 'to lende us one maske yf it be possible of allmays [Germans?], yf not of some other which you have being fayre' (John Lumley 1554).[4] The Lumleys shared an interest in the classics and an enthusiasm for sententiae; they lived in an environment astonishingly rich in the visual arts. Jane Lumley is known to have requested a copy of the sententiae which decorated the Long Gallery at Gorhambury from Sir Nicholas Bacon (Hodgson-Wright 1998: 138), suggesting her strong appreciation of both visual and verbal images. *The Tragedie of Iphigeneia* has been shown to be a play, which can be staged successfully (Findlay, Hodgson-Wright and Williams 1999a) and Nonsuch would have offered a remarkably rich range of performance options. There was a permanent banqueting house with an external platform for music and drama, possibly designed by Cawarden. In August 1558, when Elizabeth I visited Nonsuch on her first royal progress, the banqueting house was the location for an impressive series of performances.

> there the Queen had great entertainment with banquets, especially on Sunday night . . . together with a mask; and the warlike sounds of drums and flutes, and all kinds of musick, till midnight. On Monday was a great supper made for her; but before night she stood at her standing in the further Park and there she saw a course. At night was a play of the children of Pauls and their musick master Sebastian. After that was a costly banquet accompanied with drums and flutes.
>
> (Nichols 1788: 44)

The 'mask' has not been identified. While there is no record of a performance of *The Tragedie of Iphigeneia* for Elizabeth I, Lumley's treatment of the Chorus of women demonstrates her familiarity with the conventions of royal entertainments. Whereas Euripides' 'women of Calchis' are also strangers in Aulis, Lumley's Chorus are gossips at home welcoming the stranger Clytemnestra. The centrality and strict hierarchy of arrival ceremonies and

---

4. I wish to thank Stephanie Hodgson-Wright for this reference, quoted by kind permission of Mr J. R. More Molyneaux.

welcome speeches to great house entertainments are mirrored in the emphatic internal stage direction added to the Chorus's lines by Lumley: 'Let us therfore mete hir with moche mirthe, leste she shulde be abasshed at hir comminge into a strange countrye' (370–2). Clytemnestra's response: 'This trulye is a token of good luck that so many noble women meate us' (374–5), follows the same etiquette; Jane Lumley would have been the principal 'noble woman' who welcomed Elizabeth I on her visits to Nonsuch.

The Tragedie of Iphigeneia foregrounds ceremony, showing the fallacious and aborted wedding of the first half of the play evolving into the solemn ritual of sacrifice and funeral. Iphigeneia mediates between the genres when she instructs the Chorus to commemorate, rather than lament, her in song: 'Wherefore I shall desier all you women to sing some songe of my deathe' (892–3). The Chorus are temporarily bewildered: 'after what fassion shall we lament, seinge we may not show any token of sadnes at the sacrafice' (898–900), yet the dialogue makes it clear that song is envisaged at this point. This may be a further suggestion of performance; the Arundel household was a rich musical environment (Hodgson-Wright 1998: n. 141) as the entertainments devised for Elizabeth's visit indicate. *The Tragedie of Iphigeneia* is set entirely in the open air, raising the question of outdoor performance. The most intriguing possibility is a performance of the play in the Grove of Diana, which must have been a feasible location, since in 1610, 'a stand for musicans' was built there for the visit of Anna of Denmark (Dent 1970: 189). In addition to the pleasing mythological congruence, an outdoor performance in this setting would give particular resonance to Agamemnon's instruction to Senex: 'Do not staie by the pleasante springes, and tarie not under the shadoinge trees' (118–19). Nonsuch had a variety of other possible performance spaces, including the Privy Chamber, where Henrietta Maria subsequently had a fixed stage erected in 1632 (Dent 1970: 191), other extremely well-lit indoor rooms, and the two courtyards.

While Stephanie Hodgson-Wright has posited specific connections between Lumley's play and the fate of Lady Jane Grey (*see* above), the play may also carry more general resonances of the public self-staging of women martyred for their religion under Mary I, from 1555 onwards. Iphigeneia's mood of triumph in the face of death echoes the celebratory tone of the Latin Collect of the Mass for a Female Martyr with which the Catholic Lumley would have been familiar: 'O God, among the wonders of your power you have granted even to the weaker sex the victory of martyrdom . . .' (trans. Longley 1970: 348). Iphigeneia's auditors are impressed by 'the stoutenes of her minde' (932) as she approaches her death; 'stoutness' is a phrase conventionally used to describe the bravery of female martyrs in the period. After Elizabeth I's accession, John Foxe published the first complete edition of *Acts and Monuments of the English Martyrs* (1559), a catalogue of the

Protestant martyrs who had died under Mary. The Arundel household's awareness of such narratives is indicated by the presence of a copy of Alan Cope's Catholic Latin tract opposing Foxe's publication in the Lumley library by 1566 (Jayne and Johnson 1956: 44).

Foxe's account suggests that a number of women martyrs seized the public exposure of martyrdom as an opportunity to stage a scene of resistance to the Catholic religion and to the male authorities arresting them. Foxe was himself a dramatist, author of the Latin 'Comoedia Apocalyptica' *Christus Triumphans* (1556). Even if it is his formulation which imposes structure and order on more chaotic real events, he draws on dramatic imagery to do so. For example, in his account of the arrest and beheading of Lady Jane Grey, Foxe uses typography appropriate to a dramatic text, printing Fecknam's conversion dialogue with her in the form of prose lines from a play, with character headings. He also shows Jane Grey empowering herself verbally by playing on the word 'meet' in the sense of 'agree' to maintain her high social status and display her determined loyalty to her faith.

> After this Fecknam took his leave, saying that he was sorry for her: 'For I am sure,' quoth he, 'that we two shall never meet.'
> 'True it is,' replied the Lady Jane openly, 'that we shall never meet, except God turn your heart; for I am assured, unless you repent and turn to God, you are in an evil case. And I pray God, in the bowels of his mercy, to send you his holy spirit; for he hath given you his great gift of utterance, if it pleased him also to open the eyes of your heart.'
>
> (Foxe 1851: 1553)

The arrests and executions of non-aristocratic women often took place before a large public audience of onlookers and were often visually and verbally symbolic. Religious martyrs of all social classes, both female and male, appear to have utilised a number of simple shared performance strategies. They combined physical cooperation with defiant speech, demonstrated exaggerated emotion in deliberate opposition to the situation and they played out symbolic actions. In the case of women, gender and power differentials also appear to have been deliberately exploited. The case of the daughter of a husbandman, Rose Allin of Essex, in 1557 highlights this. Her calmness in the face of the officers who came to arrest the family seems to have enraged 'one master Edmund Tyrrel', who used the household candle she carried to burn her hand very severely, while heaping increasingly extreme gender and class insults upon her: 'Thou naughty housewife', 'you will burn, gossip', 'Sirs, this gossip will burn', 'Why, whore, wilt thou not cry?' 'young whore', 'strong whore', 'thou beastly whore'. Rose Allin's power came from her manifestation of oppositional emotion: 'She thanked

God, but rather to rejoice.' Like Jane Grey she engaged in defiant word-play with her male accuser, upon the word 'mend'. When she and her parents were taken to be burned alive, Foxe notes that they 'were joyfully tied to the stakes' and that they 'suffered their martyrdom with such triumph and joy' (Foxe 1851: 945–6).

Another example is the case of 'Mistress Joyce Lewes, a gentlewoman born and delicately brought up in the pleasures of the world' in 1557. Her arrest was occasioned by the act of formally and symbolically turning her back on the holy water at church. Under questioning in prison, she was 'ever found stout'. Her acute awareness of the opportunity public execution could offer for self-staging is indicated by her response to the sentence: 'the writ being brought down from London, she desired certain of her friends to come to her, with whom she consulted how she might behave herself that her death might be more glorious to the name of God, comfortable to his people, and discomfortable unto the enemies of God'. The account of her journey to execution emphasises the role of her women friends as conscious and willing fellow players in the parodic drama of resistance which she staged:

> One of her friends sent a messenger to the sheriff's house for some drink . . . after she had prayed some three several times, in the which prayer she desired God most instantly to abolish the idolatrous mass . . . she took the cup into her hands, saying, 'I drink to all them that unfeignedly love the gospel of Jesus Christ, and wish for the abolishment of papistry.' When she had drank, they that were her friends drank also. After that a great number, specially the women of the town, did drink with her; which afterward were put to open penance by the cruel papists, for drinking with her.
>
> (Foxe 1851: 950)

This publicly enacted all-female communion was certainly perceived as a blasphemous performance by the Catholic authorities who punished the women for parodying holy rites. Rather than performing 'open penance' for her actions, Joyce Lewes manifested joy at the point of execution 'when she was tied to the stake with the chain, she showed such a cheerfulness that it passed man's reason' (Foxe 1851: 949–51). 'Stoutness' and 'joy' are the consistent distinguishing features of a martyr's performance, which impress their auditors, raising thought-provoking parallels with Iphigeneia's response to her own death.

After the accession of Elizabeth I, in 1558, Catholic recusants came under the critical gaze of the state. Women played a major part in maintaining Catholic practices and networks behind the closed doors of the household; although their activities were conducted in secret, public exposure transformed their declarations of faith into significant public performances.

Margaret Clitherow, a butcher's wife, was pressed to death in York in 1586 for refusing to plead at her trial. Two accounts of her life, *A True Report of the Life and Martyrdom of Mrs Margaret Clitherow* (1586) by Father Mush, a recusant priest who was possibly the cause of her arrest, and an anonymous summary *An Abstracte of the Life and Martirdome of Mistres Margaret Clitherowe* (1619) (in Rogers 1979), suggest the ways in which a bourgeois wife and mother deployed powerful dramatic effects in her public appearances. Clitherow was a Catholic convert, repeatedly imprisoned for harbouring priests. Throughout the legal proceedings of 1586 in which she refused to plead 'having made no offence, I need no trial' (Mush 1877: 413), her behaviour was assured and defiant. She refused to engage verbally with her accusers, but consistently deployed symbolic visual strategies using costume. She first appeared at the assizes in a large hat indicating both her social status and her refusal to submit to the court's authority. She sewed a 'linen habit like to an alb' [a priest's vestment] (Mush 1877: 429) for her execution, with tapes provided to tie her hands to posts so that she could die in the shape of the cross. 'Her hat before she died she sent to her husband, in sign of her loving duty to him as to her head. Her hose and shoes to her eldest daughter Anne, about twelve years old, signifying that she should serve God and follow her steps of virtue' (Mush 1877: 432). Her accusers also used costume theatrically to challenge her at her trial. Her judges called for Catholic vestments and 'other church gear' to be brought to the court room: 'These sacred Ornamentes, were by way of *derisio* put on two fellowes backe, who with twenty antick faces, made themselves apes, to please the Judges, and the multitude . . . they asked her how she liked the vestments, I like them well (quoth shee) if they were on their backs that knowe how to use them unto Gods honour' (Rogers 1979: sig. B3v). Clitherow's interpretation of her situation was deliberately oppositional. On the morning of her execution, she 'went cheerfully to her marriage, as she called it' (Mush 1877: 430). Whenever she appeared in public she gave generous alms to the watching crowds, even when her arms were pinioned (Mush 1877: 418). As with the Protestant martyrs, her 'stoutness' and her cheerful demeanour disconcerted her auditors: 'they marvelled all to see her joyful countenance' (Mush 1877: 430).

At her execution, Mary, Queen of Scots (1542–87), actively staged herself as a national Catholic martyr. When accused of complicity in the Babington plot to depose Elizabeth I, she wrote to Bernardino de Mendoza 'I think they are making a scaffold to make me play the last scene of the Tragedy' (Fraser 1969: 521). 'Scaffold' carried the double meaning of stage and point of execution; even with a very restricted audience, Mary presented herself as a martyr rather than as a political victim. Her demeanour seems to have been less oppositional and more exclusively symbolic than some of the other women martyrs discussed here. She wore a wig and dressed elaborately for the occasion, wearing red undergarments so that when she put off her regal worldly persona and outer garments to be beheaded, she appeared in 'the liturgical colour of martyrdom' (Fraser 1969: 538). Her executioners understood her religious message as they burned every remaining item that might have become a relic, including her clothes.

Mary was well aware of the power of theatre since she had brought her experience of French royal spectacle to bear on her own court in Scotland.[5] Her marriage to the Dauphin in 1558 had been celebrated with magnificent public fetes in Paris, and after the death of her husband, Queen Mary's own royal style continued to be influenced by that of the Valois monarchy. She returned to Scotland in 1561, and 'thair began', John Knox remarked, 'the masking, which from year to year hath continewed since'. Mary introduced a full range of court entertainments: banquets, dancing, music and semi-dramatic entertainments, often taking part in these herself (Carpenter 1989: 20). The most elaborate festival was the three-day entertainment at Stirling Castle to celebrate the baptism of Mary's son, James, on 17–19 December 1566. As Michael Lynch has shown, Mary used the baptism celebration to stage royal policy. After she urged 'lufe, unitie and charitie' between Protestant and Catholic factions at a speech in Jedburgh in October 1566, these qualities were dramatised in the rituals and entertainments at Stirling. Catholic clergymen who had previously been persecuted were intended to join hands with their Protestant counterparts, as in the French royal festival at Lyon in 1564, where Protestant and Catholic children had joined hands to present an image of French harmony (Lynch 1990: 17, 7).

The Stirling festival was a state occasion, with the monarchs of France, Savoy and England all represented, and Mary exploited it to advertise her powerful royal lineage. In the banquet and entertainment on the final evening, she implicitly appropriated Elizabeth I's national imagery. The guests were seated 'at a round table like Arthur's' and in George Buchanan's play *Pompae Deorum Rusticorum*, written specially for the dinner, Mary was celebrated as King Arthur and as the goddess Astrea, the restorer of harmony among chaos. (Some of the resonance may, however, have been lost when the elaborate moving stage collapsed mid-performance!) However, the celebration of Stuart power and glory came to a dramatic climax in a mock storming of Stirling Castle with coloured costumes, cannons and fireworks (Lynch 1990: 12–13). Presiding over this entertainment, and undoubtedly participating in elements of it, Mary showed her skills in manipulating courtly dramatic production for political purposes.

---

5. I am grateful to Alison Findlay for the following two paragraphs.

The self-staging of royal and ruling figures is also explored in Mary Sidney's scrupulous verse translation of Robert Garnier's five-act French tragedy *Marc-Antoine*, with particular focus on their deaths. *The Tragedie of Antonie* (1590) is a much more self-consciously literary piece than Lumley's play and may exemplify what Diane Bornstein has called 'the silent art of translation' (Hannay 1985: 12). Much of the critical attention paid to *The Tragedie of Antonie* has been restricted to discussions of its relationship with Shakespeare's *Antony and Cleopatra* (1608) (Bullough 1966: 229–31). Mary Sidney's play has been either unfavourably compared with Shakespeare's tragedy, or fleetingly acknowledged as one of its sources (Wilders 1995: 61–2). Serious critical attention to Mary Sidney as a dramatist has largely consisted of efforts to demonstrate ways in which *The Tragedie of Antonie* embodies Philip Sidney's aesthetic and critical values, as articulated in his *A Defense of Poesy* (1595), which Mary Sidney supervised through the press after his death (Buxton 1964: 199–201). Arguably, however, Sidney's play has its own powerful and moving performance dynamic, with elements which strongly suggest potential for formal household performance.

Mary Ellen Lamb has argued convincingly for a central rationale in Sidney's selection of her several translation texts in different genres. The *Psalms*, Philippe de Mornay's *Discourse on Death*, and Garnier's play are all texts concerned with *ars moriendi*; the art of dying well (1990: 115–41). Lamb's argument can usefully be developed to encompass Sidney's particular dramatic interest in the expression of lamentation; *The Tragedie of Antonie* is a text distinguished by its extended and formal dramatisation of lament as a rhetorical and theatrical form. Lamb's reading of the play deals well with its stoic values, placing considerable emphasis on Cleopatra as the key exponent of the art of dying (1990: 129–32), including an interesting and detailed analysis of the ways in which her resolution to die exemplifies the 'heroics of constancy as these concerned women' (1990: 119). It is equally important to note, however, the tragedy's intense focus on Antonie, the eponymous protagonist; the dramatisation of his engagement with death is the catalyst for Cleopatra's decision. Indeed, as patron, Mary Sidney appears to have assigned the task of foregrounding Cleopatra's death to her protégé Samuel Daniel, in 'the worke the which she did impose', his *Tragedie of Cleopatra* (1594) (Daniel, 1594 sig. A2). Set on the day of Antonie's death, the play traces a sustained comparative exploration of the impetus towards death as experienced by both main protagonists, but undoubtedly focuses primarily on Antonie, who articulates his commitment to death in the very first sentence of the play 'It's meete I dye' (1.7). Antonie is deeply preoccupied with the process of dying, and Mary Sidney is a writer much more interested in process than event or conclusion. His first long soliloquy dramatises his internal debate from a variety of different subject positions, he speaks of himself in the first, second and third person and of Cleopatra in the second and third persons. Throughout the play, Antonie repeatedly draws attention to the immediacy of his preoccupation with death: 'Ah is not this the daie / that death should me of life and love bereave?' (3.3–4). He experiences in imagination the details of his own death in battle, characterising himself as a warrior who 'should have died in armes' (3.231) in contrast to the inexperience and effeminacy of Caesar (3.211–50). His final heroic and emphatic self-assertion is fittingly situated at the heart of the play:

> But goe we: die I must, and with brave end
> Conclusion make of all foregoing harmes:
> Die, die I must: I must a noble death,
> A glorious death unto my succour call
> (3.373–76)

a firm rejection of the preceding comparison of himself with Hercules, debased and feminised, in domestic thrall to love (3.343–68).

Sidney's choice of translation text offers the opportunity to explore a series of different versions of Antonie's death. Antonie's engagement with mortality is constant throughout the play, he imagines a variety of ways to die, yet his decision about the manner, 'some couragious act' (3.379) remains fluid until the end. Dercetus's emotional report to Caesar and Agrippa after the event highlights the complex stages experienced by 'this life-dead man' (4.303) and presents the audience with a series of interlinked scenarios of Antonie's death. Dercetus's dramatic re-enactment requires him to reproduce Antonie's last words in his own voice (4.242–53, 259–61), like an actor. His suspenseful account encompasses Antonie's death by 'this murthering sword' (4.206–7), by 'swounding with anguish' (4.268), only to revive (4.270) and finally to die of his wounds united with Cleopatra in the intimacy of her monument (4.312–13). Antonie's 'lingring death' (4.274) takes more than 140 gripping lines to narrate. Mary Sidney's interest in the sustained depiction and realisation of the shifting stages of a soldier's death may have emerged from personal experience. Katherine Duncan-Jones (1991: 292–9) details the long, lingering process of Sir Philip Sidney's death as a result of military wounds sustained at the battle of Zutphen in 1586, including the strong hopes of recovery at one point. Though Philip Sidney's military reputation did not at all resemble Antonie's compromised position, there are some suggestive similarities in the accounts of their extended deaths. Philip Sidney received a serious though not fatal wound in battle on 23 September 1586. Six days later his doctors sent 'a most comfortable letter' to England, which was received as good news. Sidney and his family at home appeared to expect that he would live. He became much worse, however, and died suddenly on 17 October (Hannay 1990: 55–8). Mary Sidney had suffered the bereavements of her father and her mother earlier in 1586; it is likely that the changing news about her brother's health from the Netherlands, culminating in his unexpected death, had intense impact. *The Tragedie of Antonie* may have offered her a way to explore a distinctive aspect of military experience: the shift from the theoretical awareness of mortality to the actual stages of an individual's encounter with its immediate reality. The play also deals at length with the personal and political impact of an individual death upon others; the resonances of Antonie's impending and actual death affect every other character in the play, including the Chorus. It is feasible that translating Garnier's play offered Mary Sidney a starting point from which to explore her own profound experiences of loss and respond creatively to the impact of her brother Philip's death.

In Renaissance terms, the play's portrayal of Cleopatra is unusually sympathetic, finding a variety of ways to excuse both her political and personal actions in relation to Antonie (Krontiris 1992: 159–60). Mary Sidney's literary education would indicate the distinctiveness of Garnier's characterisation; she must have made an active choice to translate a version of this familiar classical narrative which exonerates Cleopatra so comprehensively. Cleopatra first appears in person in Act 2; her self-construction primarily in terms of her relationship with Antonie is indicated by her naming of him in her very first line, combining elevated metaphors with rhetorical expressions of outrage, as she internalises and personalises any suspicion of treachery.

> That I have thee betraide, deare Antonie,
> My life, my soule, my sunne? I had such thought?
> That I have thee betraide my Lord, my King?
> That I would breake my vowed faith to thee?
> Leave thee? Deceive thee? yeelde thee to the rage
> Of mightie foe? I ever had that hart?
>
> (2.151–6)

Repetition, internal rhyme and the use of a subjunctive tense intensify the impact of these implied denials, followed by formally patterned and highly physical imprecations indicating the strength of her feelings:

> Rather sharpe lightning lighten on my head:
> Rather may I to deepest mischiefe fall:
> Rather the opened earth devoure me:
> Rather fierce Tigers feed them on my flesh.
>
> (2.156–60)

Throughout this impassioned opening speech, she addresses herself directly and exclusively to the absent Antonie; yet she is answered by the pragmatic Eras, whose critical questioning of her excessive emotion invokes a cross-gendered image of Cleopatra's royal ancestry as a model for stoicism. 'Come of so many Kings, want you the hart/Bravely, stoutly, this tempest to resist? (2.187–8). Interestingly, the phrasing of these lines carries echoes of the language and 'doubling of genders' in accounts of Elizabeth I's 1588 speech at Tilbury (Levin 1998: 119–20). Stichomythia is a highly focused and patterned rhetorical strategy also used effectively in this act to dramatise the moral and philosophical debates between Cleopatra and her women, whose various suggested pragmatic compromises she disregards. For example, she characterises herself as a loyal wife but strongly rejects the passive role of loyal widow (2.361–400). Cleopatra's noble and heroic stance is justified by her ingenious loyalty, asserting her commitment to Antonie regardless of misfortunes. She is presented as grief-stricken at her estrangement from Antonie, to whom she is absolutely loyal. Many phrases are both lyrical and erotic. Significantly, both Eras and Charmion have been given stronger and more compelling arguments by Sidney's transposition between them of a number of individual lines (2.191–3, 313–23). Such editorial intervention by Sidney is extremely rare in this faithful translation, and is therefore likely to indicate a strong dramatic rationale. It is also a useful reminder that Sidney has chosen not to adapt many other aspects of Garnier's text, suggesting a high level of congruence between his views and dramatic strategies and hers.

The scene shows Cleopatra prioritising her personal emotions and passion for Antonie over her political status as Queen of Egypt and imperial ally. She tellingly compares herself with Helen of Troy 'My face too lovely caus'd my wretched case' (2.194). She discriminates rhetorically between apparent political betrayal and personal loyalty to Antonie, thereby metaphorically reversing the outcome of the crucial battle (2.297–301). After Cleopatra's exit to her 'sad tombe' (2.451), the worthy Diomede, her secretary, juxtaposes celebration of her beauty and potential political power with regret for her private anguish and emotional disorder. He articulates the feminine quality of her seductive influence, commenting specifically on her eloquence in many languages (2.485). Her withdrawal into the tomb is preparation for death 'I will die, I will die' (2.416). She is single-minded about her commitment to both Antonie and death, rejecting both her political and her maternal responsibilities.

Act 5 is taken up with the gradual process of Cleopatra's death, as she anticipates it over Antonie's senseless and lifeless corpse. After his reported death in Act 4, his body is present on stage throughout Act 5 as a disturbing visual symbol: 'Now but a blocke, the bootie of a tombe' (5.146).

Cleopatra's attendants believe at first that she too is already dead; they revive her for a long invocation and final embrace with Antonie, culminating in her final orgasmic lines performed over his body. Cleopatra speaks the final words of the play from within her tomb; significantly this is the only act which does not conclude with a chorus. While she expresses longings for death, it is important to recognise that dramatically her death is still (just) in the future at the end of the play:

> O neck, o armes, o hands, o breast where death
> (O mischiefe) comes to choake up vital breath.
> A thousand kisses, thousand, thousand more
> Let you my mouth for honour's farewell give,
> That in this office weak my limbs may grow,
> Fainting on you, and forth my soule may flow.
>
> (5.205)

While Garnier's play is equally dramatically ambiguous about Cleopatra's death (Garnier 1975: 16–17), Sidney's careful choice of language emphasises the distinctively erotic dimensions to Cleopatra's performance in Act 5. In particular, she adapts the present tense of Garnier's directly phrased last lines 'mon ame vomissant', to a more lyrical and indirect future subjunctive 'forth my soule may flow'. Elsewhere in the play she translates 'vomisse' literally as 'vomited' (3.228), indicating that her formulation of the last words of the play is carefully judged.

The impact of the lack of choric closure to Act 5 is all the more significant because the Chorus's speeches are among the most lyrical and carefully crafted sections of Sidney's play, extending and universalising the tone of lamentation expressed by the protagonists.

> Our plaints no limits stay,
> nor more then do our woes:
> both infinitely straie
> and neither measure knowes.
> In measure let them plaine:
> Who measur'd griefs sustaine.
>
> (2.145–50)

In particular, Cleopatra's long central appearance in Act 2 is framed by a double Chorus, which discourse upon the human condition and the oppressed state of Egypt. This scene is the longest and most detailed in the play and also most concerned with the politics of Egypt. The second Chorus is the most explicitly political of all, lamenting the colonial status of Egypt occupied by Rome, significantly figuring the ensuing economic dependence and slavery in gendered terms as a form of rape in which the 'madly bent' (2.578) 'force' of the Roman colonists 'must us enforce' to undergo a 'doubled subjection' (2.566–70). These images of brutal power are undercut, however, by the final section which looks forward prophetic- ally to the fall of Rome, generated by hubris and mutability (2.595–627).

> One day there will come a day
> which shall quaile thy fortunes flower
> and thee ruinde low shall laie
> in some barbarous Princes power . . .
> Like unto the ancient Troie
> whence deriv'd thy founders be,
> conqu'ring foes shall thee enjoie,
> and a burning praie in thee.
> for within this turning ball
> this we see and see each daie;
> ends to first beginnings fall.
> & that nought, how strong or strange
> chaungeles doth endure alwaie,
> but endureth fatall change.
>   (2.595–8, 617–27)

Later in the play, the Chorus's anxieties about Roman dominion are real- ised when it is literally colonised by Rome, appearing at the end of Act 4 in the new dramatic guise of a group of Roman soldiers. The fact that this newly Romanised choric voice is not given the opportunity to add a qualifying coda to Cleopatra's final lamentations in Act 5 illustrates the play's ambivalent representation of Roman power, specifically effecting a metatheatrical underscoring of Cleopatra's refusal to be delimited by the imperialistic agenda of Rome.

Margaret Hannay refers to Mary Sidney's 'family's long-standing patron- age of stageable drama' (1990: 124); she herself was the patron of a number of dramatists, as well as being patron of Pembroke's Men, in the early 1590s, the very period in which she wrote and published *The Tragedie of Antonie* (Hannay 1990: 124, 1998: 146, Morris 198: 52–7). Preliminary in- dications of the play's performance dimensions come in the first and most original section of Sidney's text, 'The Argument'. She adapts Garnier freely, adding to and suppressing details of his Argument. Her most significant addition is her penultimate line 'The stage supposed Alexandria: the chorus first Egiptians, & after Romane souldiers' (Sidney 1998a: 39). She estab- lishes the main setting of the play, though Act 5 clearly requires a change of scene to the localised and intimate environment of Cleopatra's monument. She also signals the doubling of parts (and the halving of cast numbers) by her indication that the Chorus change nationality and political allegiance whereas Garnier appears to envisage two Choruses. 'Le Choeur d'Egyptien, Le Choeur des Soldars de Cesar' (Garnier 1975: 108). Garnier's word *choeur* also raises the interesting possibility that the Choruses were originally composed to be sung (Garnier 1975: 23), though no attention has previously been given to this possibility in discussions of Sidney's play. There may be a fruitful link with Mary Sidney's translation of the *Psalms*, liturgical texts which were often sung (Hannay 1990: 85, 94). The formal five-act structure of the play sequentially foregrounds each of the dramatically isolated figures of Antonie, Cleopatra and Caesar. Strikingly, the protagonists never meet in life before the audience's eyes; they are shown alternately in separate scenes in polemical debate with themselves in soliloquy, or in dialogue with minor characters. Keeping them separate is a bold structural device with the dramatic advantage of concentrating on each protagonist in turn, allowing both Antonie and Cleopatra full scope in their individual scenes, while also emphasising their political and emotional estrangement. The play reveals significant verbal conflict within each character, and with others.

The main textual innovation in Sidney's translation is the selective use of rhyme as a dramatic signifier. One of the most distinctive linguistic and performance features of her play is the selective use of flowing alternate rhyme for the choruses (and for key concluding moments in the drama), whereas Garnier uses rhyme throughout. Sidney's use of pronouns is distinctive and dramatically telling. She deploys changes of pronoun to investigate selfhood and individual autonomy, thereby linking characters who never appear on stage together alive. For example, Antonie refers to himself in the first, second and third person in his opening 148-line soliloquy, his radically shifting use of pronouns articulates several different psychological perspectives. This might invite a performance technique suggesting that he no longer has a coherent identity, but is speaking in several different voices, rather like the dramatic conventions for public theatre play portrayals of mad characters, such as Hieronimo in *The Spanish Tragedy*.[6] The main protagonists move flexibly between the first and third person, suggesting an intellectual and emotional fluidity that blurs the boundaries of the individual self. In performance, many pronouns would receive spoken emphasis within the rhythm of the sentence, highlighting both the distance and intimacy between Antonie and Cleopatra. Cleopatra's deep erotic preoccupation with Antonie leads her to constantly interrogate her own responsibility and commitment towards him, eventually integrating herself verbally with him: 'he is myself' (2.352).

---

6. Thomas Kyd was also the translator of Garnier's *Cornelie* (1594).

Other evidence suggesting the play's status as a performance text includes Sidney's use of theatrical imagery and language. She introduces two specific images of performance or entertainment, both strongly gendered and identified with Antonie. In the first, she specifically augments Garnier's imagery to emphasise Antonie's troubled sense of his own withdrawal from the masculine arenas of battle and politics to the feminised performance space of courtly aristocratic entertainment. He is speaking to himself in the second person:

> Since then the Baies so well thy forehead knewe
> To Venus mirtles yeelded have their place:
> Trumpets to pipes; field tents to courtly bowers;
> Launces and pikes to daunces and to feastes.
>
> (1.69–70)

The 'courtly bowers' are Sidney's specific addition to Garnier's text; together with the references to music, dancing, feasting and a goddess from classical mythology, they are highly reminiscent of the elaborate contemporary pastoral entertainments devised for Elizabeth I when she visited her subjects. Mary Sidney wrote a pastoral dialogue for an intended visit by Elizabeth in 1600 (*see* below) and had been present at one of the most elaborately staged such productions of the reign, the Earl of Leicester's Kenilworth entertainment of 1575 (Hannay 1990: 34–5). Antonie's reference is to a style of household performance on the grandest scale imaginable.

The second theatrical reference is the extended comparison made by Lucilius between Antonie and Hercules (3.352–68). Lucilius compares Hercules' heroic reputation adversely with his thraldom to pleasure, emphasising the astonishing image of Hercules cross-dressed '. . . with sinewy hand / Winding on spindles threde, in maides attire?' (3.359–60). Love has turned Hercules, and by implication Antonie, into a comic ungainly parody of a boy actor playing a woman's part. The syntax is intriguingly ambiguous in the concluding lines of the speech:

> The monsters free and fearless all the time
> Throughout the world the people did torment,
> And more and more encreasing daie by daie
> Scorn'd his weake heart become a mistresse play.
>
> (3.365–8)

'Play' is a primarily theatrical translation of Garnier's noun *esbats* (modern French *ebats*), meaning 'gambol, frolic, diversion'. *Ebattre*, the root verb has an active sense 'to play, frolic, gambol', which Sidney has chosen to emphasise, suggesting that Hercules/Antonie is unmanned, become either merely

35

an actor subject to a mistress's directorial imperative or a female authored text. The word 'play' refers both to the concept of acting as fiction and to a plaything or diversion. The audience, whether monsters, people, or both, is scornful of the poor production. Hercules/Antonie's masculinity and agency are gone and he now acts a foolish part in a love-comedy, rather than a heroic tragedy. Sidney introduces the word 'play' twice more into her text. She translates Garnier's *plaisirs* as 'plaies' in Caesar's criticism of Antonie and Cleopatra. '. . . both nights and daies / Their time they passed in nought but love and plaies'(4.40), suggesting the diversionary, imaginative and interactive dimensions of the love affair. Just 15 lines later she again translates *esbats* as 'play' in Agrippa's line 'Of us he made no count but as to play' (4.55), suggesting that Antonie underrated his enemies, regarding the battle as a mere charade. The literal-minded Roman view is that love has taken Antonie into the seductive realm of theatre, blurring his judgement about the distinction between fiction and reality.

A number of aspects of *The Tragedie of Antonie* are suggestive of household performance. Simple staging is indicated: 'the stage supposed Alexandria' (Sidney 1998a: 39). The most complex physical actions of the play, the suicide and hoisting of Antonie in Act 4 are reported, thereby avoiding excessive staging demands. The children, highly important symbolically in the play to represent Cleopatra's maternal and dynastic responsibilities, are in practice only required to be fleetingly present in Act 5 and speak the briefest of lines: 'Madame Adieu.' 'We come' (5.77, 81). The text contains several internal stage directions including one about Cleopatra's appearance, which also usefully details her physical actions:

> Darkened with woe her only study is
> To weepe, to sigh, to seeke for lonelines.
> Careles of all, hir haire disordered hangs
> Her charming eies whence murthring looks did flie,
> Now rivers grown, whose wellspring anguish is,
> Do trickling wash the marble of hir face.
> Hir faire discover'd brest with sobbing swolne
> Self cruell she still martireth with blowes.
>
> (2.493–8)

Lucill's weeping is equally clearly indicated in Act 3. Interestingly, there is some evidence that Garnier's play may have been performed (Garnier 1975: 17); no critical attention has yet been given to the possibility that Mary Sidney was the translator of a play with a production history. *The Tragedie of Antonie* is a lyrical investigation of loss and lamentation that could have been powerfully performed in the context of a great household.

Indeed, Mary Sidney demonstrated her interest in and competence at writing performance texts by her composition of a short witty pastoral interlude. *A Dialogue between two Shepherds: Thenot and Piers in Praise of Astraea* (*c.* 1600) is a courtly entertainment written in honour of an intended visit by Elizabeth I. Margaret Hannay defines this text as 'metapanegyric, fully self-conscious in its exploration of its own genre' (1990: 166). A key feature of the genre of great house entertainment is its attentive and subtle responsiveness to audience. The shepherds are complimenting Astraea, goddess of justice, an allegory of Elizabeth I. Their conflicting arguments, by implication, invite the audience and the Queen to judge between them. Thenot and Piers are alternate competing speakers; the comedy derives from the comparison between their verbal styles. The more extravagantly and lyrically the poetic Thenot praises Astraea, the more insistently the plain-speaking Piers undermines his imagery and proves him a liar. As in *The Tragedie of Antonie*, the main dramatic effects are achieved through language and rhyme. The rhythm of the text is fast and energetic, each speaks in three-line rhyming stanzas, a, a, b. Statement and riposte share a final end-rhyme, reinforcing the paired structure of the argument. The dialogue is humorous because Thenot's appealing but conventional courtly praise is constantly undercut by Piers' eccentric but telling and emphatic qualifications:

> *Thenot.* Astraea sees with Wisedoms sight
> Astraea workes by Vertues might
> And joyntly both do stayin her.
> *Piers.* Nay take from them her hand, her minde,
> The one is lame, the other blinde
> Shall still your lying staine her?
> (Hannay 1998b: 100)

Piers has the last word in the dialogue, he destabilises language completely by revealing its inadequacies and demonstrates that the only effective way to praise Astraea is in silence. Although this interlude may not have received its intended production before Elizabeth (Hannay 1990: 164–5), its minimalism makes it an exceptionally flexible performance text, designed for outdoor or indoor performance, with only two actors, a minimum of props and set. It may well have been intended as part of a longer sequence of entertainments. It can usefully be compared with the eulogistic tone of Mary Sidney's dedication of her translation of the *Psalms* to Elizabeth I, itself possibly intended to be spoken aloud when the written text was presented at the same projected visit.

The reign of Elizabeth I dominates the period chronologically, yet significantly between 1553 and 1603 there were three queens regnant. Queens played out a public and ceremonial role, in which presence, costume, speech and gesture signified. They were also the focus of a range of cultural entertainments at court, including drama, dancing and music. Mary I and Mary, Queen of Scots ruled over English and Scottish Catholic courts respectively, where continental influence also prevailed. Court masques, dancing and other lively performances are recorded at the Scottish court (Fraser 1969: 187–9) during Mary, Queen of Scots' reign. The accession of Mary I in England in 1553, raised initial crucial questions about the tension between gender and power. Mary I's coronation ceremonies in 1554, distinguished by lavish continental pageants, were elaborate visual spectacles, which have been read by Judith Richards to reveal detailed signs of contemporary gender confusion about women and the performance of state power. Spectators' reports are contradictory, some believed they had seen her ride in procession like a king, others carried in a litter like a queen consort (Marshall 1993: 86–90, Richards 1997: 900–2). At the coronation ceremony itself, Mary held two sceptres, the king's and the one for a queen consort (Marshall 1993: 90). On her accession, Elizabeth's coronation ceremonies of 1559 were specifically compared by observers with Mary's, a suggestive indication of informed public awareness of dramatic symbolism. A distinctive feature of Elizabeth's journey through London was her particular concern to construct herself as a deeply attentive and visibly appreciative audience to the detail and meaning of the pageants 'For her Majestie was disposed to hear all that should be sayd to her . . . her Grace . . . required that the chariot myght be removed towardes the pageaunt, that she might percyve the childes woordes' (Nichols 1788: 12). She played an active, and apparently spontaneous, part in the tableau of Truth and Time. When she enquired about the meaning of the symbols, Truth, the daughter of Time was identified. She seized the dramatic and propaganda opportunity to identify herself as the true monarch: 'Tyme? quoth she, and Tyme hath brought me hether' (Hackett 1995: 43, Wilson 1980: 7, Leslie 1998: 52).

Arguably, though each queen inherited the throne in her own right, both Mary I in England and Mary, Queen of Scots in Scotland choose the more conventional, less assertive performance model of queen consort. Each married and is recorded performing traditional female accomplishments, rather than establishing an elaborate public persona, which extended beyond her royal status. Elizabeth I, however, remained unmarried, partly by playing out elaborate ritualised extended public courtships; she is specifically identified by Helen Hackett as a dramatic performer at key points in her reign (1995: 41–9). Of the three queens discussed in this chapter, Elizabeth I is the one who engaged with dramatic production most fully and consistently. She staged herself skilfully throughout her long reign, in public appearances, audiences, pageants, and portraits, through speeches and visual signifiers. She attended numerous plays and country house entertainments staged for her and about her by her subjects. Carole Levin has shown how she developed self-staging strategies and how integral theatrical metaphors were to Elizabeth's successful performance as queen, revealing 'the importance of drama to successful rule at this time' (Levin 1998: 113). Costume was an important part of the stage management of Elizabeth's image. Her costumes were both splendid and symbolic. The link with performance is made particularly strongly by the possibility that the Rainbow portrait (*c.* 1603) represents Elizabeth in an actual masque costume (Arnold 1988: 82). It is possible to argue that Elizabeth engaged with two broad performance modes: the simple striking imagery of pageant appearances or public speeches utilised at her coronation pageants or at Tilbury and the more complex genre of elaborate multi-faceted country house entertainments prepared for her by her aristocratic subjects on her summer progresses. Examples such as Nonsuch (1558) or Kenilworth (1575), indicate that these were extended, elaborate and expensive dramatic productions lasting over several days and staged in several locations, indoors and out. They included formally staged performances, surprise encounters, music, dancing, feasting and also hunting. Hunting was one of Elizabeth's favourite sports, which was probably also stage-managed for success on these occasions.

These entertainments were a form of political compliment or flattery but also functioned as gifts to the sovereign. Such entertainments included Bisham (1592), Elvetham (1592), and *The Lady of May* by Sir Philip Sidney at Wanstead (1598). Each entertainment was different and records of only some survive, containing varying amounts of performance information. They seem to have been performed by a combination of courtiers and professional actors. It is not clear how extensive individual aristocratic hosts' roles in scripting each entertainment were, though each undoubtedly contained a number of distinctly local or personal notes.

Lady Russell's entertainment at Bisham provides an excellent example of the ways in which aristocratic women participated in these productions. It seems likely that Lady Russell's involvement in scripting the entertainment was quite extensive (Wilson 1980: 47). The arrival ceremonies of the entertainment opened on the edges of the estate where a 'wilde man' guided the queen towards Lady Russell's two daughters as performers sitting on a hillside dressed as 'two Virgins keeping sheepe, and sowing in their Samplers' (Wilson 1980: 44). The queen observed the shepherdesses, who affected not to have noticed her as they sewed and were courted by Pan, engaging in a witty and highly pertinent discussion of women and gods. Such recognition games were a common feature of royal entertainments, designed to blur the boundaries between reality and fiction and also to anticipate and enable the frequent concluding identification of Elizabeth with a goddess. The shepherdesses were engaged in embroidering the tongues of men and women onto their samplers. To deflect Pan's attempted seduction, the shepherdesses assert that the male tongues deceive 'wrought all with double stitch but not one true', but the women's tongues which contain multiple symbolic references and compliments to Elizabeth are 'wrought with Queenes stitch and all right'. The shepherdesses emphasise the sincerity of women's words, 'weomens tongues are made of the same flesh that their harts are, and speake as they think', immediately following this statement with extravagant compliments to the still unperceived Elizabeth, rhetorically validated as a monarch in her own right: 'we attend a sight which is more glorious than the sunne rising', 'the Queene of this Islande, the wonder of the world, and nature's glory' (Wilson 1980: 45). These lines allow them to perceive the queen for the first time, and Pan is comically dismissed in haste to 'give our mother warning' of the guest's arrival. Thus the Russell daughters move between their fictional and their real identities, kneeling to the queen 'that our houses may be blessed with her presence' (Wilson 1980: 45). Elizabeth, now identified as a goddess, is formally welcomed to the house in song by another goddess, Ceres, presumably a professional actor. Here a different kind of fiction applies, since the female queen was being greeted as an equal or superior by an actor who was very probably male. Royal entertainments consistently appear to have mixed female characters played by aristocratic women with female characters played by male actors. In describing 'The Queenes Majesties Entertaynment in Suffolke and Norfolke' (Nichols 1788: 2. 74–5) Thomas Churchyard reveals that the professional actors who participated in such entertainments were all male. He discusses the cast of 'the shew of Manhoode and Dezart . . . men all, saving one boy, called Beautie'. This cross-dressing raises interesting questions about the 'mirror' scenes with rival female deities often included in these entertainments, such as *The Lady of May*. Here, Elizabeth meets the Lady (presumably played by a boy), who fails to identify her but recognises 'something in your face which makes me yeeld to you' (Philip Sidney 1973: 24) as a superior deity. Elizabeth, who frequently employed masculine attributes as politically required, for example in her Tilbury speech, is thus greeted by her female mythological counterpart, who is only a fictional woman. Elizabeth is invited to participate actively in the fiction by judging between the May Lady's two suitors, and choosing her husband.

At the much more elaborate large-scale entertainment at Elvetham, which included fireworks and extensive water displays, the Queen was welcomed by a mixture of fictional and real characters: a Latin poet, the three Graces and the Hours, and finally by 'the Countesse of Hertford, accompanied with divers honourable Ladies and Gentlewomen, moste humbly on hir knees' (Wilson 1980: 105–6). Elvetham is interesting because it seems to have been a particularly female-oriented entertainment, with a high proportion of female characters including six Virgins, the Countess of Hertford, three further Virgins, Neaera, the Fayery Queen and her Maids. Michael Leslie has highlighted ways in which Elizabeth was both honoured audience and also the subject, even sometimes almost the unwilling victim of these multivalent entertainments. He analyses the spatial and political relationships between action and audience, and offers an illuminating discussion of ways in which Elizabeth performed as a resistant audience, in some cases refusing to watch the entertainment provided. Sometimes Elizabeth was the sole star of these occasions; at other times entertainments were apparently designed with some element of surprise or structured participation by the queen (Leslie 1998: 47–72). Analysis of such entertainments as dramatic productions offers important insights into the complex ways in which Elizabeth interacted with her subjects.

Elizabeth I's undated energetic alliterative translation of the first choral interlude from Seneca's play *Hercules Oetaeus*, spoken by a chorus of Aetolian women attendants, is a dramatic text, which refers extensively to court values. The passage, totalling about 120 lines, generalises about and elaborates upon the miserable lot of human beings: the cares of rulers, the superficiality of courtiers, idealising the tranquillity of the poor: 'The poor man deemeth not his happy state/till wealthy folk by fall it show' (99–100). The language of this dramatic passage is dense, rich and archaic, making this an elaborate stylised and embroidered performance text comparable to Elizabeth's complex symbolic costumes. The ruler is gendered male 'But for himself a king but few regard' (28) and courtiers are seen as wearying 'The court's lustre a stale guest made for me' (29) 'A badder sort the prince's court regard' (57). By contrast, faith is gendered female (13) and the passage idealises the simple lot of 'The wife that is y-tied to man of mean estate' (82). Though she has neither fine clothes nor jewels, she lives a life of extreme content, free from jealousy or other corrupt worldly emotions. The passage is an intricate comparative reflection upon human values and choices; Carole Levin has interpreted the passage's concluding references to the aspirational imagery of Icarus (Levin 1998: 121–2) as relevant to the political manoeuvring Elizabeth necessarily engaged in throughout her life. In conclusion, Elizabeth I's ability to move fluidly and successfully between the roles of actor, audience, author and text, is a final compelling example of the ways in which women in this period worked through the interstices of a male dramatic tradition to engage successfully with dramatic production.

CHAPTER 2

Beauty, Chastity and Wit:
Feminising the Centre-stage

STEPHANIE HODGSON-WRIGHT

This chapter will investigate the ways in which royal and aristocratic women sought to empower themselves by re-working the notions of beauty and chastity in the erudite and sophisticated forms of court masque, household entertainment, tragedy and pastoral drama. At the beginning of the period, beauty was a cultural concept defined within an aesthetic tradition dominated by masculine ideals and values and chastity was a condition imposed upon women as a means of ensuring legitimate offspring. However, the innovations by royal and aristocratic women in various forms of dramatic production chart the appropriation of beauty as a concept to be defined by women and the voluntary embracing of chastity as means and symbol of empowerment.

The period during which the masque at the English court gained its greatest significance is bounded precisely by the activities of the two queens consort. Anna of Denmark (1574–1619) presented the first Jacobean court masque, Samuel Daniel's *The Vision of the Twelve Goddesses* (1604). The last court masque, William Davenant's *Salmacida Spolia* (1640), was a joint venture between Henrietta Maria (1609–69) and Charles I, each having presented four masques independently in previous years. In the intervening time, it was the innovations of the queens which shaped the development of this type of entertainment. Both queens brought with them, from Denmark and France, a tradition of court entertainment in which women were primary activists. Queen Anna firmly claimed a place for herself and her ladies on the English court stage and introduced a rudimentary element of plot into the court masque with the antimasque innovation. Henrietta Maria not only refocused the aesthetics of court entertainments via the cult of Platonic love and the values of *préciosité*, but also established the role of women as speakers and singers on the court stage in both the masques and the pastorals in which she and her ladies acted. Furthermore, it was the court masque that provided the forum for the technical developments in theatrical presentation, rather than the public theatre. The playing space of the masque transformed directly from the flat space of the great hall to the perspective set and moveable scenery.[1]

The masque, especially in the early part of James's reign, was often used as a means to celebrate a politically significant marriage. Jacobean political rhetoric frequently likened the state to the household, especially to the partnership between husband and wife, and a masque that celebrated the joining of two important aristocratic families also celebrated the union of James and his kingdom.[2] With marriage functioning not only as a hegemonic tool, but also as an ideological mirror of the state, the masque provided a politically-charged performance medium through which Anna could claim recognition for herself and the women of the court. As queen consort, Anna was required to set up a queen's court, which, as Leeds Barroll (1991: 191–208 and 1998: 47–59) has demonstrated, acted not only as a key focus for cultural production, but was also structured as a virtual mirror image of the king's court. The gendering of the two courts effectively drew attention to Queen Anna's position as a positive female presence, with a crucial role to play in the political future of the Stuart dynasty. The key texts performed by Anna and her ladies figure the queen in variously empowered roles, shifting from an alternative locus of masculine, martial and monarchical values, to the source of beauty and the overtly feminised role as mother of the heir apparent.

Anna's first masque, *The Vision of the Twelve Goddesses* (1604) written by Samuel Daniel, figures Anna and 11 of her ladies as classical goddesses. Rather than merely reflecting and confirming the glory and power of James, as future masques would do, this masque presents feminine forces supplying the qualities that, by implication, the king lacks at the beginning of the masque. Twelve goddesses bring gifts to the Temple of Peace, in total representing the powers necessary for successful government. Juno presents a sceptre (power); Pallas presents a lance and target (wisdom and defence); Venus presents a multi-coloured scarf (love and amity); Vesta presents a burning lamp and a book (religion); Diana presents a bow and quiver (chastity); Proserpina presents a mine of gold ore (riches); Macaria presents a caduceum with the figure of abundance (felicity); Concordia presents a

---

1. John Orrell has convincingly refuted Orgel and Strong's view that plays were given deeper settings than those for masques, by arguing that, in Inigo Jones's view at least, the difference between a scenic theatre and a masking house lay in the arrangement of the auditorium, not the playing space (Orrell 1977: 17).
2. e.g. Ben Jonson, *Hymenaei* (1606); Thomas Campion, *Lord Hay's Masque* (1607).

branch in a wreath or knot (union of hearts); Astraea presents a sword and scales (justice); Flora presents a pot of flowers (the beauties of the earth); Ceres presents a sickle (plenty) and Tethys presents a trident (power by the sea). Significantly, rather than representing the ultimate queen consort, Juno, Anna chose to play Pallas, representing the two key monarchical qualities of wisdom and military prowess. Yet it is the breaking of the theatrical frame, when Iris reveals that the performers are not really goddesses, which offers the clearest a moment of empowerment. Rather than appearing in person, Pallas and her goddesses have elected to be impersonated by Queen Anna and her ladies:

> And no doubt but that, in respect of the persons under whose beautiful coverings they have thus presented themselves, these deities will be pleased the rather at their invocation (knowing all their desires to be such) as ever more to grace this glorious monarchy with the real effects of these blessings represented.
>
> (Daniel 1980: 37)

Although Anna and her ladies are playing parts, it is their very likeness to those parts which makes their representation successful. In *Tethy's Festival* (1610), Daniel's next masque for Anna (and Anna's fifth), the women performers claim socio-economic importance, representing rivers and the sea, arguably the most valuable geographical features of a pre-industrial country. There is also an emphasis upon the separateness and femaleness of Anna's court, as the main visual feature of the masque is Anna enthroned with her daughter Elizabeth at her feet, a mirror image of the prime spectators, James and the heir apparent. Once again, attention is drawn to the performative nature of the occasion, yet the difference between masquer and character is blurred:

> Behold, the post of heaven, bright Mercury,
> Is sent to summon and recall again
> Imperial Tethys with her company
> Unto her watery mansion in the main,
> And shift those forms wherein her power did deign
> T'invest herself and hers, and to restore
> Them to themselves whose beauteous shapes they wore.
>
> (Daniel 1995: 63)

This statement, by drawing the audience's attention to the likeness between the performers and the performed, asserts the validity of iconic representation of women characters by women performers.

Anna's second masque, *The Masque of Blackness* (1605) written by Ben Jonson, does not figure the queen and her ladies as presiding deities, but as foreigners, blacked-up to represent the 12 daughters of Niger. It stages three important things. First, a critique of Western European aesthetics, significantly emanating from 'Poor brain-sick men, styled poets here with you' whose values 'infect all climates' (Jonson 1995: 4). Second, the resultant insinuation of the ladies into their cultural milieu, as they search for a land ending in –tania whose ruling power (James) is 'of force / To blanch an Ethiop and revive a cor'se' (Jonson 1995: 6). The latter is readable both as an affirmation of James's divinely ordained power and as a transgression of that power. If blanching an Ethiop is of the same magnitude as reviving a corpse, then what we are about to witness is an act of hubris, not royal largesse. Significantly, the women are not magically transformed in this masque. They are enjoined to return in a year and present themselves before the king with their white complexions. Third, then, the masque makes the metatheatrical point that James's magnificent powers were incapable of solving the removal of black make-up, which rather casts doubt upon his ability to blanch the Ethiop.

One commentator, Dudley Carleton, was famously outraged by Anna's activities thus far. Of *The Vision of the Twelve Goddesses* he says 'Only Pallas had a trick by herself, for her clothes were not so much below the knee that we might see a woman had both feet and legs which I never knew before' (cited Spencer and Wells 1980: 41). As Suzanne Gosset comments 'He ignored the appropriateness of the costume to Pallas in observing its inappropriateness to Anne' (1988: 98). His reaction to *The Masque of Blackness* was more antagonistic:

> The presentation of the masque at the first drawing of the traverse was
> very fair and their apparel rich, but too light and courtesanlike. Their
> black faces and hands, which were painted and bare up the elbows, was a
> very loathsome sight and I am sorry that strangers should see our court so
> strangely disguised.
>
> (cited Barroll 1996: 180–1)

However, the Venetian ambassador Nicolo Molino sent a complimentary review, focusing upon the beauty and sumptuousness of the masque, to the Doge on 27 January 1605; just over two weeks earlier, Ottaviano Lotti, secretary to the Florentine ambassador sent a similarly complimentary review to his government, focusing upon the magnificence and, perhaps most significantly, rare inventions of the masque. The French ambassador M. de Beaumont wrote to Villeroy on 12 January that he had been entertained by a 'superbe ballet' (Barroll 1996: 185–6). Carleton based his criticism upon the fact that Anna presented herself as something other than her royal personage; put simply, she was acting. If Stephen Orgel's assessment of the state of European theatre is accurate, presumably the foreign dignitaries were used to such performances, and hence did not find Anna's efforts shocking (Orgel 1996: 2).

The Masque of Beauty (1608) features the same characters returning to thank the king for their new complexions. It is here that Anna appropriates the concept of beauty to underscore both the active presence of the female performer and the political importance of the female aristocrat. The daughters of Niger, now white and joined by four similarly blanched sisters, occupy a floating island where, by virtue of their beauty, they are the presiding forces. The community is not exclusively female; the 'naughty' poets of *Blackness* have chosen to reside there, as do the 'best of youth' from the court, including the heir apparent Prince Henry, apparently accepting female rule. Moreover, the four newcomers have received their whiteness from their sisters.

> And, that the influence of those holy fires,
> (First rapt from hence) being multiplied vpon
> The other *foure*, should make their beauties one.
> (Jonson 1970: 186)

This is the key point of the masque: the women are not merely beautiful, they determine and bestow beauty. Its elements are defined as abstract concepts rather than visual images: Splendour, Spring/Fertility, Serenity, Gladness, Temperance, Loveliness, Dignity, Perfection, Harmony. Abstract beauty is constructed as a site of political contest and a form of cultural power innate to women:

> stray'ing, vncertayne, floting to each shore,
> And to whose hauing every *clime* laid clayme,
> Each *land*, and *natione* vrged as the ayme
> Of their ambition, *beauties* perfect *throne*,
> Now made peculiar, to this place, alone . . .
> Long may his light adorne these happy *rites*
> As I renew them; and your gracious sights
> Enjoy that happinesse, eu'en to envy, 'as when
> *Beautie*, at large, brake forth, and conquer'd men.
> (Jonson 1970: 193)

Anna and her ladies thereby create a female presence upon the stage by claiming beauty as innately feminine, a quintessential quality not easily imitated by male actors.

In *The Masque of Queens* (1609) men impersonating women are actually dismissed from the stage. Anna's innovative false masque, or antimasque, is presented by Jonson as 12 hags or witches who pose a chaotic threat to the peace and harmony of the masque-world. Professional actors would have played the witches, who perform a travesty of the courtly masque dance. Crucially, it is at this point that the queens assert their supremacy. The transgressive power of witchcraft, so often celebrated by latter-day feminists, appears to be uncomfortably compromised here as the queens, drawn from classical mythology and European history, seem to subscribe to masculine values and collude with patriarchy to suppress it. Yet Jonson's elucidation identifies these queens variously as great beauties, dedicated mothers, efficient governors, learned in languages and, in the case of Queen Valasca of Bohemia, positively opposed to men, as she led her women to slaughter all their husbands to escape their tyranny. Anna played a version of herself, Bel-Anna, 'of whose dignity and person the whole scope of the invention doth speak throughout. . . . The name Bel-Anna I devised to honour hers proper by, as adding to it the attribute of Fair, and is kept by me in all my poems wherein I mention her majesty with any shadow or figure' (Jonson 1995: 50–1). Notwithstanding the association of some of the queens with masculine values, the epitomising character once again, as in the previous masque, enacts beauty as well as power. If we read the masque not simply in terms of what was performed, but in terms of who was performing, when the witches are banished from the stage, male performers impersonating a stereotype of female transgression are banished by female performers whose power is epitomised by inimitable beauty.

The continuing significance of Anna's innovations can be seen in Robert White's *Cupid's Banishment* (1617). It was performed for Anna by 'the young Gentlewomen of the Ladies Hall in Deptford' (White 1996: 83), who, by imitating many of Anna's themes, claim a place for themselves in the political and cultural future of the court. The women performers show their determination not to collude in Cupid's power, which he claims will continue 'As long as there are things called women' (White 1996: 85). Cupid is excluded from the marriage and coronation ceremonies of the king and queen, arriving to watch the latter, only after being disarmed by Jupiter. The queen is 'attired all in silver tinsie showing that she was one of Diana's train' (White 1996: 86), re-figuring Diana as a collaborator in dynastic marriage, being the protectress of unmarried aristocratic female virginity. A reconciliation is attempted, but fails when Cupid realises 'What, a marriage, and Cupid no actor in it?' (White 1996: 86). His outburst is followed by humiliation at the hands of wood nymphs who 'chase him forth into the woods by violence and banish him that presence' (White 1996: 87). The final appearance of Diana's nymphs simultaneously emphasises chastity, sexual/procreative promise and dynastic importance, as they are 'attired all in white tinsie to show their defiance to Cupid . . . their hair dishevelled, their breasts naked [but adorned] with rich jewels and pearls' (White 1996: 88). By the time Anna died in 1619, her example and her innovations had been well established. The masque recently styled 'The Visit of the Nine Goddesses' (McGee 1991: 371), probably the last performed by women in front of King James, draws heavily upon *The Vision of the Twelve Goddesses*. Performed by the daughters of Sir John Crofts, it entails a group of classical goddesses giving gifts to King James. McGee sees in it only the affirmation of patriarchal power, as 'a pastoral of a King's power and a father's potency' (McGee 1991: 378). However, if it is interpreted in the light of Anna's masque of 1604, we can see the same radical statement being made: the goddesses do not celebrate James's divine powers, they bestow them.

When tracing the transgressive and provocative effects of the Stuart queens' theatrical activities at court, feminist scholars have tended to pay more attention to Henrietta Maria than to Anna. Two influential essays, by Suzanne Gosset (1988: 96–113) and Sophie Tomlinson (1992a: 189–207) have identified two pivotal moments in Henrietta Maria's activities. Gosset's essay focuses upon the point in *Tempe Restored* when Circe, played by Madam Coniack, says to Pallas, played by a professional male actor 'Man-maid, begone!' (Townshend 1995: 162). This, Gosset claims, is crucial in pointing out the anomaly of having a woman character played by a woman sharing a stage with a woman character played by a man, which the audience were clearly expected to interpret at the same level of fictive representation. The symbolic representation of the woman by the male player is clearly demonstrated as inadequate next to the iconic presence of the female player. Tomlinson highlights the more theatrically consistent, but nonetheless culturally innovative, all-female productions of pastoral plays staged by Henrietta Maria and her ladies. In 1626 they performed Racan's *Artenice*, to a select audience. As Tomlinson notes (1992a: 189), this constituted a transgression of multiple proportions: breaking the taboo of royalty speaking on stage, taking the role of women on the court stage into the realm of spoken parts and the cross-dressing necessitated by an all-female cast. Although some English noblemen might have found the experience less than edifying, the foreign envoys, and the King himself were greatly impressed (Hamilton 1976: 72). Moreover, the occasion marked itself as one that could address a pan-European audience, drawing upon the sentiments of d'Urfe's *L'Astree* and figures from Ripa's *Iconologia*, as Hamilton argues (1976: 73). By stressing the European nature of her entertainment, Henrietta Maria was, like Anna before her, putting the case for harmonising England with the rest of Europe, where noble ladies and those of a less exalted class were no strangers to performing arts. Furthermore, one could argue, especially in relation to *The Masque of Queens* (*see* above) that the command 'Man-maid begone' was effected through spectacle in Anna's masques. Henrietta Maria, while bringing innovations of her own to the court stage, built upon her predecessor's legacy. Her *préciosité* and Platonic ideals, which she had largely imported from French salon culture, can be seen actively to reinforce the themes of Anna's masques earlier in the century.

During the 1630s, Henrietta Maria's presence was particularly felt upon the court stage. Walter Montagu's *The Shepherd's Paradise* (1633), performed in English, retained an all-female casting policy. The play politicises both beauty and chastity. The shepherd's society, which has gained certain political and legislative independence from the state, is based upon the chastity of its members. Its queen is chosen on the grounds of her beauty and only the women members are allowed to vote in this election. Men are therefore both politically and culturally disenfranchised. When Moramante opposes Gemella's admission to the society, on the grounds that she is a Moor and can therefore never be thought beautiful enough to be queen, Bellesa reprimands him:

> The Darkenes of the night may be as faire.
> for it, as can the dayes serenest ayre
> And soe this coulour of it selfe may bee
> Lovely as our's in it's owne Degree;
> And for the exclusion of her selfe from hope of being Queene, she
> doth noe more then all of vs, submitt to the opinion of the most, &
> whoe knowes what one day may be called beauty? since wee see the
> opinion of it alter every day.
>
> (Montagu 1997: 54–5)

Here Bellesa identifies female beauty as an unstable concept, not easily pinned down to particular characteristics. This politicised beauty is one that cannot be 'boy[ed]'(*Antony and Cleopatra* 5:2:216) for general entertainment. As the text makes clear, it is not simply a blazoned recipe that can be imitated with wigs and make-up; it is beauty subject to the changing views of aristocratic women.

The politicisation of female beauty and chastity is reiterated in Henrietta Maria's masques. All four of her masques, Ben Jonson's *Chloridia* (1631), Aurelian Townshend's *Tempe Restored* (1632) and William Davenant's *Temple of Love* (1634) and *Luminalia* (1638) maintain the theme of feminine virtue tempering masculine force. In *Chloridia*, the threat posed by the disgruntled Cupid bringing Jealousy, Disdain, Fear and Dissimulation out of hell is dispelled 'by the providence of Juno' (Jonson 1995: 151). Chloris thereby retains her virtuous fame:

Who hath not heard of Chloris and her bower?
Fair Iris' act, employed by Juno's power
To guard the Spring, and prosper every flower
Whom Jealousy and hell thought to devour?
(Jonson 1995: 153)

Davenant's masques reiterated the theme of the feminine tempering the masculine. For example, in *The Temple of Love*, Charles is implicated in the masque as the partner to Henrietta Maria's character, in this case Indamora, Queen of Narsinga, whose beauty will establish the Temple of Chaste Love. Charles, 'the last and living Heroe (Indamora's royall lover)' is invited to 'helpe and witness the consecration of it' (Davenant 1634: A2ᵛ). Like Anna, Henrietta Maria plays a queen in her own right, whose political and religious power stems from her beauty, rather than from her marriage to a king. The masque asserts equality in their relationship:

To Charles the mightiest and the best,
And to the Darling of his breast,
(Who rule b'example as by power)
May youthfull blessings still increase,
And in their Off-spring never cease,
Till Time's too old to last an hower.
(Davenant 1634: C2ᵛ)

The plural form of the verb in line three is significant, as is the wish for offspring. This method of perpetuating the *status quo* cast women in a leading role, sharing the responsibility with their husbands.

Tempe Restored is the most dramatically complex and performatively transgressive of Henrietta Maria's masques, offering two significantly juxtaposed departures from previous masque conventions. Women performers sing the main characters in both the antimasque and the masque and the structure of the masque marks a shift away from the established formula of masque proper unproblematically overcoming antimasque, toward a more ambiguously nuanced dramatic plot and characters. The Fugitive Favourite, who has deserted the sensual delights of Circe's household, identifies himself, not Circe, as the cause of his former profligacy:

'Tis not her rod, her philtres nor her herbs
(Though strong in magic) that can bound men's minds,
And make them prisoners where there is no wall:
It is consent that makes a perfect slave.
(Townshend 1995: 157)

When Circe enters, she is presented as a powerful desiring subject played, for the first time in an English court masque, by a professional woman singer, Madam Coniack. The 'antimasque' in which she appears is actually fictionalised as an entertainment commissioned by Circe herself as a distraction from her loss. The masque proper does not therefore dispel the antimasque; Circe and her nymphs merely retire once their entertainment is over. The main masque, in which Henrietta Maria represented Divine Beauty, is heralded by 14 'influences' and Harmony, also played by a woman, Mrs Shepherd. The main dance ends with the queen seated next to Charles, identified as Heroic Virtue:

> In Heroic Virtue is figured the King's majesty, who therein transcends as far common men as they are above beasts, he truly being the prototype to all the kingdoms under his monarchy of religion, justice, and all the virtues joined together.
>
> So that corporal beauty, consisting in symmetry, colour, and certain unexpressible graces, shining in the Queen's majesty, may draw us to the contemplation of the Beauty of the soul, unto which it hath analogy.
>
> (Townshend 1995: 164)

It is the combination of Divine Beauty and Heroic Virtue that dissolves Circe's enchantments, enacted when she publicly resigns her power to Pallas, Jupiter and Cupid. The return of an antimasque character during the main masque is unusual, making the scene function like a comedic resolution in which Circe ultimately accepts the superior power embodied in the union of Divine Beauty and Heroic Virtue, but not without the occasional disruptive remark towards Pallas and Jupiter.

Circe's disruption stems from her desire, which has been imposed upon her by Cupid. She is not, then, a mere allegorical figure, but the subject of a dramatic plot. Circe herself does not need to be excised; rather it is the masculine response to the desire that she represents, which must be tempered with reason. It is perhaps no accident that such a dramatically interesting female court masque character was the first to be represented by a female performer. In an arena that had already seen female performers taking dramatic roles, clearly the complex role of Circe demanded representation iconically by a woman, rather than symbolically, by a boy. Martin Butler has identified in *Tempe Restored* a 'discomfort with the formal prescriptions within which other Caroline poets were happy to work' and that it is 'the only court masque from this period to share much common ground with Milton's *Comus*' (Butler 1993: 135–6). Part of that common ground is the unmasque-like sense of drama and conflict created within and among the characters. Another shared aspect (though not that necessarily implied by Butler) is the opportunity each provided for women performers: Lady

Alice Egerton played the leading female role in the masque at Ludlow, which included song and spoken dialogue. As masque slides from spectacle into drama, the woman performer gains a voice.

As in the court, in the country house women can be seen to gain a voice at the point when the structured formality of Stuart court masque is least visible. The surviving examples of entertainments without royal auspices are few (Lindley 1995: xvii), those which survive are probably the smallest fraction and many others, due to their very nature, will have perished. Nevertheless the *Records of Early English Drama* collections catalogue evidence for women performing in and commissioning entertainments, for example in the household of Joyce Jefferys 1638–40 (Klausner 1990: 190–3). *The Entertainment at Ashby* (1607) by John Marston also survives (Huntington Library MS EL 34 B9). This is a woman-centred celebration of female lineage that was offered by the Countess of Huntingdon for her mother the Countess of Derby. The verses themselves are of particular significance, because they were spoken by the noblewomen present on the occasion (Knowles 1988: 489–90), to 'dignify the central marital strategy of the family' (Knowles 1989: 173). In recent years, the authorship of the verses appended to the Huntington manuscript has been in dispute, although James Knowles has convincingly argued the case for Sir William Skipwith (1989: 137–92). He also argues for Skipwith's involvement 'not simply as the provider of verses and chancery bills, but as host. Indeed, it is conceivable that the verses or the bill or both were part of the Skipwith hospitality' (1989: 172). If this speculation is correct, then the manuscript evidences an aristocratic community in which women not only commissioned entertainments, but were also called upon to perform in them.

Among the surviving manuscripts of Lady Rachel Fane (1631–80),[3] there are four entertainments, one plot revision for an entertainment and one play-fragment. Each has stage directions and was probably performed during the 1630s. The pieces clearly address the context of the Fane household at Apthorpe, both in terms of their concerns and their production values. The entertainment that might be styled 'Temperance and Mirth' has an antick dance by 'ye gentleman usher ye taylor ye buttler ye koocke other wilse translated in to an ase [ass] an ape a fox & a catte' (Sackville MSS U269 F38/3, item 3 fol. 4v). The 'Christmas Entertainment' was performed by nine younger members of the household, including four of Rachel's brothers and her sister Frances. It uses pastoral conventions, but within the context of an English country house, having among its *dramatis personae* a jester, a shepherd, a group with a maypole and a man with a mattock

---

3. Her writings are preserved in the Kentish Studies Centre, Maidstone. My thanks to the late Jeremy Maule for alerting me to the importance of this material.

(agricultural tool) and spade. The jester is the master of ceremonies for the occasion and he 'puls a book out of his pokit & opens it, wherein is birds beasts flowers' (fol. 2r). Each member of the audience receives a 'litel toye' from this book, accompanied by an appropriate verse. Light-hearted references are made to Lord Despencer's appetite, his wife's pregnancy, Elizabeth Fane's unmarried state and Francis Fane's predilection for study. The gentle-women of the household are also included, most interestingly the French Lady Voisin, who is encouraged to stay in England 'For ye makers sake' (fol. 2v). Venus, Cupid and Urania appear in a brief entertainment that deals with issues of love, chastity and procreation, articulating similar sentiments to those expressed in both *Cupid's Banishment* and Lady Mary Wroth's play *Love's Victory* (*see* below). Venus promises the company that they shall go free from 'my sons iniury', which seems a blessing at first, but then she reminds them 'When yo dye, yr Posterity / Soe long as mortels life'. Urania seems to represent chaste love, identifying herself as 'not of ye chaste dianes trane / But I doe honor her & her name' (fol. 3r), yet also ready to obey Venus, who invites her to dance. Afterwards Venus recants her earlier words and Cupid acknowledges his mother's superiority:

> I come for to acord
> to what my mother had done
> For yt I know
> Her wisedom is soe
> Yt she cane more good
> Yn I unto yo shew.
>
> (fol. 3v)

The entertainment based around a 'Wishing Chair', in which the four seasons are called up in turn by the occupant of the chair, mixes English folklore and dance with some of the formality of masque. The types of dance are distinguished: 'Yn ye springe & ye sumer wth 2 of ye sheaperdisses & ye gide yt brought ym in take out ye companie for cuntrey dances, wch shall be 8 dances yn ye spring ye sumer wth ye 2 others dance their masking dance' (fol. 9v). Significantly, the entertainment is introduced by a 'Fantastical Man' who assures the company that they will not be witnessing a form of political propaganda:

> I'm sent to entertaine, & wait upon a lovely traine
> Start not beautys but be free, wonder not but sit & se
> All we do to honnor yo,
> No loose toung nor spye com heere, to direct yr eye or eare
> Everything yt shall apeere, be delight, to fill this night
> Full of pleashewr light & cleere.
>
> (fol. 8v)

This would seem to be a deliberate attempt to distance the entertainment from the court masque, and in fact the entertainments as a group deviate from the typical court masque structure. Nevertheless, as John Creaser has commented on *Comus*, it is possible that a dynastic agenda underlies the entertainment, and that 'the children . . . are portrayed *becoming* masquers' (Creaser 1984: 130).

Rachel Fane's interest in writing a fully formed dramatic plot is evidenced by a fragment of a play that was probably performed in much the same context as her entertainments. It opens with 'Enter fore warner' who asks leave of the 'pattrens of this sacred seat' to perform (Sackville MSS U269 F38/3, item 1, fol. 1r). The conversation between the duchess and her gentlewomen, which opens the play, is firmly set in the domestic context of a noble household, as they talk of needlework and the preservation of fruit. It is also comically self-reflexive, as the duchess chides her second gentlewoman for producing nothing 'but playe books & toys' (fol. 1r). They are interrupted by news of the duke's death, at which the duchess orders a performance of her grief:

> take away my iewels pull downe thes
> things & lete my Chamber & bed be
> hung wt blake & let all things be
> prepared for soe desolate a creatur
> as my selfe . . .
> I will goe In & make my moene to ye gods yt
> they may send me sum releves or
> end my endles greafe.
>
> (fol. 1v)

However, when she next appears, she is pragmatic and determined to manage the state in which she and her son now find themselves:

> this besi world gives noe time
> to griefe therfore we must poses our witts & memory
> to contrife in sum maner to bring this inventhion to pase.
>
> (fol. 1v)

Although there is little more than these opening scenes remaining, Fane demonstrates the necessary and possible shift between two different forms of management, the household and the state, which noblewomen could be called upon to make.

Given the amount of dramatic activity involving aristocratic women, we might read the two surviving play-texts by women of this period in the context of court and household auspices. It was doubtless to these that Elizabeth

Cary (1585–1639) and Mary Wroth (1586/7–1651/3) addressed themselves when writing *The Tragedy of Mariam* (1613) and *Love's Victory* (*c.* 1621). *The Tragedy of Mariam* directly inverts the dynamics of Anna's court masques and the country house entertainment. As Mary Erler has recently pointed out in relation to the *Entertainment at Ashby*, a household entertainment turned upon arrival and departure: 'First the coming of the longed-for guest is signalled spatially; and second, one of the principles of power frequently invoked is the guest's ability to transform the waiting, ordinary space and those within it in some important way' (Erler 1991: 5). Conversely, *The Tragedy of Mariam* turns on the unlooked-for and unwanted return of King Herod, who transforms the liberated Judea into a site of misery and destruction. Furthermore the play inverts Anna's innovative masque and antimasque structure, as the largely benevolent 'chaos' of individual freedom in the first part of the play is shattered by the reinstatement of a tyrannical patriarchal order. Bearing these influences in mind, it is feasible that, although no record of a performance exits, the text was written with a performance agenda.[4] Indeed, the play deals with the issues of dissembling by and objectification of women. However, the play also offers an in-depth analysis of beauty and chastity, demonstrating tension between the political meanings that each concept accrues, and their meaning to the individual subject.

The most spectacular aspect of the play is Mariam's beauty (in every sense of the word). It is speculated upon by almost every character in the play, including Mariam herself. Yet, on close examination, this beauty turns out to be politically charged. Deriving from her inherited genes, rather than her marriage to Herod, Mariam's beauty also signifies her innate royalty. *The Tragedy of Mariam*, like Anna's masques, politicises beauty and constructs it as a site of dynastic contest. In 1.2 the conflation of beauty and lineage is made clear as Alexandra emphasises the monarchical legitimacy of Mariam's descent and compares it with the aesthetically and politically offensive Herod. In recalling her pursuit of Mark Antony on Mariam's behalf, Alexandra casts Mariam as political prize, aesthetically superior to Cleopatra, a comparison Mariam herself will make in 4.8 as she contemplates her impending death. Mariam's beauty also has the power to retain social order; it does not inspire desire in those of a lower social rank. Sohemus, although devoted to Mariam says:

> Thy brow is table to the modest law,
> Yet though we dare not love, we may admire.
> (3.3.93–4)

---

4. For further discussion of the performative aspects of the play, *see* Findlay, Hodgson-Wright and Williams (1999a and 1999b).

Doris acknowledges that 'Mariam's purer cheek / Did rob from mine the glory' and asks 'Was I not fair enough to be a queen?' (2.3.9–10 and 21), conflating her social inferiority with aesthetic inferiority. In a similar vein, Herod, when bewailing Mariam's death in Act 5, conflates her aesthetic superiority to women of darker skin with her status as his queen:

> Why shine you sun with an aspect so clear?
> I tell you once again my Mariam's dead.
> You could but shine, if some Egyptian blowse,
> Or Ethiopian dowdy lose her life.
> This was (then wherefore bend you not your brows?)
> The king of Jewry's fair and spotless wife.
>
> (5.1.193–8)

The opposition between dark and fair is deliberately problematised in the play, most overtly in Salome's reference to Silleus as 'the fair Arabian' (1.4.20). Similarly, although Salome is identified by Herod as 'a sun-burnt blackamoor' (4.7.106) and 'an ape' (4.7.104) in comparison with Mariam, Silleus calls her 'fair' (1.5.1). Pheroras, determined to reject a dynastic marriage because he is in love with the slave Graphina, exposes Mariam's beauty as an effect of dynastic privilege:

> For though the diadem on Mariam's head
> Corrupt the vulgar judgements, I will boast
> Graphina's brow's as white, her cheeks as red.
>
> (2.1.38–40)

In *The Tragedy of Mariam*, beauty is simultaneously in the eye of the beholder and ideologically constructed according to political interest.

Although standing outside of the dynastic beauty contest, Graphina becomes drawn into it as the object of Pheroras's gaze. For Graphina, as a slave, submitting to the absolute gaze of a prince is obligatory by virtue of her social status. To be constructed by Pheroras as desirable enough to rival Mariam herself is therefore advantageous, rather than disempowering. Furthermore Graphina has asked to remain chaste before her marriage to Pheroras, a request which he has honoured, although, as she makes clear, he could have taken her by force: 'Though you so weak a vassal might constrain / To yield to your high will' (2.1.62–3). For Graphina, then, chastity is a condition to be aspired to, perhaps because it is a key strategy for preserving the legitimacy of heirs and therefore a signifier of social status. For Doris, such chastity is not enough. Despite her virtues as a wife, Herod divorced Doris and denied her the status as mother to the heir apparent. For Alexandra and Doris, the status that comes with lineage and dynastic marriage is all-important: both are mothers who draw their status from their children. Salome's lack of chastity is linked to her scorn for such status. She is never referred to as a mother; she alone feels the brunt of Mariam's scorn, and seeks revenge only for herself. Marriage is not a dynastic tool for Salome; she changes husbands with her desires and in the case of Constabarus and Silleus, chooses those who cannot effect her political advancement in Judea. Salome trades the external status afforded by dynastic marriage for power within alliances that are based upon desire. Conversely, Mariam is fiercely and self-consciously chaste, yet unlike Alexandra and Doris, gradually shifts away from linking this with political advancement. When arguing with Alexandra in 1.2, she puts the case that her son Alexander is Herod's appointed heir, notwithstanding Antipater, his son by Doris. But then Alexandra retorts with:

> Why? Who can claim from Alexander's brood
> That gold-adornèd lion-guarded chair?
> Was Alexander not of David's blood?
> And was not Mariam Alexander's heir?
>
> (1.2.65–8)

Herod may be king *de facto*, but Alexander's status as heir apparent – 'born to wear the crown in [Herods'] despite' (1.2.72) – is conferred by Mariam's genes. Mariam then appropriates chastity as a strategy for avoiding dynastic alliances:

> Not to be empress of aspiring Rome,
> Would Mariam like to Cleopatra live:
> With purest body will I press my tomb,
> And wish no favours Antony could give.
>
> (1.2.121–4)

Yet, however much Mariam protests her chastity and we, the audience, are given no reason to suspect her, the play shows that chastity, as a passive quality of non-commission, has to be performed by other means. Chorus 3 gives a particularly stringent formula for wives to follow in order to demonstrate their chastity, although the ultimate directive is potentially subversive, suggesting that women should withhold at least part of themselves from their husbands:

> No sure, their thoughts no more can be their own,
> And therefore should to none but one be known.
>
> (Ch. 3, 23–4)

Mariam's outspoken nature, particularly towards Herod, against whom she has many grievances, is identified as a sign that compromises her claim to chastity. Salome has already used this to 'slander hapless Mariam for unchaste' (1.3.52). Having learned that Herod is returned, Mariam determines to reject him in spite of Sohemus' advice to her to be temperate and affable. For Mariam, seducing a man she does not love, even if he is her husband, is tantamount to unchastity:

> I know I could enchain him with a smile
> And lead him captive with a gentle word. . . .
> To be commandress of the triple earth,
> And sit in safety from a fall secure,
> To have all nations celebrate my birth,
> I would not that my spirit were impure.
>
> (3.3.45–6 and 57–60)

The corollary of Mariam's argument, as indicated in line 60, is that dynastic marriage, unless accompanied by love, is a form of unchastity. Like Salome, Mariam seeks to act upon the desires of her own body, although those desires are very different. She manipulates the notion of chastity in order to reclaim possession of herself and deny herself to any man, even her husband.

Once Herod returns, he becomes the absolute audience whose gaze constructs the performance of the other characters, particularly Mariam and Salome. Mariam does not accept his power over her, believing 'Mine innocence is hope enough for me' (3.3.62). She refuses to let his response to her beauty – 'Thou art by me beloved, by me adored' (4.3.33) – be the sole determinant of their relationship. She will not respond to his endearments, upbraids him with the murder of her grandfather and brother and barely defends herself even after Salome's 'poison cup' plot has been implemented. Her refusal to perform chastity by other means, (which she herself later identifies as 'humility' (4.8.35)), allows Herod to construct her, wrongly and ironically, as unchaste. Yet Mariam may as well be unchaste; she behaves as a desiring subject, rather than a desired object, even though her desire is towards abstinence rather than indulgence. In a dynastic marriage, the point of wifely chastity is to ensure the production of legitimate heirs. Once Mariam rejects Herod, she threatens the production of heirs *per se* and the issue of legitimacy becomes irrelevant. Mariam's chastity is only of value if accompanied by the necessary performance of wifely submission to Herod. As Skiles Howard perceptively describes it, Mariam's chastity is 'unescorted' (1998: 99), self-possessed rather than possessed by the legitimating authority of her husband. Mariam's refusal renders her as disruptive to patriarchal order as Salome. Salome, however, is a consummate performer, pragmatically accepting the *de facto* superiority of Herod's gaze and tailoring her performance to manipulate him. Compliance with patriarchal authority is exposed as something that can easily be performed by the subversive unchaste woman. Patriarchal authority itself is exposed as an unimaginative audience that cannot distinguish between dissembling and integrity and which therefore requires the enslavement of beauty and chastity (figured literally in the character of Graphina) in order to function effectively.

In Mary Wroth's *Love's Victory*, beauty is less prescribed and chastity less fatal. Nevertheless, as with *The Tragedy of Mariam*, elements of *Love's Victory* are drawn from the court and household traditions; for example, the gift-giving ceremony at Ashby and Rachel Fane's book of little toys can be seen in another format in Arcas's book of fortunes. Furthermore, *Love's Victory* demonstrates values conversant with the *préciosité* and Platonism popular in the salon culture of early seventeenth-century France, which were to emerge in Henrietta Maria's theatricals. Several scholars have also noted that Mary Wroth's own experience of performance would certainly have rendered her capable and probably disposed towards staging the play privately. She was a dancer in the masques of *Blackness* (Lindley 1995: 281) and *Beauty* and probably observed many more (Waller 1993: 228).[5] Jonson cast her in his lost pastoral *The May Lord* and also dedicated the first folio edition of *The Alchemist* to her (Roberts 1983: 164–5). Furthermore, a copy of *Love's Victory* was once owned by Sir Edward Dering (1598–1644) who was a great collector of plays and involved himself in amateur theatricals with his friends and family (Brennan 1988: 14–15). Finally, if it was performed, there is evidence to suggest that Wroth envisaged casting according to gender. In *Urania*, she uses the example of a boy playing a woman declaring her love on one occasion to emphasise the lack of effect a female character has upon a man (Wroth 1621: 60) and on another as a simile for an unconvincing show (Wroth MS Newberry: fol. 30 2v). Josephine Roberts points out that the

> presence of stage directions in the Huntington manuscript of *Love's Victorie*, particularly the abbreviation *ex*: used to mark the departures of characters from stage, indicates that it was not a closet drama, but the type of well-crafted pastoral that would have interested Dering and his circle of amateurs.
>
> (Roberts 1983: 163–4)

Indeed, some more adventurous critics have suggested imagining, or experimenting with performance. Barbara K. Lewalski comments that: 'Stylistically it is competent and often charming, especially when we imagine (as I think

---

5. *See also* Orrell (1979: 16).

we should) a performance in which the all-pervasive songs and choruses are set to music. The dialogue, rendered in heroic couplets, is usually natural and easy' (1993: 304). Carolyn Ruth Swift argues that if ever Wroth staged *Love's Victory* 'she may have used the great hall of Penshurst and its balcony', that the verse 'Meadows, paths, grass, flowers' (1.1.17–24) 'well suits Elizabethan melodies I have tried, such as "Blow, Blow thou Winter Wind"' and that 'Wroth sometimes achieves brilliant lyricism even in the demanding test of reading aloud' (1989: 173–4).

The view of the play as designed for a private, coterie performance lends some support to a reading of it as a type of *roman à clef* for two generations of the Sidney family and this has proved to be a popular approach among recent critics.[6] The identification of Musella with Mary Wroth/Penelope Rich, Philisses with William Herbert/Philip Sidney, Simeana with Susan de Vere/Mary Sidney, Lissius with Philip Herbert/Matthew Lister and Rustic with Robert Wroth/Robert Rich has virtually become a critical convention. For example, Swift suggests that if Lady Mary played Musella and the Earl of Pembroke Philisses, perhaps in *Love's Victory* 'they fulfilled their own dream of a relationship accepted by society' (1989: 187). Furthermore, Cerasano and Wynne-Davies claim that 'an awareness of Mary Wroth's biography is essential to the understanding of her work, for the characters in her romances, poems and plays represent the people she knew, those she loved and those she despised' (1996: 91). While this is useful as an initial approach to the text, it is excessively limiting to read the play merely as a dramatised wish-fulfilment of Mary Wroth's family circle, however culturally powerful that circle might have been. Barbara K. Lewalski has suggested that we should turn away from Wroth's life and *oeuvre*, arguing '*Love's Victory* is much more usefully contextualized in relation to pastoral tragicomedy, a mixed genre especially popular at the Renaissance courts of Italy, France, and England' (1991: 89). It is more productive to combine both approaches, reading with awareness of Wroth's biography, yet unfettered by the aim of finding representation of historical personages, in order to understand the text as Wroth's reworking of her own experience and of established literary models, in a feminist adaptation of an aristocratic male-dominated genre. One of the remarkable features of *Love's Victory* is that it apparently has no single literary source. There are certain 'theatergrams' (Campbell 1997: 103–24) drawn from pastoral texts by previous

---

6. e.g. Roberts (1983: 166–7); Cerasano and Wynne-Davies (1996: 91–4); Swift (1989: 171–88). Such an approach also draws support from the clear contemporary allusions drawn in *The Countess of Mountgomerie's Urania* (Brennan 1998: 5), which drew the wrath of Edward Denny, Baron of Waltham upon her and forced the withdrawal of the book from sale.

writers, but the story is original to Wroth.[7] Wroth's pastoral world is, on the whole, positive and owes this characteristic, in large part, to female characters. In writing a pastoral play, which has an original plot, it is feasible to argue that Wroth adopted the method which is commonplace among modern writers – that she utilised material from her own experiences. Far from being simply a *roman à clef*, Wroth's play draws on a variety of behaviours and character types from the various cultural milieux in which she lived. Having set up her pastoral world, Wroth seeks to interrogate not only the cultural conventions, which were associated with the pastoral,[8] but also the prescribed behavioural modes for women of her own social standing and the literary codes which stripped women of cultural agency.

The play presents Venus and Cupid presiding over the amatory fortunes of supposedly rural shepherds and shepherdesses, plus a forester and a former shepherdess, now a chaste devotee of Diana. The play opens with Venus voicing her discontent that the inhabitants of the play-world no longer hold love in high regard and instructs Cupid to cause mischief among them, so that they will once again come to respect the power of love. For the first four acts, Wroth deals with three modes of female behaviour: performing silent wooing, professing unattainable chastity and the self-affirming communicative group. On two occasions in the play, women are instructed to place themselves in a position where they might perform to a selected audience. In 3.1, Silvesta instructs Musella how to create an audience–spectator dynamic that will prompt Philisses to declare his love. Musella says she has often been on the point of speaking to him but 'straight forbear, / Knowing it most unfit' (3.1.77–8) and Silvesta agrees 'Indeed a woman to make love is ill' (3.1.79). Nevertheless, out of this seeming compliance with the dominant cultural codes of Jacobean England, Silvesta wrests for Musella an opportunity for agency:

---

7. Nevertheless, there was no shortage of generic exemplars which Wroth may have consulted. Along with fellow playwrights Samuel Daniel *The Queen's Arcadia* and John Fletcher *The Faithful Shepherdess* she could have taken inspiration from Tasso's *L'Aminta* (1580), which was rendered into English by her aunt's client Abraham Fraunce as *The Countess of Pembroke's Ivychurch* (1591) or from Battista Guarini's *Il Pastor Fido* (1590). Lewalski points out, however, that Wroth's play differs in tone from both plays: 'Guarini's pastoral world is much darker than Tasso's, but Wroth's is lighter than either' (1993: 299).
8. Lewalski points to Wroth's departure from the conventional narrative ending into something more potentially theatrical. Following the narration of Philisses and Musella's deaths by Silvesta and Simeana in 5.5, there is 'a dramatic scene assembling all the company in the Temple of Venus for a Kommos-like finale' (1993: 204). This use of the classical Greek term also signals the inherent theatricality of this scene, which is redolent of the finale of many plays for the public theatre, when the just deserts of the characters are doled out by a presiding power.

He, poor distressed shepherd, every morn
Before the sun to our eyes new is born,
Walks in this place, and here alone doth cry
Against his life and your great cruelty.
Now, since you love so much, come here and find
Him in these woes, and show yourself but kind.

(3.1.81–6)

In 4.1, Musella duly does this and gains Philisses. In 3.2, a more assertively experienced source, Dalina, gives similar advice about dealing with men:

Let them alone, and they will seek and sue,
But yield to them and they'll with scorn pursue.
Hold awhile off, they'll kneel, nay, follow you,
And vow and swear.

(3.2.147–50)

Climeana chooses not to follow this advice and is duly rejected by Lissius. Simeana, however, remains behind when the others leave the stage, thereby placing herself before Lissius and allowing him the opportunity to speak his love. Perhaps Wroth is drawing upon the experience of herself and many more young women at court, as the decorated performers placed before a range of single men in order to catch the eye of a potential husband. Wroth first went to court in the last years of Elizabeth I and her earliest experiences, according to Rowland Whyte, were of performance and display, having 'dawnced before the Queen two galliards with one Mr Palmer, the ablest dawncer of this tyme; both were much comended by her Majestie; then she dawnced with hym a corante' (cited Waller 1993: 227). Although the match which was made for Wroth was far from a love match, perhaps she was indicating that the performance of the single woman at court can carry a personal agenda which goes beyond her apparent objectification.

The literary objectification of women, of which Petrarchanism is the supreme exemplar in the early seventeeth century, also undergoes scrutiny. Philisses, who is identified as a poet, is initially presented as silenced, unable to speak either his love to Musella or his misgivings to Lissius. The Petrarchan lover cannot communicate. When he does eventually communicate, it is because Musella has acted as a desiring subject, rather than merely a desired object. The character of Silvesta effects an insightful interrogation of the figure of the Petrarchan lady, not despite, but precisely because she remains chaste and unattainable. Throughout the play, Silvesta exhibits a great deal of personal agency, and more involvement in the development of the plot than any of the mortal characters. When Silvesta first enters (significantly before the Forester), she tells her own story in a quasi-soliloquy and her speech is the longest in the play thus far. Wroth thereby gives the audience the opportunity to see and hear Silvesta outside of the limiting gaze of the Forester. Indeed, in 2.1 the Forester's attempts to fix Silvesta within his gaze fail abjectly as she refuses to allow him to look at her, on the grounds that even this will compromise her chastity. The defeated Forester then disappears from the play until 5.6. Meanwhile, Silvesta remains within the action, first to demonstrate her knowledge of the love-game in her advice to Musella in 3.1. Silvesta also becomes Venus's ordained instrument to provide the potion that apparently kills Philisses and Musella, and then declares herself willing to undergo death as a result. In this sense, Silvesta is the true heroine of the play, offering her advice, aid and finally her life for her friends. Being the unattainable object of the Forester's affections is the least important part of Silvesta's character and is secondary to her other vital functions within the play. However much she might figure as the unattainable Petrarchan lady within the Forester's world-picture, Silvesta has an agenda, and the agency to act upon it, outside and beyond his limiting construction.

The cooperative community of women, in which Silvesta plays a key role, might also be seen to reflect the community in which many aristocratic women found themselves. Marion Wynne-Davies perhaps offers one of the most useful insights as she draws a parallel between an incident in Mary Wroth's life and an incident in the play. In Act 3, the shepherdesses find themselves alone and Dalina instigates the 'game':

> Now we're alone let everyone confess
> Truly to other what our lucks have been,
> How often like and loved, and so express
> Our passions past; shall we this sport begin?
> None can accuse us, none can us betray,
> Unless ourselves, our own selves will bewray.
>
> (3.2.21–6)

Wynne-Davies likens this to Anne Clifford's diary entry describing the sojourn of several aristocratic ladies, including Wroth herself, at Penshurst in the summer of 1617:

> Penshurst, like all familial houses functioned as a place where noble women could find pleasure in one another's company without the darker and more dangerous intrigues of the early seventeenth-century court. The picture drawn by Clifford toys with the idea of a female 'academy'; it is an image decorated with the embellishments of literary texts and toned to the liking of a companionate body of female wits.
>
> (Wynne-Davies 1998: 61)

However, rather than reading the incident in the play as a dramatised version of this very encounter, we may read it as a dramatised version of this type of encounter. The fact that the shepherdesses are alone in Act 3, perhaps indicates the extent of slippage between game-play and autobiographical narrative. Dalina suggests this as 'sport', when in fact they are relating real incidents. However, staging the stories as sport also protects the speaker from her own narrative, as the setting puts a fictional frame around her story. If the play is to be read as a *roman à clef*, then Dalina's game would also serve as a metatheatrical reference to the status of the text itself.

The second scene of Act 4 demonstrates a rift in the divine power-base, which has overseen all the action thus far. Venus is content with the outcome and feels that the lovers have suffered enough, but Cupid is not so easily satisfied:

> I mean to save them; but some yet must try
> More pain, ere they their blessings may come nigh.
> (4.2.13–14)

The priests also entreat Cupid to stop the lovers' tribulations in significantly politicised terms, delineating where beneficent rule ends and tyranny begins:

> Love, thy pow'rful hand withdraw;
> And [All] do yield unto thy law,
> Rebels, now thy subjects be,
> Bound they are who late were free. . . .
> They your images do prove,
> In them may you see great Love;
> They your mirrors, you their eyes,
> By which they true Love do spy. . . .
> Greater glory 'tis to save,
> When that you the conquest have,
> Than with tyranny to press,
> Which still makes the honour less.
> (4.2.17–20, 27–30 and 33–6)

At this point, the controlling female force in *Love's Victory* is threatened by a usurping male. Cupid's power apparently takes over from Venus's and threatens to turn the play into a tragedy. Rather than the self-affirming contests, as in 1.2, 2.1, 3.2 and 4.1, this act is centred on the staged suicide of two of the protagonists. Musella enters in 5.1 and in conversation with Simeana explains that her mother is insisting upon her marriage match with Rustic, the crude, insensitive, clown-like figure who has been the focus of much of the humour in the first four acts. This match was 'Agreed on by my father's will, which bears / Sway in her breast and duty in me' (5.1.13–14).

Philisses and Musella agree that they will sacrifice themselves to love and determine to commit suicide at the Temple of Love. In the next two brief scenes, the other shepherds and shepherdesses meet up to consider the news of Musella's impending marriage. In 5.2 Dalina vaguely implicates Arcas in the destructive turn of events, and it turns out, upon the confession of Musella's mother in 5.5, that:

> Arcas first plotted it with skilful art,
> To ruin me and, living, eat my heart;
> He told me that Musella wantonly
> Did seek Philisses' love. Alas, only
> The speech of that did inly wound me so,
> As stay I could not, nor the time let go.
> But sent for her and forced her to consent.
>
> (5.5.126–32)

Fortunately, the pair are not really dead. Just as Musella is about to stab herself in 5.3, Silvesta intervenes and offers the lovers a potion which apparently kills them. She knows that this means death for herself, and in the final scene, as all the characters gather around the bodies of Philisses and Musella at the Temple of Love, she is condemned. This allows the Forester, who enters having been woken by a dream in which he sees Silvesta burned at the stake, to offer his life for hers and thus demonstrate the depth of his love. Rustic disclaims all rights to Musella, now that she is dead, which allows for the final miracle, the revival of Musella and Philisses. Venus reveals that she has orchestrated the happy ending, which, in her opinion, has been too long in coming:

> Lovers be not amazed! This is my deed,
> Who could not suffer your dear hearts to bleed. . . .
> Then, all rejoice, and with a loving song
> Conclude the joy hath been kept down too long.
>
> (5.7.67–8 and 73–4)

Cupid is curiously silent throughout the entire denouement, apart from one brief speech:

> Now my wars in love hath end,
> Each one here enjoys their friend;
> And so all shall henceforth say
> Who my laws will still obey.
> Mother, now judge Arcas' fault,
> All things else your will hath wrought.
>
> (5.7.135–40)

Throughout the entire play we have been told that Cupid will cause mischief among the lovers, although the text never actually shows the character engaged in this type of action. While it is possible to assume, and even imagine in staging, Cupid aiming his bow at Philisses and Lissius, his precise role in Simeana's jealousy is more difficult to determine. This seems to be the responsibility of Arcas, which suggests that Arcas is an agent of Cupid. Such a reading would also explain Cupid's promised disruptions of Act 5, though it is Arcas who acts as the villainous troublemaker. If the relationship between Cupid and Arcas is one of master and servant, or power and agent, then Arcas is made the scapegoat for Cupid's machinations, allowing Cupid's stature as a divine being to remain uncompromised. This treachery between male figures would stand in contrast to an unlikely, yet vital, alliance between female figures. Venus chooses the devotee of her natural opposite, Diana, as the agent of her beneficent interference, and happily shares the glory with her:

> Silvesta was my instrument ordained
> To kill, and save her friends, by which sh' hath gained
> Immortal fame, and bands of firmest love
> In their kind breasts where true affections move.
>
> (5.7.71–4)

The unlikeliness of the alliance between Silvesta and Venus is underscored by the fact that Silvesta remains a chaste devotee of Diana and does not complete the set of happy couples by requiting the Forester's love. The text thereby signals chastity as one of a range of positive life-choices for women, alongside the various partnerships embarked upon by the other women characters.

When comparing *The Tragedy of Mariam* with *Love's Victory*, Naomi Miller makes the implicitly unfavourable analysis that 'the varied voices of Cary's female characters are framed by the experience of male tyranny, [whereas] Wroth extends the opportunity for her female characters to find voices of their own with reference to a wider range of gender relations than appear in Cary's play' (1996: 52). However, Miller does not pay due attention to the difference in genre between the two plays. *The Tragedy of Mariam* is grounded in harsh realities, being a dramatisation of historical events; *Love's Victory* plays with the comedic possibilities of a fictional world that rejects and defeats the intrusion of patriarchal oppression. Yet Miller's analysis is valuable in that it indicates the change in focus of dramatic production by women throughout the period. What is especially characteristic, and for our purposes significant, about the dramatic production by women in the early seventeenth century was the manner in which the construction of feminine power changed. It is possible to detect a shift in focus away from the aristocratic woman identifying herself in relation to a man and/or to values ideologically constructed as masculine. Towards the middle of the period, the dramatic activities begin to demonstrate women identifying themselves in relation to a variety of others, both male and female, and, perhaps more significantly, beginning to evolve a sense of an empowered feminine self. At the beginning of the seventeenth century, women were identified in relation to men in practical and ideological ways. If a woman were to claim any value for herself, it had to be in terms that were, in the seventeenth century, gendered masculine. The culturally feminine virtues (chastity, silence and obedience) were passive, the first being notoriously hard to prove, and the latter two being completely at odds with the social, economic and political power held by royal and aristocratic women. What we find throughout women's dramatic activity in the early seventeenth century is an initial seizing of masculine prerogative, followed by a gradual shift towards the validation of feminine virtues and values on equal terms with masculine virtues. Silence and obedience are rejected as appropriate feminine virtues and chastity is reclaimed as a chosen, rather than imposed state. Chastity, once dramatised as a threat to be enforced, is recreated as an opportunity for self-determination, either as a single woman or as an equal partner in a chaste marriage. Erica Veevers draws particular attention to Peter Paul Rubens's allegorical painting (1629–30) of Charles I as St George rescuing Henrietta Maria (1989: 186–90), making the very significant observation that Henrietta Maria is actually the focal point of the painting. A comparison of this image of Henrietta Maria with Paul Van Somer's portrait of Anna (1617) epitomises the movements effected in women's dramatic activity in the early Stuart period. As Orgel notes, Anna appropriates masculine modes of dress (1996: 84) and claims a share in James's favourite activity, hunting. Yet the image also has associations with the chaste and autonomous goddess Diana and in so doing, signifies self-sufficiency. By being pictured with her husband, Henrietta Maria is deliberately and distinctively gendered female, her beauty offsetting Charles's martial prowess and it is she, not he, who takes centre-stage.

CHAPTER 3

'Upon the World's Stage': The Civil War and Interregnum

ALISON FINDLAY

On 2 September 1642, Parliament ordered the closure of public theatres because stage plays or 'Spectacles of Pleasure, too commonly expressing lascivious Mirth and Levity' seemed out of joint with 'the distracted Estate of England, threatened with a Cloud of Blood by a Civil War'. The population should turn to solemn 'Repentance, Reconciliation, and Peace with God' while 'these sad causes and set Times of Humiliation so continue' so as to return the land to peace and prosperity (Firth and Rait 1911: 26–7). The legal closure of the public playhouses did not mean a cessation of dramatic activity, however. Dale Randall (1995) and Susan Wiseman (1998) have pointed out that professional playwrights and performers continued to stage entertainments through the years 1642–60. The sense of these 18 years as a *tabula rasa*, an empty stage awaiting the entrance of Restoration theatre, is partly the creation of literary critics with limited ideas of what constitutes drama. Such an exclusive viewpoint was, ironically, fostered by some seventeenth-century practitioners who were anxious to mask their own contributions to culture under the protectorate when the Restoration heralded a new beginning (Potter 1989: xi). During the troubled years of the English Civil War and its aftermath, theatre, like other fundamental elements of English society, suffered a tempestuous sea change rather than extinction. As with government and religion, the events of these years produced dramatic fragmentation and reconstitutions.

Undoubtedly the closing of the public theatres curtailed a rich theatrical tradition, but from women's point of view, the loss had the advantage of creating a newly-levelled playing field. Men and women were now equally excluded from the commercial stage; in an environment in which drama became increasingly self-politicised, other 'private' and non-official playing arenas offered alternative theatres of war. The ways in which women

participated as authors, directors, actors and protesters in various performances and rituals suggests that they understood the power of drama as
a means of self-presentation or persuasion. This chapter will examine a
selection of different theatrical 'texts', ranging from scripts written by noblewomen to religious and political demonstrations and personal testimonies,
in order to argue that drama was used strategically, and self-consciously by
women from across the political spectrum.

Drama has often been categorised as a specifically royalist form. The
reason it carries such strong associations during the Civil War period can
be partly attributed to the continuity of private performances in aristocratic
homes, which maintained an easily recognisable form of theatre. Sometimes
professional (male) companies were invited to give performances to the
gentry; James Wright reports that 'in *Oliver*'s time, they used to Act privately,
three or four Miles, or more, out of Town, now here, now there, sometimes
in Noblemens Houses' (Wright 1699: 9). In nostalgic revivals of professional
plays, women could draw on a tradition of household performance to take
the parts previously played by boys. On 10 July 1654, for example, Dorothy
Osborne writes to William Temple informing him of the large company of
people assembled at her father's house, 'the most filled of any since the Arke'
and tells him 'They will have me Act my Part in a Play, the Lost Lady it is,
and I am she[,] pray God it bee not an ill Omen' (Osborne 1987: 206). The
play to be staged in this amateur performance is Sir William Berkeley's *The
Lost Lady*, first presented in 1638 by the King's Men at Blackfriars (Berkeley
1987). Dorothy Osborne (1627–94/5) regards playing the lead as a dramatisation of her own apparently hopeless romantic attachment to Temple,
fearful that all would be lost. Perhaps the tragicomic ending, where the hero
discovers that his lady is still alive, encouraged her to imagine a more hopeful
future. In fact Dorothy and William married on Christmas Day in 1654.

Romance, pastoral and tragicomedy, especially in their dramatic forms,
were literary genres that 'belonged specifically to the royalists', Lois Potter
has argued (1989: 74). In the two dramatic scripts of the sisters Jane
Cavendish (1621–69) and Elizabeth Brackley (1626–63) these forms are used
to explore female responses to the traumatic experiences of the English Civil
War. Cavendish and Brackley were the daughters of William Cavendish,
leader of the royalist army in the north of England until the defeat at
Marston Moor in 1644, when he went into exile on the continent. Since his
first wife, Elizabeth Bassett, died in 1643, his daughters Jane, Elizabeth and
Frances were left in charge of managing his estates at Welbeck Abbey and
Bolsover Castle, which were besieged and taken by the parliamentary forces
(Starr 1931).

In their father's absence, probably in 1644–5, Jane and Elizabeth composed *A Pastorall* and a play, *The Concealed Fancies*, which were included in a

handsome manuscript presentation volume (Cavendish and Brackley *c.* 1645). Even though the scripts were unpublished and were obviously intended for a limited coterie audience, that of the Cavendish family circle, there is nothing self-effacing about them. Margaret Ezell points out 'the women had no desire to hide their literary accomplishments', but saw themselves as active participants in the literary and dramatic circle headed by their father. William was a noted literary patron who encouraged all his children, male and female, to write. He had authored or co-authored several plays himself and commissioned entertainments to be performed at his family homes, so his daughters' choice of dramatic genre is not surprising (Ezell 1998: 248-9). We have no evidence to prove that either of Jane and Elizabeth's co-authored texts were performed although, as I have argued, there is strong internal evidence to suggest they wrote with multi-dimensional performance in mind and expected their audience to appreciate the theatrical effects built into the scripts (Findlay, Hodgson-Wright and Williams 1999a and 1999b).

In *A Pastorall,* Cavendish and Brackley appropriate a recognised royalist genre to dramatise the sufferings caused by the Civil War. In spite of its idyllic dream of withdrawal to a simple Arcadian world, pastoral was a highly politicised form (Patterson 1987). During the Civil War, pastorals looked back nostalgically to the royalist illusion fostered by entertainments like Montagu's *The Shepherds' Paradise* and its subsequent destruction under parliamentary rule (Randall 1995: 187-9). Jane Cavendish and Elizabeth Brackley's entertainment personalises the tragedy of a threatened pastoral territory. The authors rewrite the conventional masque form to enact their sense of loss at the absence of their exiled father and brothers. The script is built round a tension between the protagonists' desire for withdrawal, typical of pastoral, and their inability to escape the harsh realities of the war. *A Pastorall* opens with prologues by each author to the all-important father figure, William Cavendish, whose presence or absence in the text functions like that of the monarch at a masque. A theatrical dimension is indicated by Jane's request to 'Give leave now to rehearse; / A Pastorall.' She assures Cavendish that with his approval ''twill ne're decay', initiating a thread of imagery connecting the landscape, the daughters, and their creative efforts (Cavendish and Brackley *c.* 1645: 49).

The two antemasques represent the chaos of the Civil War in metaphysical and then local terms. The first, by Jane, presents five witches to symbolise the atmosphere of danger. The three speaking roles, Hag, Bell (probably Belladonna) and the younger Prentice, express delight in the inversion of normal family bonds where all kindred 'hath their devisions of hatred' (52). Witchcraft was often blamed as a supernatural cause of the Civil War in ballads and broadsheets, but in adopting the trope, Jane

Cavendish ironically mocks such scapegoating. Unlike the weird sisters in *Macbeth*, these witches are feminised and subjugated figures, keenly aware of their status. Prentice comments 'wee are but the people that's talked on, to serve others designes, and our pride to our selves makes us thinke wee are Actours' (52). The lines draw attention to women's symbolic role in the war, their exclusion from the armies in which their fathers, brothers (or husbands) fought. If the *Pastorall* was written for Jane, Elizabeth and their younger sister Frances to perform, as seems likely, the irony is all the more pointed. It is only as 'Actours' and writers that the Cavendish sisters can intervene. The witches celebrate 'how hansomely wee tye Ladyes Tongues' (53), but the play allows those ladies an opportunity to express their experience of war.

The second antemasque, by Elizabeth, shifts to a concrete perspective on the war, again introduced through female figures. The country wife Gossip Pratt explains to Naunt Henn how she has smuggled a pig into the captured aristocratic household, and sent it to the lord's daughters imprisoned there (an obvious parallel to the authors' own situations). The daughters are invited to lift up the pig's tail to find it farting (58), a piece of obscenity which seems odd since Gossip Pratt is obviously a royalist sympathiser. The crude gesture disguises a sophisticated coded communication, however, since porcine terminology was used to describe penthouses used in siege warfare (Gravett 1990: 32).[1] In the English Civil War, where siege artillery played a considerable role (Blackmore 1990: 82), William Chillingworth built wooden siege towers known as 'sows' because of the soldiers' legs hanging down like teats (Carlton 1992: 158). Priam Davies, a parliamentary captain who defended Brampton Bryan, noted 'those engines of war which the enemy had prepared to undermine us. They termed them "hoggs"' (Historical Manuscripts Commission 1904: 27). Gossip Pratt seems to be using the code to inform the ladies of some impending royalist military action. Cavendish and Brackley draw on it to amuse a knowing coterie of friends, their intended audience. Although women appear to be confined to the domestic arena of food provision, they perform a vital role in communications, the play suggests.

The localised effects of the Civil War are explored in a conversation with Goodman Rye and Goodman Hay, who bring news of the arrival of satyrs in the district. The country wives are apprehensive about their crops and livestock, but the men characterise the satyrs as 'very loveing people' who 'understand not that phrase Plunder' (59). They are to be welcomed as friends, 'though they take our kine & sheepe from us', says Gossip Pratt

---

1. I am grateful to Gillian Waters and Chris Gravett of the Royal Armouries for their help with this point.

(59). The curious identification of royalist troops with satyrs suggests that Cavendish and Brackley, and their intended audience, were familiar with an earlier anonymous pastoral, *Time's Distractions* (*c.* 1643). In *Time's Distractions*, the 'rugged satyrs' capture the monster Danger, and are commanded by Juno to 'triumph over Danger in your dances' so that the goddess can restore 'peace and happiness' to Arcadia (*Time's Distractions* 1976: l.785–97). If Cavendish and Brackley or one of their family did not write this anonymous play, then they may have seen it in manuscript, passed from one royalist household to another, or in a domestic performance.

Unlike *Time's Distractions*, Cavendish and Brackley's *Pastorall* does not end optimistically. At the end of the second antemasque the country folk join 'in a songe of all our losses' (60), contrasting sharply with the usual pastoral landscape of plenitude. The masque scenes continue the theme. Cavendish and Brackley recreate themselves and their sister Frances in the persons of three shepherdesses, Innocence (Jane), Chastity (Elizabeth) and Ver or Spring (Frances), but adapt the form to create a deliberately failed pastoral. Throughout the drama, these heroines practise an extended process of reversed anthropomorphism, identifying with the landscape as though they wish to efface themselves in its various features. The shepherdess Prologue introduces a feminised terrain of which she and her sisters are part:

> We're now become a fine coule [cool] shady walke
> Soe fit to answeare Lovers in their talke
> And if sad Soules would mallencholly tell
> Let them then come, to visitt, where wee dwell
> For wee're become a fine thick Grove of thought
> Soe fresco even our selves with teares full fraught . . .
> And this our Groto; soe who lookes may have
> A welcome to a sad Shee Hermetts Cave.
>
> (65)

The identification of woman as territory was a common feature of courtship literature, most famously in Donne's 'Elegy: To his Mistress Going to Bed' where she is 'my America, my new found land', to be explored and colonised by the lover (Donne 1990: 13). In the cases of heiresses the metaphor often took concrete form since their dowries involved the transfer of estates. Cavendish and Brackley simultaneously adopt and defy the convention, maintaining the sexual innuendo behind geographical features like 'thick Grove' and 'Groto', while taking a firmly anti-romantic stance. Innocence tells her shepherd suitor 'I dedicate my selfe to each sweete feild / For to your Sex I'm very loth to yeild' (68). The shepherdesses are determined to retain control of the pastoral landscape and their bodies, just as the authors mould the genre to suit their own purposes.

The shepherdesses' rural duties are rewritten as expressions of grief for the absence of the Cavendish sisters' exiled family. Innocence and Chastity are dressed in garments of 'pure white' (66), the colour of the uniforms of William Cavendish's troops, and they model themselves on their sheep as icons of suffering. Retreat to the pastoral world is therefore a withdrawal to religious sanctuary, to pray and mourn, rather than a carefree escape to romance. The heroines dedicate themselves to the loyal love of their father and brothers. The young Ver (Frances) can only listen to the birds, hoping for an end to her sadness (71), while Chastity, a 'shee Priest' (73), remains icily chaste even though she is married. Her suitor complains 'You owne your selfe to bee a wife / And yet you practice not that life' (73). Elizabeth Brackley probably wrote this part for herself since she was married to John Egerton before the Civil War, but was 'too young to be bedded', according to Margaret Cavendish (1872: 123–4). Chastity gives voice to the helplessness undoubtedly felt by some wives and daughters left behind as their men went to fight:

> I'm now bicome a Bracken, branch & stalke
> Soe sadnes dim recrutes mee to a walke
> Thus joyed news did pensell mee with sweete greene
> But now not soe griefe shal bee all my Queene.
>
> (73)

As these lines show, the landscape of Cavendish and Brackley's *Pastorall* is barren. The heroines' emotions arrest the natural seasonal pattern; the untimely withering of royalist family life is presented as the freezing of female fertility. Ironically, the sisters' own dramatic endeavours are the result of an uncreating and uncreative process. Innocence claims her father's absence 'makes a Chaos sure of me' (77), and Chastity's song laments 'The Winter of a Summers coulder yeare' (67). She retreats to the Temple of Love with Innocence and Ver, to rehearse their daily anthem of grief. The grotto, so suggestive of female sexuality, has been transformed into a convent of chastity. The sisters are confined to a winter of discontent and only a miraculous return of the family can release them from the icy grip of this emotional paralysis: 'Our Summer is, if that could bee / Father, Brothers, for to see' (78).

The *Pastorall* refuses to grant such a release. The shepherd suitors take on a feminised quality themselves as their attempts to win their mistresses prove fruitless and they collapse in a 'Hee cave' or 'could Groto' (79). The arrival of a fourth shepherd named Freedom seems to promise a happy resolution. He is admitted to the female grotto and advised by Chastity on how to conduct his wooing (80–1). Her view that he should woo briefly rather than formally is echoed by the heroines of *The Concealed Fancies*, so possibly Jane and Elizabeth took this opportunity to communicate their preferences to their romantic partners. In spite of Freedom's willingness to learn, the deadlock caused by the wider context of Civil War cannot be broken. He persuades the shepherds and a fourth shepherdess called Jearer to take part in a dance with 'Country Lasses' (82), but the sister-protagonists refuse to join the celebrations. The shepherd Careless points out their reasons:

> Now could wee[,] Ladies[,] have but such a dance
> That would but fetch your freinds now out of Fraunce
> You then would well approve of this our mirth
> But since not soe, you doe appeare sad Earth.
>
> (83)

These concluding remarks underline the identification of the shepherdesses and the Cavendish sisters with a failed pastoral. As disapproving observers, they point up the absence of the central figure: their father. This household entertainment deliberately frustrates the court masque's pattern of harmonious resolution, where the royal spectator joined in the final dance. Without William Cavendish to dance, there is no festive ending, no hope of romance in the future. The entrance to the grotto will remain firmly shut. In an epilogue Jane tells her father:

> My Lord it is your absence makes each see
> For want of you what I'm reduc'd to bee
> Captive or Shepherdesses life.
>
> (84)

Cavendish and Brackley depict themselves as trapped within the masque, just as they were captives in the Cavendish homes. Without the presence of a paternal spectator, they are unable to cross the boundary from the fictional roles of chaste retirement they have created for themselves.

Their play *The Concealed Fancies* offers a more optimistic resolution to their problems. Its semi-autobiographical nature is made explicit since the identities of heroines, actors and authors are self-consciously elided. Attention is immediately drawn to the female performer in the first prologue which begins 'Ladies, I beseech you blush not to see / That I speak a prologue, being a she' (Cavendish and Brackley 1996: Prologue 1–2). Such a spectacle is to be approved rather than reprehended, the prologue asserts, going on to suggest that female authorship in 'our new play' also 'become[s] a woman's wit' (Prologue 8). Scripting, directing and performing the drama gives Cavendish and Brackley a fantastic control of events, which was largely denied them in real life, especially when their two family homes were over-taken by the enemy.

Welbeck Abbey was captured on 2 August 1644 by the Earl of Manchester who reported 'Newcastle's daughters, and the rest of his children and family are in it, unto whom I have engaged myself for their quiet abode there' (Starr 1931: 803). Ten days later, Colonel Muschamp's royalist troops were forced to surrender Bolsover Castle, leaving behind 'six pieces of ordnance and three hundred firearms' (Faulkner 1985: 42). On 17 April 1645, Jane and Frances wrote to Lord Fairfax from Bolsover, appealing for it to be disgarrisoned, but to no avail (Starr 1931: 804). Welbeck Abbey fared slightly better, being briefly recaptured by Colonel Fretchville and Major Jammot in July 1645, but it was under parliamentary control again by November.

Unsurprisingly, *The Concealed Fancies* is full of military references. The two household settings imply the two Cavendish homes, both ruled by Lord Calsindow, who is obviously meant to represent the authors' father. The first house, occupied by the sisters Luceny and Tattiney, is under royalist control, but the Castle of Ballamo is taken by the parliamentarians. The Ballamo plot opens with a discussion of the royalists' floundering attempts to defend the castle (3.1.1–37). The servants Mr Friendly, Mr Proper and Mr Divinity seem to be based on Mr Whitehead, Mr Butler and Mr Bamford, members of the Cavendish household whose behaviour is caricatured in a poem by Jane (Cavendish and Brackley *c.* 1645: 23), while the 'old man' (3.1.6) in charge of the defence is a dramatic sketch of Major Jammot. The representation of the very people with whom the authors were besieged lends a note of documentary realism to the play; the gentle mockery of these figures serves as a form of comfort and amusement in the face of defeat at Welbeck Abbey.

In the two parallel plots, Cavendish and Brackley explore the opportunities and restrictions that the war offered to noble or gentle women. The authors cast themselves as controlling figures in the roles of Luceny (Jane) and Tattiney (Elizabeth), whereas in the Ballamo plot, they give a different image of themselves and their sister Frances, in the parts of Cicelly (Elizabeth), Sh. (Jane) and Is. (Frances). The three cousins, whose names are never given in fuller form in the manuscript, are apparently helpless when their castle falls under the parliamentary siege. Nevertheless, the passive image of woman is challenged in scenes where Sh. and Cicelly make fun of the roles they are expected to play:

Sh. Pray, how did I look in the posture of a delinquent?

Cicelly. You mean how did you behave yourself in the posture of a delinquent? Faith, as though you thought the scene would change again, and you would be happy though you suffered misery for a time.

(3.4.4–10)

The exchange pinpoints a significant difference between woman as object to be looked at, and as self-conscious, role-playing subject. While at the mercy of their captors, Sh. and Cicelly deliberately theatricalise their status as victims. Sh. remarks that she has 'practised Cleopatra when she was in her captivity' (3.4.13–14) and would rehearse the role again if the parliamentary commander determined to lead her in triumph. Rather than playing in a 'gallant tragedy' (3.4.17) by a man, she anticipates an alternative script of royalist victory, a fantasy which *The Concealed Fancies* itself will become. The metatheatrical dimension is all the more resonant if we imagine these lines being spoken by Cavendish and Brackley in performance. Authors as well as actors, they advertise their power to change the scene according to their will instead of following a military scenario determined by men.

Paradoxically, the female protagonists enjoy an unprecedented freedom even when they are confined within their homes. In their father's absence, they are responsible for running the households. The cousins at Ballamo take the opportunity to break into his locked cabinets and plunder the fruit and cordials stored there. They discuss their raids like military commanders; Sh. telling Cicelly 'this day shall be yours, and tomorrow mine' (3.4.67–8), where she will lead a campaign to break into her father's 'magazine of love' (3.4.73). The cousins' liberty contrasts with the imprisonment of two royalist prisoners, Action and Moderate, who complain bitterly about their loss of property and their confinement (3.6). Conventional gender positions are reversed in the portraits of busy female characters, and frustratedly passive men.

The play registers the new-found status many noblewomen enjoyed as commanders of the little commonwealth in their menfolk's absences. In defending their homes, women of both warring factions exercised 'masculine' strength, sometimes even intervening physically in military action (Carlton 1992: 165–6). At the same time, they exploited their position as the weaker vessel for tactical purposes. For example, Lady Brilliana Harley, besieged in Brampton Bryan in Herefordshire, told Sir William Vavasour that she could not possibly surrender it without the permission of her husband. However, Priam Davies reported that she 'commanded in chief, I may truly say with such a masculine bravery, both for religion, resolution, wisdom, and warlike policy, that her equal I never yet saw' (Eales 1990: 171–3). The Cavendish sisters advertise such female policy in the figures of the cousins, who deliberately overplay their expected roles as helpless victims in juxtaposition with a celebration of their freedom. When the siege is lifted, they sing joyously about being 'at liberty' (5.1.3) and resolve not to think 'of duty' (5.1.7) even though they will be married. They are rescued by their suitors in traditional romantic fashion. However, when the Stellow brothers burst in to save Sh. and Cicelly, their exaggerated account of their sufferings 'in hell' (5.1.10) sounds humorously hollow to an audience who have witnessed the fun they have had as prisoners. The Stellows become the unwitting victims of a private joke as the women undercut their status as conquering heroes.

When we consider the autobiographical quality of the play, the overlap between the two households gives a curiously introverted tenor to the rescue. The siege at Ballamo is lifted by a military attack from the other Cavendish household led by Colonel Free (probably based on Colonel Fretchville). Since the Stellows are brothers to Luceny and Tattiney, Cavendish and Brackley effectively depict themselves as being saved by their own brothers. The betrothals between the Stellows and Cicelly and Sh. present an introverted image of family love and loyalty, rather like that which concludes *A Pastorall*. It is as though Cavendish and Brackley cannot think or love beyond their immediate family while imprisoned in their homes with their father and brothers in exile.

The main romantic plot re-enacts the military skirmishes as a battle of wits between the sexes. Although Wiseman cautions that we cannot view the Cavendish family dramas as the basis 'for a full argument about women's acting' in the 1640s and 50s (1998: 96), the play shows its authors' consciousness of the Civil War period as a turning point, what Trubowitz calls 'a transforming, if embattled, moment in the history of gender relations' (1992: 129). Luceny and Tattiney determine to remain mistresses of themselves as they are wooed, betrothed and married to Courtley and Presumption. The suitors' wish to subjugate their wives is parried by the heroines using a variety of techniques. Their servant Pert remarks 'this lady that I mean will have her several scenes, now wife, then mistress, then my sweet Platonic soul, and then write in the like several changes of mistress, not only to confirm love, but provoke love' (4.5.55–9). The plot advertises its heroines' abilities to manage relations with men; and behind that, the Cavendish sisters' own skill, as writers and performers, to manipulate events on stage and in the household beyond.

First, Luceny and Tattiney mock the artificial poses adopted by their suitors. Luceny complains that she has been besieged in her chamber by Courtley and when he begs a ribbon, she retorts 'I thought you had learned better manners than to offer to plunder me of my favours' (1.4.95). Her military imagery highlights the savage nature of courtly love discourse in which the lady is reduced to a material object like a castle, to be conquered by a supposedly suppliant wooer. Discourse of love and war is intertwined again in Act 2 Scene 1 where Corpolant, another suitor to Luceny, is mocked for his incompetence. He plans to win Luceny's hand by negotiating with Colonel Free, her cousin and then her father; then turns to advise

Free to 'correspond' or negotiate with the enemy who have taken Ballamo (2.1.78). Corpolant's belief that marriage, like military operations, can be arranged exclusively between men and that Luceny's love can be bought, shows complete indifference to her feelings. As one might expect, Cavendish and Brackley's script challenges such male-centred attitudes. The grotesque nature of arranged marriages to unattractive, worldly men is figured in Corpolant, whom Luceny ridicules in an insulting song, calling him a fool, 'an ugly sot' and 'a clog of dun[g]' (2.3.70–93). At the end of the play, Corpolant is appropriately matched to the socially ambitious Lady Tranquillity, who has been trying to promote herself as a bride for Lord Calsindow. Like Corpolant, Lady Tranquillity is a comic figure, possibly a parodic portrait of the Cavendish sisters' stepmother-to-be, Margaret Lucas.

It is the absence of Lord Calsindow that allows Luceny and Tattiney the freedom to negotiate with their suitors. In seventeenth-century England, a considerable number of women arranged marriages themselves in families where the father or menfolk were absent, a situation that obviously became more common during the years of civil war (Ezell 1987: 17–34). The numerous metatheatrical references in *The Concealed Fancies* suggest that its authors used the dramatic form to advertise their own autonomy, as self-fashioning subjects rather than passive objects of male desire.

To escape from their suitors, Luceny and Tattiney retire to a convent like the shepherdesses in *A Pastorall*, vowing to mourn their 'dear and absent friends' (4.1.52) who are in exile 'in a far country' (4.1.13). The 'sacred church' (4.1.49) setting probably draws on the history of Welbeck Abbey, which had been a premonstratensian monastery. The reference to a 'holy stone' or altar (4.2.21) suggests that the authors designed this scene for the house chapel at Welbeck, perhaps replaying their prayers for the safe return of their father as part of a domestic performance there. Sexual and national politics are neatly intertwined in this act where Courtley and Presumption invade the nunnery disguised as two poor men and complain that they have been rejected by their mistresses (Findlay 1998: 262–4). Their idea of love as a romantic conquest is contrasted with the loyal love of two poor women for their exiled 'friends'. Luceny pointedly counsels the men to 'grow wiser' (4.1.8) and 'whip your folly away' (4.1.18), while she sympathises with the women, giving one a 'bow of hope' (4.1.15) and the other a laurel 'as a promising hope of conquest' (4.2.20). It is not just a royalist victory that is imagined here, but a triumph of female wit over the patriarchal dominance prescribed by Presumption as the recipe for a successful marriage (3.3.7–44). Unsurprisingly, when Courtley and Presumption remove their disguises, their protestations of love are firmly rejected by the heroines.

In the resolution of the romantic plot, theatre creates a space for royalist victory, traditional male supremacy, and yet also allows the heroines to triumph in the battle of wits. Courtley and Presumption finally win their mistresses by styling themselves as gods who bring back Lord Calsindow from exile. Cavendish and Brackley seem to announce to interested parties that only a miraculous restoration of their father could bring them out of their cloistered grief to contemplate romantic love and marriage. The play moves into the realm of fantastic spectacle typical of the court masque, as Lord Calsindow returns to command his household and give his daughters away. The appearance of an angel in Act 3 to save the heroines from suicide and despair prepares for the miraculous conclusion. Cavendish and Brackley employ supernatural elements in a highly sophisticated way, however. On one hand, the authors' and the heroines' deepest desires are tied into a rigidly patriarchal framework. The magical restoration of Lord Calsindow to the household carries with it a royalist ideology in which the figures of father, king and husband are celebrated as divinely appointed commanders in the microcosm of the home and the macrocosm of the kingdom. Calsindow's return is dependent on an imagined royalist victory and the price to pay is the elevation of Courtley and Presumption to god-like status, each as a *deus ex machina* who can bring peace and happiness.

The heroines' proto-feminist ideals cannot easily be reconciled with such absolutism. Cavendish and Brackley use theatre to negotiate a path through the network of conservative and radical principles to which they, their heroines and their household adhere. The self-conscious theatricality of the masque ending undermines the image of male supremacy. It is too fantastic; Luceny and Tattiney doubt what they see, asking their suitors 'are you god-cheaters?' (5.4.9) and implying that the authority of their husbands-to-be is no more substantial than the costumes they have donned for the occasion. Domestic performance conditions, where resources would presumably have been limited, would have heightened the potential for subversive parody. Indeed, Cavendish and Brackley may have deliberately exploited the limitations of their own production in order to give a deliberately ironic picture of the husband as a divine commander (Findlay 1998: 264–5). Luceny and Tattiney do not internalise the idea of female inferiority or subjugation. Far from regarding their husbands as gods, they remain true to their ideal of being mistresses of themselves.

Performance is a tool that allows them to pay lip service to conventional gender roles when it suits them, while outwitting their partners and asserting their own wills. The heroines' acting skills expose a gap between the model of wifely submission and the reality of relations between the sexes. The circumstances of war, in which noblewomen were often obliged to take on more 'masculine' forms of behaviour in their houses, widened this gap. Cavendish and Brackley's play pushes the process one stage further by deliberately theatricalising male dominance and female subjection as a form of mimicry, an insubstantial performance (Findlay 1999b). On her wedding morning, Luceny prepares for marriage by contemplating an image of herself in her mirror and revealing how she plans to mimic obedience to her husband. Her song summarises the heroines' constant rejection of attempts to subjugate them. Instead of becoming silent images, they will shift in and out of the wifely frame as mischievous performers, to fool the men who try to dominate them:

> *Luceny [Sings].* Now do I view myself by all so looked upon,
> And thus men whispering say, 'faith, she's already gone,
> For wit or mirth I plainly see,
> That she a wife will be.'
> 'No sir,' say I 'a wit above
> Is Hymen's monkey love.'
>
> (5.4.12–17)[2]

Luceny determines to 'appear' a wife 'in show' (5.5.3), reproducing the behaviour expected of her like a performing monkey. In their first epilogue, Luceny and Tattiney recount the success of such a technique, its power to replace an ideology which claims 'husbands are the rod of authority' with the ideal of 'an equal marriage' (Epilogue 85–8). In *The Concealed Fancies* theatre itself, especially heightened artificial forms like song and masque, allows Cavendish and Brackley to replay conservative royalist traditions and simultaneously to embrace the new possibilities for female autonomy offered by the Civil War context.

The musical elements of *The Concealed Fancies* look forward to other entertainments in which well-born women were involved. On the continent, Henrietta Maria and Prince Charles strove to maintain a tradition of theatrical activities in spite of severely limited financial resources. *The Nuptialls of Peleus and Thetis* (1654) was acted in Paris six times with Princess Henriette Anne (*b.* 1644) taking the role of Erato. In true royalist tradition, the princess declared:

> . . . he who loudly would complain
> of *Princes* falls and *Peoples* raign,
> Of angry starrs, and destiny,
> Let him but cast his eyes on me.
>
> (Howell 1654: A4v)

---

2. I have added speech marks to clarify the opposition between male and female voices which Luceny quotes here.

Erato, the muse of mimic imitation, introduces an ironic note on the displaced English monarchy who are reduced to performing authority on the stage. The text points out that the part 'fell to her by lott' (A4v), but it may have had subversive effect in performance, like the use of mimicry in *The Concealed Fancies*. Erato's lines immediately follow Apollo's arrogant declaration that no queen or muse would refuse his love. As the muse of mimicry, Henriette implicitly hints at the performative nature of female subservience. The English edition of the play, translated by James Howell, was dedicated to Katherine, Marchioness of Dorchester and published just after Cromwell was made Lord Protector. Such timing demonstrates, as Randall remarks, a remarkable freedom of expression for royalist sympathies during the protectorate (1995: 169). In England, the tradition of household performance was kept alive in two operatic entertainments by Davenant. Mrs Coleman, wife of the actor Edward Coleman, sung in the chorus of *The First Day's Entertainment at Rutland* (1656) along with another woman; in *The Siege at Rhodes* (1656), Mrs Coleman sang the role of Ianthe and another, unnamed woman was employed to play Roxana. Both pieces were performed at Davenant's home, Rutland House, but since he charged admission to the shows, the appearance of the women moves a stage closer to the introduction of the professional actress in 1660 (Randall 1995: 170–1). As Michel Adam notes, though, the lines between amateur and professional are especially difficult to establish in this period (Adam 1993: 31).

The large country house was not the only arena in which women were able to take an active part in dramatic productions during the years 1642–60. The closing of the public theatres can be seen as an opening of other public spaces for performance and a democratisation of dramatic activity. Women as well as men took advantage of opportunities to represent themselves in public speech and spectacle, from religious or political platforms. As Susan Wiseman points out, 'some radical and many critical stances were, indeed, compatible with and expressed in the dramatic structures usually seen as the property of "royalists"' (1998: 41). The proliferation of theatre into these non-official arenas – in the streets or market place, in places of worship or in the courtroom – gave women space and time to express ideas which were often radical.

The growth of religious sects in the Civil War and Interregnum opened an important platform to women. Female preaching was an activity that seemed to contradict Scripture (I Corinthians 14: 34–6), yet separatist churches allowed figures like Katherine Chidley (a Leveller) and Mrs Attaway (a General Baptist) to make a name for themselves by addressing congregations that were sometimes reportedly as large as those who had attended the theatres. Unsurprisingly, the sectaries' meetings were criticised in exactly the same terms as the theatres by more mainstream Puritans. Thomas

Edwards' *Gangraena* (1646) commented 'In their Ch[urch] meetings and Exercises there is such a confusion and noise, as it were at a Play' (Edwards 1977: 92). Women preachers were the focus of intense public curiosity, sometimes arousing the same contempt as actors.[3] In *The Old and Good Way Vindicated* (1645), for example, Elizabeth Warren complained of those who 'intrude into this weighty work, having neither due calling, nor fit abilities, for a sincere or conscientious discharge of the duty; some of such persons being merely mechanick, who leap from the limits of their lawfull station, affecting a dignity transcending their desert, and feeding like chameleons on the air of popular applause' (15). Women who set themselves up as ex-egetes were often perceived as 'merely mechinick' or insincere actors of the holy word, who could only 'affect' the dignity of God's true ministers.

It is difficult to establish incontrovertible evidence to support Warren's view that female preachers were conscious of playing to an audience, 'feeding like chameleons on the air of popular applause', but the account in *Gangraena* of one of Mrs Attaway's sermons in Bell-Alley, London, does suggest a carefully rehearsed scene. Rachel Trubowitz rightly observes that 'in the Civil War period the desire for change and the nostalgia for tradition achieve a fragile equilibrium, one that enables women to occupy centre stage, but that compels new behind-the-scenes tactics for . . . exploiting and obscuring female power and authority' (Trubowitz 1992: 129). Women preachers appear to have employed such behind-the-scenes tactics at their meetings, working together to stage conformity to cultural norms alongside religious nonconformity, in order to legitimate their entry on to the religious platform. In the Bell-Alley sermon the three women 'came forth out of an inward roome or chamber' carrying 'Bibles in their hands' to meet the expectant audience. They took their places around a table and 'the Lace-woman' began the meeting:

> turned her self first to this Gentlewoman, (who was in her hoods,
> neckelace of Pearle, watch by her side, and other apparell sutable) and
> intreated her to begin, extolling her for her gifts and great abilities; this
> Gentlewoman refused to begin, pleading her weaknesse; and extolling
> this Lace-woman who spake to her; then the Lace-woman replied again
> to the Gentlewoman, this was nothing but her humility and modesty, for
> her gifts were well knowne; but the Gentlewoman refused it again, falling
> into a commendation of the gifts of the Lace-woman; whereupon this
> Lace-woman turned her self to the company, and spake to some of them to

---

3. *See* Sue Wiseman, 'Margaret Cavendish among the Prophets: performance ideologies and gender in and after the English Civil War', *Women's Writing* 6 (1999), 95–111, which appeared in print as this book went to press.

exercise, excusing her selfe that she was somewhat indisposed in body, and unfit for this worke, and said if any one there had a word of exhortation let them speake; but all the company keeping silent, none speaking: Then the Lace-woman began with making a speech. . . .

(Edwards 1977: 84–5)

Attaway and her companion work in consort to promote images of themselves as models of female modesty, conscious of their physical and mental weakness, while simultaneously advertising their 'gifts and abilities' as a prelude to their speech. Alongside the words, the Bibles and the gentlewoman's 'sutable' apparel, including her pearl necklace, project a visual message of respectability, purity, sober wisdom. In addition, the third woman's silent testimony to her sisters provides an on-stage exemplar for the rest of the congregation to follow. The exchange of invitations to speak and polite refusals, cleverly builds up audience anticipation at the same time as undermining criticisms of female forwardness. Finally, the seeming modesty of the Lace-woman's challenge to the audience appropriates the authority of the preacher at a marriage service ('if any man can show any just cause why they may not lawfully be joined together, let him now speak, or else hereafter for ever hold his peace'). She boldly outfaces objectors, co-opting approval for what she is to say. The combination of rhetorical devices and non-verbal signifiers makes this a skilfully orchestrated performance by the three women. The 'laughing confusion and disorder' which followed are, arguably, evidence of the novelty of the occasion and the women's need to prepare, rather than a response to their poor performances (Edwards 1977: 86).

In religious sects like the Baptists, Quakers and Ranters, women's right to pronounce on religious matters drew on the radical principle that anyone, regardless of social class or gender, was equally open to the immanence of the Holy Spirit and called upon to show it through preaching or prophecy. Women sectaries of the Civil War had a recent model in the infamous figure of Lady Eleanor Davies whose religious insights were often broadcast in dramatic ways. In 1626, she had followed her prediction of her first husband's death by donning mourning clothes at dinner (Cope 1992: 42). Ten years later, she had joined with a group of women in Lichfield to stage objections to the Laudian reforms in the Cathedral. In opposition to changes to the church furniture, Lady Eleanor and her companions appropriated the space for themselves, first occupying seats in the choir, then those reserved for the wives of the senior clergymen. The climax to this performance came when Lady Eleanor sat on the bishop's throne, declared herself archbishop and bishop, and spoiled the new altar hangings (Cope 1992: 83–4). She continued to express her controversial opinions in print until her death in 1652, in spite of being committed to Bedlam as insane (Davies 1995: 371). Sir John Lambe's label of 'never so mad a ladie', and the High Commission's view of Davies's prophecies as 'divellish practizes' was a legacy that haunted other female visionaries in the Civil War period (Cope 1992: 70–1).

Women who were called by the Holy Spirit to broadcast their visions were inevitably thrust on to a public stage, either in or out of doors, to enact the divine message, which drove them. They repeatedly claimed that their role as God's messengers was a type of anonymity, a wish to transcend the self and sometimes they spoke from trance-like states as in the cases of Anna Trapnel and Sarah Wight (*b.* 1632, Wight 1647). Nevertheless, as Phyllis Mack has sensitively argued, the visionary's public testimony was an attempt 'to make something *universal* of her personal experience'; she expressed her spiritual enlightenment in terms that were both 'profoundly *social*' and 'intensely *physical*' (1992: 8). The communal, social and physical dimensions made visionaries' performances theatrical. Paradoxically, it was often the exhibition of self that attracted critical attention. This was most obvious in the Quaker practice of 'going naked as a sign', where display of the body was read not as a demonstration of God's message, but as a blatant transgression of conventional images of woman and her exclusion from the public stage.

One of the earliest examples of 'going naked as a sign' was the appearance of a woman in Whitehall Church during the sermon of Peter Sterry, on 17 July 1652. Sir Ralph Burgoyne reported 'she stripped herself of all her apparel' and 'ran into the middle of the congregation, over against the pulpit, and cried "Welcome to the Resurrection"' (Keeble 1994: 203). In spite of remaining totally anonymous, the woman provoked David Brown to define her as an impudent strumpet, using the same derogatory terms applied to women who appeared on stage. Her invasion of the church is a continuation of the female theatrical traditions begun by Anna of Denmark and Henrietta Maria:

> the like shamelesse spectacle hath not been so publickely and impudently shewed nor acted in all the vile shewes, and whorish masks, (where many thousands of pounds have been spent in one night) even to provoke God to wrath, and mankind to wickednesse, amongst the grossest either heathenish or Popish Tyrants of these Nations in former times . . . a bold woman of about 30 years old, sober in her speech, came in a most Strumpet-like posture, mocking you, and that your Sermon of the Resurrection, and all that honourable Congregation, consisting of the chief States of this Land, who were conveened neither to hear nor behold any sports, masks, playes, shewes, yea nor to fulfill sinfull lusts.
>
> (Brown 1652: 9)

Brown reads the woman's behaviour as a deliberate, flamboyant exhibition of the self, 'a defyance to God' (10) rather than a duty. The minister and his congregation are also implicated as spectators whose silence lends legitimacy to the performance. Brown compares them to the audiences of masques at Whitehall and plays at the theatres, pointing out that 'all honest men' expected a 'thorough and full Reformation' of behaviour 'when all the Playhouses in *London* were quite discharged, and also that great Timber barn in the Palace of *Whitehall* it self demolished, which was erected for the vile exercises of masks and playes' (11–12). Even though the performance has changed, the naked woman's spectators continue the tradition of gazing at 'vile exercises'.

Brown's condemnation of shows at Whitehall draws an implicit parallel between the naked woman and Queen Henrietta Maria, whose court performances provoked William Prynne's infamous condemnation of actresses as 'notorious impudent, prostituted strumpets' (Cerasano and Wynne-Davies 1996: 170). In spite of the huge social gap between the two women, their willingness to 'publickly' represent themselves makes them both 'lewd-like' (9–10). As if to press home the point, Brown begins his tract with the example of Queen Vashti, who refused to appear before guests at her husband's feast in spite of her beauty (Esther 1: 5–12). Having compared this queenly model of 'modesty, sobriety and chastity' with the naked woman's shameless presumption (6), Brown concludes by condemning the 'spirituall evils' of high church 'antichristian worship' encouraged by the 'late Queen' (14). The parallel between the nameless woman and the queen as ungodly performers is subtly, but unmistakably pressed home.

The naked woman would probably have rejected any such parallel, insisting that her act was part of a radical Puritan tradition, which was firmly opposed to theatrical insincerity. As Michael McKeon has argued, however, the realms of art and religion overlapped in disturbing ways during the seventeenth century. The growth of rival sects and the decline of religion as an absolute 'is not only coincident with, but also a function of the rise of the aesthetic' (1987: 37). Belief in the indwelling of the Holy Spirit was an explicitly aesthetic phenomenon in which the signifier, the female messenger, was herself an embodiment of God's presence. Diane Purkiss has shown how the woman prophet 'theatrically staged' both her body and her voice as a living text to be read by her audience (1992: 151). The theatrical elements of prophecy are important. R. F. Bauman points out that 'striking nonverbal enactments' or 'the performance of "signs" was seen by the early Quakers as an appropriate and efficacious means of delivering reproofs and prophecies to the sinful world' (1983: 84–5). The dramatic 'happening', an experimental theatre form of the 1960s, provides a suitable model with which to read women's religious enactments.

Charles Marowitz traces the origins of 'happenings' in the ideas of Artaud who argued that 'to link the theater to the expressive possibilities of forms, to everything in the domain of gesture, noises, colors, movements etc., is to restore it to its original direction, to reinstate it in its religious and metaphysical aspect' (Artaud 1958: 70). Although not anthropologically correct, Artaud believed he had found in Balinese ritual, 'a sort of spiritual architecture, created out of gesture and mime but also out of the evocative power of a system' (Artaud 1958: 55). Quaker and Ranter enactments were a similar type of theatre, spiritually inspired yet rooted firmly in physical spectacle as well as vocal proclamation. Perhaps our attachment to verbal script and concrete buildings as the foundations of drama explains why they have not been accorded a place in the dramatic tradition. Like 'Happenings', enacted 'signs' rejected a specific performance site in favour of diverse public arenas, dissolving the boundaries between theatre and life so that ' "social behaviour" is drama . . . in certain dramatized situations "people" are actors' (Marowitz 1972: 183). By combining 'the free and the ordered; the prearranged and the immediate' such forms of theatre raise audience awareness about the performance of ideologies in other contexts: 'Are we members of an audience watching scenes "laid on" for us or simply eye witnesses of accidental events?' (Marowitz 1972: 184). The public testimonies of visionary women inevitably highlighted the performative nature of gender during the Civil War period (as Cavendish and Brackley's play *The Concealed Fancies* did in another arena), calling into question the traditional exclusion of women from authoritative public roles.

The female visionary's behaviour was legitimated by its divine inspiration. The problem for those who were not participating in the religious rituals was that there was no way of knowing the truth – of either experiencing the message directly or knowing whether those involved were genuine. As Phyllis Mack has noted, the female visionary occupied no fixed position in the cultural scale and could slip easily from an admirable instrument of divine truth to a self-proclaiming strumpet (1982: 23). Underlying the prosecutions of religious performers like Martha Simmonds and Mary Gadbury was a dislike of acting as false, subversive, socially destabilising and dangerously appealing. Their daring simulations deconstructed the metaphysics of divine paternal presence. While undoubtedly believing in God, they reproduced the spirit in ways which look forward to the postmodern world theorised by Baudrillard, where religion as an 'absolute' or grand narrative, is replaced by a series of aesthetic representations. Since God can only be represented on earth, divine presence is 'not unreal but a simulacrum, never again exchanging for what is real, but exchanging in itself, in an uninterrupted circuit' (1988: 170). Baudrillard claimed that religious iconolaters 'possessed the most modern and adventurous minds since, underneath the idea of an apparition of God in the mirror of images, they already entered into his death and his disappearance in the epiphany of his representations' (1988: 169). Radical visionaries like Martha Simmonds and Mary Gadbury produced religious representations of just this kind, which simultaneously declared the presence and absence of both God and themselves.

Martha Simmonds (1623/4–65) was called to Quakerism in London in 1654 and participated in strikingly theatrical manifestations of the indwelling spirit. At Colchester, Simmonds gave a solo performance of Revelation 11:3, being 'moved to walke in sack cloth barefoote with her hayre sprred & ashes upon her head, in the Towne, in the frosty weather, to the astonishment of many' (Cadbury 1948: 41). She was also involved in a more extended collaborative production with two female companions, Dorcas Erbury and Hannah Stranger, who cast themselves as disciples of the Quaker leader James Nayler, re-enacting elements of Scripture. In Wells and Glastonbury they 'strewed their *garments in the way* as this Impostor *Nailer* rode along' (Farmer 1657: 3–4). Although it was Nayler who was proclaimed as Lord and Christ, it was in fact Simmonds who was the controlling figure. Richard Hubberthorne reported that Nayler was 'much subject to her' after she visited him in prison in Exeter (Carroll 1972: 43). Earlier, in London, she had dramatically crushed Nayler's attempts to condemn her outspokenness, demanding justice of him and apparently causing him to fall down 'in exceeding sorrow for about three daies, and all that while *the power arose in me*' (Farmer 1567: 10).

On 24 October 1656, Martha Simmonds and her companions staged the entry of Christ into Jerusalem as they accompanied Nayler into Bristol. The procession was headed by a naked man; Nayler's horse was led by Simmonds and Stranger who held the reins 'singing, *Holy, holy, holy, Lord God of Israell*' and '*Hosanna*' in front of a 'great concourse of people' (Farmer 1657: 3). The Quaker group were arrested and examined by the magistrates. The examinations gave the three women another public stage on which to continue their performances. Asked why she sang to Nayler and fell down to worship him, Martha proclaimed 'He is Lord of Righteousness' and 'He is anointed King of Israell' (16). Dorcas Erbury claimed that he had raised her from the dead in Exeter gaol (19). The drama continued in London, to which the prisoners were removed. On 25 November 1655, Hubberthorne reported 'the women are exceeding filthy in Acting in Imitations & singing' and that crowds came to wonder 'at the Imitation which is Acted Among them as often they will kneel before him &c.' (Carroll 1972: 47). The 'Imitation' by Martha Simmonds, Hannah Stranger and Dorcas Erbury was a continuation of the Passion story. When Nayler was put in a raised pillory and branded on 27 December, Simmonds, Stranger and Erbury placed themselves around him 'in imitation of Mary Magdalen and Mary the Mother of Jesus, and Mary the Mother of Cleophas' by the cross (Deacon 1657: 35).

Martha Simmonds appears to have directed these dramatic productions. Writing to her at Bristol, her husband Thomas called her '*the* chief leader in that action' and Farmer reports 'Thus you see here, this *Martha Simonds* is a considerable person' and an 'active spirrit'. He even suggests that 'the story of her prevailings upon Nailer at the first' give ground to the accusations of witchcraft raised against Martha (Farmer 1657: 21–2, 11–12). Peter Elmer has pointed out that charges of witchcraft were frequently levelled at the early Quakers. Their fits, trances, and actions imitated the behaviour attributed to witches, while their social vision (including their ideas of spiritual equality between the sexes), 'was nothing less than a Satanic inversion of the godly commonwealth' (1996: 159).

The demonisation of women like Martha Simmonds, Mary Gadbury and Anna Trapnel whose actions inverted the gender order, is testimony to the power of the inspired visionary. When the spirit was 'materialised' in a woman she acquired an extraordinary authority. McKeon points out that the elision of signifier and signified in seventeenth-century religious discourse produces a mediator of the divine so immediate that it comes 'to constitute its own mode of discourse and must be relied upon to make truly one sense in and of itself' (1987: 42). The female visionary threatened to become a dangerously autonomous subject, what Baudrillard calls a 'perfect simulacra forever radiant with [her] own fascination' (1988: 169). Mary Simmonds was deemed an anti-artist, 'that disturbes the scaene, and *spoils the play*' of the Quaker foundation (Farmer 1657: 10). She was condemned by her husband as an actor who had stepped out of '*the wisdome and counsell of the Lord*' to produce her own inauthentic script '*And hence comes all your* Cumber *and* Trumpery *without; which my soul was grieved to see it, abundance more hath been acted amongst you since I came away*' (Farmer 1657: 20).

Even more overtly theatrical was the behaviour of the Ranter Mary Gadbury, a needlewoman from Watling Street, who, in 1649, left her husband to travel with a married man, William Franklin, declaring themselves to be incarnations of Christ and Mary. Humphrey Ellis, who recorded their courtroom confessions in a pamphlet *Pseudochristus* (1650), had no doubt that their elaborate roles were nothing more than a sham, 'plotted by them, that they might deceive the better' (12). The pamphlet makes extensive use of theatrical imagery, setting the scene with the words 'This County of *Hamp-shire* is to be the stage, whereon they intend to play the rest of their parts' (13). Entrances and exits were carefully devised by the couple. After some initial preaching, William Franklin left Mary 'alone to act her part by her self' (18) and define him as the living Christ. This she did by declaring herself 'The Lady Mary' (title page), the mother and spouse of Christ. The inn to which they were guided by a revelatory vision was, fortuitously, called 'The Starre' (17), and here Mary staged a personal nativity, appearing 'taken as a woman in travail' and claiming that this was a spiritual labour, and that she would 'travail in birth till Christ were formed in them' (20–1).

Mary Gadbury's 'travail' did not produce any physical spectacle beyond Mary herself (although she did become pregnant by Franklin). She chose her venue carefully, however. As well as recalling the scene at Bethlehem, the 'Starre' inn was a ready-made theatre, a 'place of great entertainment', where 'multitudes of persons' from the town and the wider county could 'resort to her' (18). The pamphlet grudgingly acknowledges Mary's skill in manipulating her audience, varying her performance for sceptical and gullible members: 'very sly would she be in disclosing any thing' to the former, while to 'any that she saw were credulous' or 'easily to be wrought upon by her, to these she would freely speak and deliver her self, and use all means to win upon them to the seducing of them' (19). She would even single out individuals and play directly to them, 'pretend[ing] her travail to be for such a one' (21).

Like an actor preparing the entrance of the protagonist, Mary proclaimed a newly-embodied Christ 'with much earnestnesse' (18), specifying the time and appearance of his incarnation 'which so well agreed to *William Franklin* . . . that many presently deemed he was the person in all this held out by her to be the *Christ*' (19). In particular, she prophesied to her audience that he would be 'a plaine man in gray cloaths' (19). Mary made use of costume herself, reporting that in an early vision she was told '*put on your beautiful garments, O Daughters of Sion; for the marriage of the Lamb is come*' (15). At the inn, another vision was more specific, directing her '*Thou shalt be clothed in a white robe which I will give thee*' (27), so she promptly asked the innkeeper and his wife for white linen and made 'her an outer-garment with it, that it might shew forth her inward purity' (27).

Discontinuity between inner being and outer appearance was exactly what the court was anxious to expose when Gadbury and Franklin were brought to the Southampton assizes. To discredit them, they had to be revealed as actors. It is therefore not surprising that Mary had to face up to insults conventionally levelled at female performers – that their painting or make-up was a sign of their lewdness and insincerity. The judge held up a candle and told her that she looked so fair 'he did scarce believe it to be natural'. However, Mary took up the challenge, 'stept forth presently, and very boldly put her face very near to the candle and said, That she was glad the glory of God did shine so bright in her face, that they were forced to admire it' (42). Her readiness to present herself as a spectacle, and, furthermore, to suggest that this is not shameful or unnatural, looks forward to a time in which women have as much right to take the stage as men.

The assizes, conducted at night, drew attention to the courtroom as another kind of theatre. Neil Keeble has pointed out that courtroom scenes with their 'clearly defined conflict, claustrophobic location and increasing suspense' are 'intrinsically dramatic'. The accused 'casting themselves as protagonists, conducted themselves very much as actors upon the stage' (1987: 53). Mary Gadbury certainly saw the dock as an opportunity to extend her active role. Far from being a reluctant deponent, 'She was very forward of her own accord' to recount her experiences, 'discoursing so at large, as she did of her Visions, Revelations, Voyces' so as to make her testimony over two hours long (44). She describes a voice, which 'spake forth from her, and said *It is the Lord, it is the Lord*; but she could not say it was her own voyce' (10). Playing both her own voice and that of God allows Gadbury to transcend the position defined by her gender and her status as a prisoner. She testifies that 'the Voice spake forth aloud, as the voice of a man roaring out in speaking *I am the Lord of Hosts*, JEHOVAH *is my name, the high and holy one*' (16). As an instrument of divine communication, Gadbury claims an authority that upstages the judges who appear to sit in power over her. When one referred to Franklin as '*Fellow*', Mary held up an accusing hand and, in the 'height of confidence', said '*Thou dog, how darest thou call thy Saviour Fellow; thou art not worthy of a crumb*' (35).

Other women functioned as important extras in this spiritual drama. Goody Waterman, initially sceptical about the pair, was won over in a dramatic conversion (29) and proclaimed herself '*the Kings Daughter, all glorious within*' in court (40). When Mrs Woodward was summoned to testify, Mary Gadbury hailed her across the courtroom with the words '*Come in my Elect Lady*' (40). Those attending the assizes seem to have appreciated the trial as a form of entertainment. When Mary Gadbury was accused of adultery with Franklin, she 'denyed any whoredom', arguing that 'she companied not with him for carnal copulation . . . but as a fellow-feeler of her misery; at which last the whole Court laughed exceedingly, some saying *Yea, we think you companied with him as a fellow-feeler indeed*' (50).

Like the public theatres, the courtroom was a male-controlled space and overarching script; women were only given major roles when attempting to defend themselves against serious charges like witchcraft, but even within these tight parameters, some were able to negotiate a space to represent themselves. This is certainly the case with Anna Trapnel (*c.* 1622–, *fl.* 1654). *Anna Trapnel's Report and Plea* (1654) is an autobiographical account of the author's spiritual testimonies in London and Cornwall, and her judicial trial. Part of the latter is set out as a play, in which the words of the judges and Trapnel herself are labelled with speech prefixes. Bibliographic eccentricity suggests that this is a later addition to the text, as though Trapnel wished to highlight pivotal points in the proceedings.[4] One of the most important is over performance:

> Justice *Lobb* told me *I made a disturbance in the town*: I asked *Wherein?* He said *By drawing so many people after me.* I said, *How did I draw them?*: he said *I set open my chamber doors and my windows for people to hear. A. T. That's a very unlikely thing that I should do so, for I prayed the maid to lock my chamber door when I went to bed, and I did not rise in the night to open it:* I said *Why may not I pray with many people in the room, as well as your professing woman that prays before men and women, she knowing them to be there; but I know not that there is anybody in the room when I pray: and if you indict one for praying, why not another? Why are you so partial in your doings?*
>
> (Trapnel 1654b: 28a)

Trapnel counters accusations of exhibitionism – setting open doors and windows – with the deliberate adoption of dramatic form, as if to assert her right to a public voice. She wryly reminds readers that the courtroom was itself an exhibition space; far from being a '*very unlikely thing*' for Trapnel, her outspoken self-defence in that theatre is a performance, a form of self-staging or 'disturbance', which paradoxically enacts Lobb's view of her. Even while she was denying the charge, she was confirming it. Trapnel uses dramatic form to control reader-response just as surely as she did the trial itself. Sceptical or hostile readers are addressed in the 'you' applied to Justice Lobb and accused of being '*partial in your doings*'. Like the original audience in the courtroom, readers can witness her innocence.

Trapnel's appearance in court is 'framed by her encounters with crowds who, when they witness her for themselves, change their view of her', as Hilary Hinds rightly observes (1996: 168). The 'rude multitude' who had come to marvel at a witch came out saying '*Sure this woman is no witch, for she speaks many good words*' (28a). Throughout the text, Trapnel relies heavily on her audience to promote her message. She describes the spectacular presentation of herself at '*Foy*-Town' (Fowey), 'set in a chair' surrounded by men, women and children, who 'sitting on a high wall' like a theatre gallery, gave 'a great shout' when she finished speaking. To justify her performance, she told spectators 'I came not into the Countrey to be seen and taken notice of' (28b), that she was 'onely a voyce and Christ the sound' (29). Trapnel's

---

4. The British Library copy of the text contains two extra leaves (d and d2) so pagination is erratic, jumping from p. 28 back to p. 25 and then continuing in sequence. I thank Stephanie Hodgson-Wright for alerting me to this. In the following extracts (28a) is from the first p. 28 and (28b) is from the second page labelled 28.

insistence on herself as 'onely a voyce' – the conduit of Christ's word – creates an unmistakable contradiction between self-assertion and self-effacement in her actions and writings. Hinds' sensitive study *God's English-women* (1996) points out that it is difficult for feminists to locate a powerful authorial presence in such visionaries, who are neither 'authors nor narrators', located both inside and outside their texts (92).

Thinking about Trapnel in theatrical terms allows us to resolve the contradictions. As the many cues within her writings suggest, Trapnel is not the autonomous author of her radical messages, nor a passive vessel, but an *actor* of God's word. As in other dramatic productions, the script may not be hers, but the performance is, and this involves a creative energy, what McKeon, in another context, calls 'an internalization of divine as human creativity' (1987: 49). Trapnel draws attention to her ambiguous position in *The Cry of A Stone* (the title itself a teasing contradiction): 'thy Servant is made a voyce, a sound, it is a voyce within a voyce, anothers voyce, even thy voyce through her' (Trapnel 1654a: 42). In *A True Report and Plea*, Trapnel attributes her performance skills to God. She tells how she publicised her spiritual autobiography in Truro, acutely conscious of being the focus of sympathetic, critical and curious gazes: 'but the Lord taught me how to speak before them all: as in the presence of the great God I spake, who is my Father, who alwaies shewed me kindness, and did then before those several sorts of people' (1654b: 15–16). God functions as a director, guiding her through the unfamiliar territory of performance as both her inspiration and her most important spectator. Her own efforts, as a talented pupil, are still visible within the larger framework of spiritual testimony.

Phyllis Mack correctly remarks that Trapnel's public voice 'was as much the fruit of her own intelligence and political activism as it was the product of a disembodied trance state' (1982: 119). In *The Cry of A Stone*, Trapnel exploits the ballad, another genre designed for performance, in order to promote the radical social messages of the Fifth Monarchist sect. The printed text records 'something spoken in *Whitehall*' to '*Governors, Army, Churches, Ministry, Universities*' and opens with the names of significant witnesses to her 'Prayers and Spiritual Songs', including 'Colonel *Sidenham*, a member of the Council', and 'Colonel *Bingham*, Captain *Langdon*, Members of the Late Parliament', and 'Mr *Peak* the Minister, Lady *Darcy*, and Lady *Vermuden*' (1654a: 2). Like an inspired bard, Trapnel addresses her audience spontaneously, her flow of song outstripping the pace of the scriptors trying to jot down her messages. The simple ballad forms depersonalise her ideas, making them part of an anonymous, popular voice. This is in tune with her aim to speak out for the 'poore, fatherlesse and widow' (1654a: 36), the nation's dispossessed. She openly admonishes spectators with spiritual, military and political authority for their failure to bring '*relief to the poor*' (19–20). Even

Cromwell should be 'ashamed of his great pomp and revenue, whiles the poore are ready to starve' (50).

Trapnel's use of spiritual inspiration to address political leaders on worldly matters was characteristic of other women's prophecies, such as the appearance of Grace Barwick (*c.* 1618–1701) before the parliamentary officers (Barwick 1659) or Elizabeth Poole's dramatic appeal to the 'Generall Council of the Army' to caution them against harming Charles I (Poole 1648). Women's petitions to Parliament during the Civil War also drew on theatrical traditions. For example, on 8 and 9 August 1643, a large group of women demonstrated their anger at the defeat of the House of Lords' proposals for peace by arriving *en masse* at Westminster costumed with white ribbons on their hats and breasts, some apparently carrying children. The white ribbons, a traditional symbol of peace, also signalled purity, thus tacitly pre-empting the slanders of whore or fishwife levelled at these women because of their behaviour. As Keith Lindley notes, 'the drawing up of a petition and the wearing of white ribbons indicate a fair degree of coordination and direction behind the women's actions'. Apparently, Lady Bruncard of Westminster led the demonstrators on 9 August and other 'ladies' coordinated the distribution of ribbons (1997: 352–3).

Women sympathetic to the Leveller cause made more extensive use of costume. When Robert Lockyer was executed for leading a rebellion against Parliament's military campaign in Ireland, his funeral became a politicised theatrical event in which the Levellers 'manifested their strength as a political party' (McEntee 1992: 102). The funeral ritual allowed women a point of entry into the political arena. On 29 April 1649, Lockyer's coffin was decorated with sprigs of rosemary dipped in blood to signify martyrdom. The column of male and female mourners wore ribbons of the customary black and the sea-green colour that was associated with the Leveller cause. On 8 May, the women acted alone, putting on sea-green ribbons and dresses and marching to the House of Commons to demand retribution for Lockyer's execution. The costumes proclaimed their identity as a political collective. *Mercurius Militarius* described them as 'bonny Besses / In Sea green dresses. . . . marching down Battalia to give the members of Westminster a second charge with the artillery of a Petition' (McEntee 1992: 102). Like the rosettes and sashes of British suffragettes, the costume functions as a uniform to help transform the women into the political equals of men. The paper *Mercurius Pragmaticus* regarded their early attempts at female suffrage seriously, warning Parliament not to 'jeer Woemen with their *Huswifery*, when their business is *Liberty*' (McEntee 1992: 103).

These varied examples of dramatic activity by women demonstrate that, from a feminist viewpoint, the closing of the public theatres during the Civil War and Interregnum can be seen as a journey 'to liberty, and not to banishment' (*As You Like It* 1.3.132). The spilling over of theatrical activity into arenas such as the courtroom, the church, the household and the town and country outside, combined with a tumultuous environment in which fixed cultural models were often inverted or hollowed out. The servant Care in Cavendish and Brackley's *The Concealed Fancies* observes 'the world's turned upside down since I was young' (5.5.18). In a world where the divinely-appointed father of the kingdom could be tried and executed, the rigid demarcation of gender roles was also open to question. Different types of dramatic production by women challenged the exclusion of the sex from a range of public arenas, including the theatre itself.

After her trial for witchcraft, Anna Trapnel wrote 'I am forc't out of my close retired spirit, by Rulers and Clergy, who have brought me upon the worlds stage of Reports, and Rumors, making me the worlds wonder, and gazing stocke and as some have said they thought I had been a Monster or some ill-shaped Creature, before they came and saw, who then said they must change their thoughts, for I was a woman like others that were modest and civill, and many commending words they uttered' (1654b: 49). Trapnel would hardly have thought of herself as a pioneer of feminist theatre, yet her words show a dramatic consciousness. By appearing 'upon the worlds stage' Trapnel confronts the worst prejudices against female performers: the audience assume she is monstrous. However, her absolute conviction in her part obliges spectators to acknowledge that a woman who presents herself to be gazed on as 'the worlds wonder' is something natural. Far from being lewd, she is 'a woman like others that were modest and civill'. During the Civil War, performers like Anna Trapnel indirectly prepared the way for women's entry into mainstream professional theatre.

CHAPTER 4

'No *Silent Woman*': The Plays of Margaret Cavendish, Duchess of Newcastle

GWENO WILLIAMS

Margaret Cavendish, Duchess of Newcastle (1623–73), an aristocrat by marriage who wrote prolifically in almost every known literary and scientific genre, published 19 plays, mostly comedies, in two handsome folio collections in 1662 and 1668 respectively. These volumes were sold commercially: 'Twenty one[1] Plays, Written by the thrice Noble, Illustrious and Excellent Princess, the Lady Marchioness of Newcastle . . . These are sold by J. Martin; J. Allestry; Tho. Dicas; at the Bell in S. Pauls Church-yard'[2] were advertised in *The Kingdoms Intelligencer* of 3–10 February 1662. Cavendish also presented numerous copies of her publications to institutions and individuals; the dramatist Thomas Shadwell acknowledged 'the Noble Present of all your excellent Books' in his dedication of the play *The Humorists* (1671) to her (Kewes 1998: 196). Despite this public evidence of Cavendish's status and desire for recognition as a dramatist, her protofeminist plays have no recorded performance history until the 1990s, when their stageability has been clearly demonstrated to counter two centuries of dismissive critical comments (Williams 1998; Findlay, Hodgson-Wright, Williams 1999a and 1999b).

Cavendish's career as a dramatist exemplifies a significant tension between placing women centre stage and claiming a place within the male dramatic tradition, where she located herself from the start by publishing her works in the folio format, which distinguished the highest status male canonical drama of the century. Arguably, this publication format, which implies an established theatre pedigree, might have been selected to bypass

---

1. Each part of a two-part play has been counted as a separate text here.
2. I am most grateful to Carol Breakstone for this reference.

questions about the performance status of her plays. For example, half the plays in her 1662 folio are in two parts, presumably mimicking the commercially motivated two-part plays by dramatists such as John Marston, Thomas Dekker and William Davenant. Her relationship with the male dramatic canon was deeply ambivalent, however, revealed by her project of rewriting plots and key motifs from the plays of Jonson, Shakespeare and other male public theatre dramatists, with the evident aim of foregrounding women's dramatic status. Cavendish's extensively intertextual strategies position her plays in engaged relationship with the published dramatic canon, challenging the 'ventriloquizations of women' (Harvey 1992: 5), which doubly dominated the male-authored public theatre tradition in which female characters were personated by boy actors until the Restoration. In the Prefaces to her 1662 collection, Cavendish distinguishes between 'mercenary Players', discussing the break in the male professional acting tradition occasioned by the closure of the theatres (1662: sig. [A3+1]v), and 'the nobler sort' for whom she emphatically defends the educational value of acting (1662: sig. [A4+1]r). The final category refers specifically to the traditions of court masque and performance established by Henrietta Maria (*see* Chapter 3). Indications of household performance possibilities within individual plays support a reading of her plays as actual or potential performance texts for aristocratic women. Indeed, Cavendish's achievement lies in the repeated, multi-faceted ingenious staging of women as vocal protagonists, consistently allotted the largest parts and the most lines, including numerous lengthy monologues which critics have often been at a loss to evaluate. Male characters are subsidiary, relegated to the margins of the dramatic action, with a limited number of lines. As a dramatist, Cavendish reappropriates the ventriloquised voices of women usurped by male writers and performers.

The Publick Wooing (1662), a protofeminist reworking and extension of the Portia sub-plot from Shakespeare's *The Merchant of Venice* (1596), illustrates her discriminating strategies of reversal. The main protagonist, the aristocratic heiress Lady Prudence, is 'Virtuous, Young, Beautiful, Graceful and hath a supernatural Wit . . . she lives magnificently, yet orders her Estate prudently' (1.2). She is also notably independent and unconstrained by patriarchy; her vow to find a husband through a process of public wooing is, unlike Portia's, made of her own volition, not at the 'will of a dead father' (1.2.25). She plays a key part as both protagonist and judge in the formal comparative performances before an on-stage audience which constitute the 'publick wooing' scenes '*there being two standing places opposite each other a purpose, one for the Suter to wooe and plead his sute, and another for the Lady to stand whilst she gives her Answer*' (1.6). As in *The Merchant of Venice* the successive male suitors are generic figures, barely individualised. Lady Prudence is articulate and dignified throughout whereas the nine suitors' parts, largely written by William Cavendish, are often visually or verbally comic. Cavendish introduces a high level of erotic suspense when Lady Prudence suddenly falls passionately in love with a beggar, a figure of fun, '*her strange Wooer, a man that has a wooden Leg, a patch on his Eye, and Crook-back'd, unhandsome snarled hair, and plain poor Cloaths on: He takes the Wooers place, and the Assembly about gazing with smiling faces at the sight of such a Wooer*' (3.23). The effective extreme visual contrast between the couple signals the economic and class discrepancy. The society of the play universally condemns Lady Prudence's choice, particularly when the 'strange wooer's' behaviour at his wedding bears a marked resemblance to that of Petruchio in *The Taming of the Shrew* (1594).

> *Enter the Lady Prudence as a Bride that's very finely drest in glorious Apparel, her Bridegroom in poor old cloaths: He leads her as to the Church, limping with his Wooden Leg. The Bridal Guests seem to make signs of scorning as they follow . . .*
> 2 *Gent.* There was no time to make him Wedding-cloaths, because he came not till his Wedding-day.
>
> (4.36)

Cavendish creates intense dramatic and sexual tension in a pivotal scene set in the bridal chamber on the wedding night. Courtship is the play's main subject, a strand of comic scenes satirising the shallow superficiality and verbal inconsistency of minor female characters: Parle, Trifle, Vanity, Fondly, in their frantic quest for husbands are contrasted with Lady Prudence's eccentric proceedings. These worldly characters are appalled and prurient about observing the consummation of this incongruous love affair.

> *Fondly.* Come away, the Bride is going to bed. . . .
> *Parle.* To bed, say you? If I were she, I would first choose to go to my Grave. Hymen and Cupid bless me from such a bed-fellow as the Bridegroom.
> *Trifle.* Prethee let us watch, to see if we can descry whether he hath cloven feet.
>
> (4.38)

Undressing for the bridal bed becomes a scene of visual revelation and relief to all as the misshapen wooer sheds his beggarly properties with his clothes, '*he then appearing very handsome*', vindicating Lady Prudence's judgement. In romance tradition, the wooer is also revealed as a lost prince, the final scenes stage their elaborate wedding, theatrically celebrated with antimasks, masks, song and dance. *The Publick Wooing* foregrounds and develops Shakespeare's romance plot by making Prudence the agent of her own happiness, choosing a lover with integrity and free from ambiguous loyalties.

This brief analysis of a single play highlights some of the distinctive and successful features of Cavendish's dramatic practice. She frequently appropriates a motif from the male dramatic canon and significantly changes the emphasis by validating the voices, opinions, dramatic agency and stage presence of her independent, witty, and empowered female protagonists. Her strategies of reappropriation contest the 'ventriloquism [which] is an appropriation of the feminine voice [which] reflects and contributes to a larger cultural silencing of women' (Harvey 1992: 12). Indeed, the dominance and centrality of female voices and discourse is the most significant feature of her plays, as Jacqueline Pearson has noted, though suggesting that Cavendish's plays were 'not designed for the stage' (1985: 44). Marta Straznicky goes further in defining Cavendish's plays as 'closet drama', asserting that Cavendish 'expressly intended them for private reading rather than public performance' and that a 'performance bias fails to do Cavendish justice' (1995: 355). This chapter addresses the issue of female discourse from a performance perspective, foregrounding Cavendish's staging of these vocal women. Cavendish's plays explore ways in which the life of the mind can counterbalance the constrained circumstances of women's material lives, formally staging the linguistic and verbal expression of their imaginative capacity before an on-stage audience. The physical action of a play frequently comes to a halt while one woman discourses fluently at length. These set-piece monologues can appear undramatic, unless viewed as verbal manifestations of women's creative imagination. In Cavendish's plays speech, particularly women's speech, takes precedence over action or characterisation.

She often images the world as a theatre where women can perform to advantage. Her short witty didactic play *The Female Academy* (1662), dealing with themes later expanded in *The Convent of Pleasure* (1668), deploys extensive verbal and visual images of a dedicated female theatre-space, reconfiguring female education as performance, in a gender-reversal of its source, *Loves Labours Lost* (1594–5). Shakespeare's all male 'little academe' (1.1.13) becomes an elite 'female academy' resembling a convent, in which marriageable young women are 'strictly enclosed' by their mothers to be trained in rhetoric. There are also suggestive parallels with the Ladies Collegiate in *Epicoene*. The obverse sexual connotations of such single-sex confinement are emphasised by reiterated jokes about brothels. The women articulate their education in lengthy elegant public philosophical discourses, which function as theatrical set-piece performances subject to the male gaze of their anxious and frustrated would-be suitors: '*Enter a company of young Ladies, and with them two Grave Matrons; where through the Hanging a company of men look on them, as through a Grate*' (1.2). The female intellect is staged through increasingly fluent and creative discourses on a variety of topics, which draw ever-increasing audiences, illustrating women's empowerment through education. The comic impotence and fury of the male characters leads them to turn their adjacent auditorium into a stage for a competing and much less successful academy, where they discourse crudely and obsessively on a single topic, the 'Female Sex'. Waning audiences find the men's discourses 'simple, childish and foolish' (4.21). The longest and most articulate male discourse (3.14) is actually a cross-gendered reworking of the arguments of Kate's final speech from *The Taming of the Shrew* (1594). Finally, and metatheatrically, theatre itself becomes the assigned topic for female discourse, as women claim theatre as their own specific arena of linguistic empowerment.

> A Theatre is a publick place for publick Actions, Orations, Disputations,
> Presentations, whereunto is a publick resort; but there are only two
> Theatres, which are the chief, and the most frequented; the one is of War,
> the other of Peace; the Theatre of Warr is the Field; and the Battels they
> fight are the Plays they Act, and the Souldiers are the Tragedians, and the
> Theatre of Peace is the stage . . . but the difference of these Plays Acted on
> each Theatre, is, the one is real, the other feigned, the one in earnest, the
> other in jest . . . on the Poetical Theatre I will only insist, for the Theatre
> belongs more to our persons, and is a more fitter Subject for the discourse
> of our sex than Warr is, for we delight more in Scenes than in Battels . . .
>
> (4.22)

The unsuccessful male academy has been consistently ignored by the women who were its intended audience, so the men decide to 'leave off talking'; in a hilarious finale they noisily demonstrate their loss for words by trying to drown out the women's accomplished performances with trumpets (5.27). Of their own volition, the women appear to compromise and agree to admit suitors. The play constructs women as consummate verbal performers in the theatre of the world, well able to outperform and out-manoeuvre men.

Cavendish's explicit awareness of the novelty and gender implications of her practice is revealed by the Introduction to her 1662 volume, an important bridge between the extensive prefatory materials and the plays. It is a Jonsonian-style dramatic induction, metatheatrically staging three male theatre-goers discussing the contemporary gender monopoly on wit. With astonishment, they consider the controversial idea of going to see 'a new Play' by a woman playwright with a distinct resemblance to Cavendish's construction of herself, 'a Lady who on my Conscience hath neither language nor learning but what is native or naturall' (1662: 1). Gender is defined as the primary obstacle to the reception of a play by a woman: 'the very being a woman condemns it, were it never so excellent and rare, for men will not allow women to have wit' (1662: 1). Cavendish's entire dramatic *oeuvre* reveals her particular concern with claiming the cultural ownership of wit for women as authors, performers, initiators; plays such as *The Female Academy* investigate wit as an empowering manifestation of the female intellect. Four plays have wit in the title: *Wits Cabal I* and *II* (1662); *Nature's Three Daughters, Beauty, Love and Wit* (1662); *The Several Wits* (1662); *The Sociable Companions* or *The Female Wits* (1668); Mihoko Suzuki has written insightfully about the important function of wit as an aspect of satire in a number of these plays (Suzuki 1997). 'Wit' is a quality admired by both William and Margaret Cavendish: she calls him 'a Wittie Poet' (Cavendish 1653: 214), he is author of the play *Witts Triumvirate* (Kelliher 1993), Margaret's epitaph on her tombstone, composed by William, defines her as 'A wise wittie and learned lady' (Battigelli 1998: 115). Wit is crucial in her definition of a successful dramatist, but also a particular kind of verbal performance opposed to the feminised quality of bashfulness.

Cavendish's prose plays are comedies of female manners; she typically utilises a dramatic structure with comparative or triple plots running in parallel and consistently intercut. Plays build up contrasting examples, acutely satirising the values and manners of the age. Constructions of femininity are explored with reference to particular issues: war, intellect and education, marriage and courtship. Cavendish's characters have universalising emblematic aptronyms (Lady Happy, Monsieur Mode, Lady Victoria, Lord Singularity) in order to emphasise particular themes. Her plays often combine allegorical plots with relatively realistic settings to explore divergent possibilities for women's speech and behaviour. A number of plays rework the same important topics, staging a variety of unusual and emancipatory gender perspectives, and exploring alternatives to the unequal power balance offered by early modern marriage relations. Cavendish's creative capacity to imagine otherwise is a distinctive feature of all her writings, evident in *Poems and Fancies* (1653), her utopian fiction *The Blazing World* (1666) and also in her plays where she represents alternative versions of women's lives. Yet the resolutions of Cavendish's plays are consistently conformist, revalidating the status quo, particularly marriage. This suggests that her radical protofeminist alternatives can only be explored within the constraints of the stage. Her project is temporarily to stage rather than permanently realise woman-centred alternatives.

Her plays illustrate both a larger dramatic and political ambition and a particular family literary context. *The Epistle Dedicatory* to *Plays*[3] (1662) identifies her husband the royalist dilettante dramatist William Cavendish,

---

3. All quotations are taken from the University of Leeds Brotherton Library Special Collection copies of Cavendish's plays.

Duke of Newcastle (1593–1676), as her inspiration: 'And as for this Book of Playes, I believe I should never have writ them, nor have had the Capacity nor Ingenuity to have writ Playes, had not you read to me some Playes which your Lordship had writ, and lye by for a good time to be Acted, wherein your Wit did Create a desire in my Mind to write Playes also . . .' (1662: sig. A3r).

His wit is the engendering parent of her writing in this privileged genre. William was also her literary collaborator, contributing poems, speeches and scenes to her plays, particularly poetic or bawdy material; his contributions are clearly and deferentially identified by Cavendish in her published text with the annotation 'Written by my Lord Duke' in print or on hand-written cancel slips. In 1668 Lorenzo Magalotti visited England and noted, 'The Duke of Newcastle has printed a famous book on the management of horses. He writes plays, in which he avails himself greatly of the aid of his wife, who is said to have written two herself' (Magalotti 1980: 144).[4] Cavendish's career as a dramatist was undoubtedly closely bound up with her personal and literary relationship with William Cavendish.

A cultured literary figure posthumously described as 'our English Maecaenas' (Langbaine 1691: 386) and as 'a moving force in the literature of his day and generation' by his literary biographer (Perry 1918: 170), William Cavendish was a supportive patron to Ben Jonson, James Shirley, Richard Brome, John Ford (Rowe 1994). His life-long engagement with drama included mounting two expensive great-house entertainments by Jonson for royalty on his English estates in 1633 and 1634 (Trease 1979: 68–71, Brown 1994), another in exile in Antwerp in 1657–8 (C. S. P. Domestic 1657–8: 275–6) and one in London (Hulse 1995: 373–4). He wrote or co-authored at least four comedies, some of which were performed in the public theatre (Hulse 1996: vii); he was inattentive about their publication status. He established an aristocratic literary milieu within his own family including a reciprocal writing relationship, which encouraged the children of his first marriage to write plays and poems from their earliest years (Ezell 1998); *see* the detailed discussion of Jane Cavendish, and Elizabeth Brackley's plays in Chapter 3.

He appears to have engaged in a similar tutelary relationship with Margaret (Rowe 1994: 197), who was only a little older than his own daughters when they met and married in Paris in 1645. Each was in exile, she as a maid of honour with Queen Henrietta Maria's court, he as the military general held responsible for the significant royalist defeat at the battle of Marston Moor (1644), after which he fled abroad. In Paris he wrote plays

---

4. I wish to thank Alison Findlay for this reference.

for the English Company of actors. They married despite some opposition to their courtship from the queen (Battigelli 1998: 23), eventually settling in Antwerp where they rented the spacious and elegant Rubenshuis, a strong cultural and artistic statement in itself. Cavendish's 1662 plays were probably written in Antwerp in the late 1650s with publication delayed by the loss of the original manuscript at sea (Battigelli 1998: 25). They returned to England at the Restoration, retiring to their country estate in Nottinghamshire when they failed to find favour at Charles II's court. Both William Cavendish's lifelong passions involved public display and showmanship; one was theatre, the other 'manege', the training of horses (Trease 1979: 174–5).

Cavendish's experience of different types of theatre was considerable, extending significantly beyond the public theatres, which she writes about attending in London with her own family before the Interregnum in her autobiographical text *A True Relation of my Birth, Breeding and Life* (Cavendish 1872: 160). She had considerable contact with women performers and theatre practitioners in a variety of different dramatic contexts. Her audience experience and her contact with play production encompassed the feminocentric 'precieuse' theatrical culture of Henrietta Maria's court (*see* Chapters 2 and 3), reading drama aloud, including commenting on women readers of her own plays (Fitzmaurice *et al.* 1997a: 172–3), watching women performers in visual physical popular entertainments in Antwerp (Cavendish 1664: 406–7) and enjoying royal entertainments organised and hosted by her husband at which women performed (Tomlinson 1992b: 139–40, Hulse 1996). (Although she indicates that she spoke neither French nor Flemish, continental influences on her plays also appear significant. In particular, a number of suggestive similarities between the representation of women in her plays and in those of Jean-Jacques Molière (1622–73) would seem to repay investigation.)

Cavendish was perceived by her contemporaries as an inveterate self-publicist, appearing in public in extravagant self-designed costumes with eccentric gestures to perform 'the theatre of Margaret' (Tomlinson 1992b: 159). Yet she consistently defined herself as bashful and ill-at-ease in public situations. Despite contact with the public theatre available through William, her plays were apparently not performed in the Restoration public theatre, although Samuel Pepys attended a performance of *The Humorous Lovers* by William Cavendish in 1667, believing it to be by Margaret, and viewed her receiving extravagant applause from the auditorium (Pepys vol 7: 163). It may well be that her plays received household productions in exile or after the Restoration, however.

One important argument for Cavendish's plays as performance texts is that they reveal an informed and confident dramatic imagination. She deploys visual and verbal elements, attends to entrances and exits, indicates location, scenery or properties, exploits a wide range of physical action and surprise. She creates varieties of comedy, emphasising witty dialogue and exploiting erotic and gender effects. She deploys metatheatrical effects and masque conventions. Most of her characters are aristocratic; women predominate, but she also characterises servants and other lower-class characters well. Some plays, in particular *The Presence* (1668), dramatise her own experience or that of William Cavendish.

Her ambitious publication strategy may have pre-empted attention to her plays as performance texts. As Jeffrey Masten has insightfully argued, Cavendish's decision to publish her attentively edited plays solely in the prestigious format of folio collections, bypassing the more usual individual smaller quarto editions, which could serve as actors' copies, can be read as an attempt to define herself primarily as a literary dramatist, claiming equal status with male master-dramatists of the previous generation, Jonson (1613), Shakespeare (1623) and Beaumont and Fletcher (1647) (Masten 1997: 115, 156–64). She was the first woman to publish criticism of Shakespeare (Fitzmaurice *et al.* 1997a: 169–71).

William Cavendish initiated the comparison between her writings and those of male canonical dramatists in his fulsome verse dedication, printed as the first poem in her first publication *Poems and Fancies* (1653):

> Your New-borne, sublime Fancies, and such store,
> May make our Poets blush, and write no more.
> Nay Spencers ghost will haunt you in the Night,
> And Jonson rise, full fraught with Venom's Spight.
> Fletcher, and Beaumont, troubl'd in their Graves,
> Looke out some deeper, and forgotten Caves.
> And Gentle Shakespeare weeping, since he must,
> At best, be buryed, now, in Chaucers Dust.
>
> (1653: sig. A1r)

In *A General Prologue to all my Playes* (1662) Cavendish responds to his compliment by ostensibly denying these influences, but in a way which validates her own work. She boldly establishes her own literary credentials by simultaneously invoking and rejecting these models from the male dramatic canon, headed by Ben Jonson:

> NOBLE Spectators, do not think to see
> Such Playes, that's like Ben. Johnsons *Alchymie*,
> Nor *Fox*, nor *Silent Woman*: for those Playes
> Did Crown the Author with exceeding praise . . .
> . . . my Playes have not such store of wit,

Nor subtil plots, they were so quickly writ . . .
But Noble Readers, do not think my Playes,
Are such as have been writ in former daies;
As Johnson, Shakespear, Beamont, Fletcher writ;
Mine want their Learning, Reading, Language,Wit.
(1662: sig. A7r–v)

As Masten has emphasised, the rhetorical apologies for her own 'poor Playes' here are cleverly undercut by the repeated comparison, and implied equality, with the established giants of English drama (1997: 159). Cavendish's insistent claims in this same prologue that her dramatic writings are original: 'All the materials in my head did grow, / All is my own and nothing do I owe:' (1662: sig. A8r) are problematised by attentive readings of individual plays, which reveal extensive intertextual evidence of her frequent practice of rewriting or reversing elements of the male-authored dramatic canon. Cavendish directs her attention particularly towards plays by the dramatists most closely connected with William Cavendish, above all Ben Jonson. Julie Sanders' informed and detailed discussion of Cavendish's 'responses to the Jonsonian theatrical inheritance' signposts the way to a consideration of 'a more comprehensive field of literary influence and interaction between the dramatists of the time [and] functions to reclaim Cavendish's drama for critical attention within the context of the dramatic mainstream' (Sanders 1998: 294, 302).

This chapter complicates the argument by drawing particular attention to Cavendish's multi-valent refashionings of the figure of the 'Silent Woman', as an aspect of her challenge to the male canon and her interest in the oppositional potential of female dramatic performance. She wittily appropriates the central trope of Jonson's cross-gendered comedy of misogyny, *Epicoene* or *The Silent Woman* (1616), which was extremely popular in the Restoration (Holdsworth 1996: xxi) staging at least three silent women and one silent man in her dramatic *oeuvre*, to counterpoint her numerous highly vocal female characters. Her reclamation of the figure of the silent woman should be read in the light of Harvey's political and ethical argument that 'transvestite ventriloquism expresses a cultural suppression of the feminine voice' (1992: 12). Jonson's Epicoene is a boy actor playing a boy disguised as a woman, a ventriloquised and fraudulent dramatic construct of femininity, used to trick and expose misogynistic men. Cavendish's 'silent' characters on the other hand are self-motivated discriminating critics of society usually rewarded by true love.

Dramatically she experiments with degrees and versions of silence, from voiceless and apparently dumb characters, to bashful women whose linguistic confidence fails by contemporary court standards, using language and silence to explore questions of decorum and gender. Two silent characters are named 'Bashful' (*Loves Adventures*, *The Presence*), one 'Mute' (*The Publick Wooing*), one 'Dumb' (*Loves Adventures*). All are taken for fools by modish society; in each play the undervalued silent character is ultimately shown to have better judgement and be altogether more worthy than the satirical and shallow members of fashionable society. *The Publick Wooing*, for example, explores aspects of silence and voicelessness in the dumb show performance of a bashful suitor and in the sub-plot featuring a silent woman, the apparently dumb Lady Mute, undervalued and mocked by society and her intended husband, Sir Thomas Letgo, until she is rescued by the noble Sir William Holdfast.

As the title of this chapter suggests, Cavendish asserts herself as a prolific successful playwright, very far from silent dramatically, who amply demonstrates that 'a woman may have wit'. She creates numerous vocal female protagonists who can attract and hold an audience. It also suggests that she constructed herself as both heir and antagonist to Ben Jonson, to whom she so frequently refers in her writings (Fitzmaurice *et al.* 1997a: 173). It is possible that she found his literary influence oppressive because of his extensive historic connections with her husband.[5]

Cavendish's informed and witty symbolic challenge to Jonson was clearly recognised and understood by her earliest readers such as F. F. (probably Francis Fane) in his commendatory verses of 1676:

> Then why should we the mouldy Records keep
> Of Plautus, or disturb Ben Johnson's Sleep?
> *The Silent Woman* Famous heretofore
> Has been, but now the Writing Lady more.
>
> (Perry 1918: 262)

Critical perplexity about the status of Cavendish's plays as theatre scripts has been particularly fuelled by the apparently contradictory statements about performance contained in the exceptional number of largely self-authored prefatory materials to the 1662 *Plays*. On the very first page of the volume, *The Epistle Dedicatory* asserts that her plays' inferiority to her husband's 'is the reason I send them forth to be printed, rather than keep them concealed in hopes to have them first Acted' (1662: sig A1r). She then complicates the argument by simultaneously imagining and rejecting the idea of public theatre performance, personifying her plays as actresses publicly labelled as whores, the most disempowered female image to appear anywhere in her dramatic writings:

---

5. I wish to thank Nick Rowe for fruitful initial discussion of this idea.

I am out of the fear of having them hissed off from the Stage, for they are not like to come thereon; but were they such as might deserve applause, yet if Envy did make a faction against them, they would have had a publick Condemnation; and though I am not such a Coward, as to be affraid of the hissing Serpents, or stinged Tongues of Envy, yet it would have made me a little Melancholy to have my harmless and innocent Playes go weeping from the Stage, and whipt by malicious and hard-hearted censurers . . .

(1662: sig. A3r–v)

This image implicitly challenges prejudice against women theatre practitioners by its invocation of William Prynne's controversial definition of female actors as 'notorious whores' in 1633, which had so offended Henrietta Maria (*see* Chapter 3), emphasising Cavendish's personal connection with the queen. Significantly, Cavendish never stages the figure of a prostitute or whore in her plays, yet reiterated verbal references to prostitutes shadow her assertive female protagonists.

Cavendish's plays are unlikely to be staged since she is a royalist and the public theatres have been closed by the parliamentarian faction and because her plays are automatically gendered female. In imagination, Cavendish the playwright becomes meta-audience to a scene, which mutates from indoor theatre to outdoor punishment arena as her feminised plays undeservedly incur the penalty imposed as public spectacle upon prostitutes (Sharpe 1990: 23). 'Stinged Tongues' refers to the 'cat-o'-nine-tails' whip; the conjunction with 'hissing serpents' conflates the hostile theatre audience with envy embodied as Medusa. The affirmative female heroic figure of Minerva, representing justice, who carries Medusa's vanquished head on her shield, is crucially absent from the scene. Notably, the 'Statue' frontispiece by Abraham van Diepenbeke to *Plays Never Before Printed* (1668) stages Cavendish flanked by Minerva and Apollo (Chalmers 1997: 333) in an image based on the garden archway at the Rubenshuis; Cavendish takes the central place occupied by Hercules in the original.[6] This is a visual signifier of the protofeminist content of Cavendish's plays where women displace men centre stage. In the words of the French feminist critic Helene Cixous 'Woman must put herself into the text – as into the world and history – by her own movement . . . woman must write woman' (Cixous 1991: 334–5); female intellect displaces masculine values.

Regardless of the plays' merits, the audience is imagined already prejudiced against them. Cavendish mistrusts all kinds of public opinion and

---

6. One of the few original structures remaining at the heavily reconstructed Rubenshuis in Antwerp.

'faction' is a politicised term, which she commonly uses to represent parliamentarianism in her writings. She allegorises faction as a character in *The Comical Hash* (1662), Lady Faction is a satirical embodiment of the parliamentarian revolution 'of a strange busy Nature, she runs into every House, takes upon her to govern everyones Family, yet cannot rule her own; she condemns all Actions, be they never so Just or Prudent; all Officers, be they never so worthy, or fitly placed; all laws be they never so beneficial, or expedient for the Common-wealth; all Customs, be they never so antient or harmless, indeed all peaceable, wise and well-ordered Governments she hates and delights in nothing but disordered change' (2.5). Her defensive preoccupation with the Newcastles' own displaced and marginal status during the Interregnum is revealed, since the passage also exploits the trope of negative audience reaction used in contemporary newsbooks to belittle William Cavendish's military performance (Wenham 1970: 191).

> It is certified that the Catholik Marquesse of Newcastle is gone from Amsterdam to Flanders, and from thence intends for France. It is no great matter whither, unlesse he will doe us the courtesie to come and help Rupert to another beating: never did any Stage-player act his part worse than he hath done, to be hist off the Stage by both Parties.
> (*Mercurius Britannicus* 76, Monday 24 March–Monday 31 March 1645)

Cavendish exploits the idea of war as performance affirmatively in a number of plays. Anna Battigelli (1998: 44) has suggested that her earliest published works were written at a period of intense personal melancholy as a response to exile and loss, the personal consequences of the particular historical crises and adversity of 'these Unhappy Wars', which so profoundly changed the lives of 'not only the family I am linked to . . . but the family from which I sprung . . .' (Graham *et al.* 1989: 91; Battigelli 1998: 44). Some of her plays, however, reconstruct such events as opportunity and enfranchisement for women. The comedy, *Bell in Campo I* and *II* (1662), is an energetic and empowered rewriting of the English Civil War dealing with the war experiences of women, particularly Lady Victoria, Cavendish's most actively heroic protagonist. The triple plot contrasts the attitudes of three aristocratic wives from the allegorical Kingdom of Reformation whose husbands go to war against the Kingdom of Faction. Lady Victoria's unconventional decision to accompany her husband the General to the battlefield for love is contrasted with the stay-at-home marital obedience of Madam Jantil and Madam Passionate, who are soon widowed. In a series of verbal allusions to the alternative shadow construction of femininity, a conformist wife specifically reminds the audience that prostitutes or 'trulls' are the only women who usually accompany men to war (I.2.6). Once at war, the chaste and idealistic Lady Victoria's loyalties develop away from her husband, in sharp and outraged response to the male army's secret and deceitful decision to confine the women away from the action, in a garrison town; she evolves into an Amazonian authoritative and charismatic orator to a highly responsive separatist female army, her long speeches are rhetorical performances in their own right, invoking strong audience responses (I.2.9 and II.3.8).

The play sharply contrasts active and passive modes of women's symbolic and gendered self-staging. Lady Victoria's heroic, vigorous, active, military and increasingly masculine role is indicated by the permanent wearing of battle armour (I.3.11), in which she resembles Minerva or Pallas, to whom prayers are regularly offered on the battlefield. Madam Jantil appears at home in a symbolic shroud, staging her own extended death and funeral rites within her husband's tomb. Madam Passionate is depicted in her chamber, surrounded by food and drink (II.11.12). Social class is sharply and effectively delineated in the play through the commentary and realistic interactions of the female servants who form a Chorus which links the two sub-plots.

Lady Victoria acquires a series of feminised heroic titles: 'Generalless', 'Instructress', 'Commanderess', while the ordinary women become 'Heroickesses', in terminology reminiscent of the French aristocratic tradition of the 'femme forte' (Chalmers 1997: 332–3). The play explores the controversial and also comic possibility that women may be more competent at warfare than men. Victoria may also embody elements of Henrietta Maria, offering an ironic comic perspective on the Queen's military priorities, in the retelling of a documented incident of a lost dog (I.1.4). The play's puzzling title is probably best translated as *Beauty on the Battlefield*, taking account of Cavendish's avowedly imperfect language skills, with possible resonances of *De Bello Gallico*, echoing the frequent affirmative cross-gendered parallels with Caesar in Cavendish's writings.

As her name suggests, Madam Jantil is a model wife who becomes a model widow, devoting herself totally to the stylised formal memorialisation of her dead husband in grave architecture and biography. She single-mindedly enacts her own immolation by severing contact with the world, almost ceasing to eat, and obliterating herself in the elaborate tomb complex, which she has had constructed: 'thus will I live a signification, not as a real substance but as a shaddow made betwixt life and death' (I.3.21). She is self-absorbed into becoming a living monument, an extended tragic reworking of Hermione in *The Winter's Tale* (1610) and also possibly of George Chapman's comedy *The Widow's Tears* (1612). Her identity is subsumed in that of her dead husband; she plays out excessive and highly visual and symbolic funeral and death scenes, so extreme that they could possibly become comic in performance. Madam Passionate is a more obviously comic figure, a 'musty widow' (I.5.23) who is a caricature of John Webster's 'lusty widow' in *The Duchess of Malfi* (1614). She is caricatured as foolish, greedy and lascivious, in highly humorous scenes revealing her abundant physical appetites. The tone changes abruptly when she remarries and is maltreated by her new young husband.

Lady Victoria's female army become energetic and highly successful soldiers who can afford to donate their surplus victories to the men. At the end of the play, their military achievements are marked by a staged public triumph before citizens' wives, in which Lady Victoria rides onto the stage in a carriage pulled by eight horses. The on-stage horses seem to be a direct reference to James Shirley's public theatre play *Hyde Park* (1632)[7] and also a specific compliment to William Cavendish's interests. Since William Cavendish often showed his horses to visitors or prospective purchasers at the Rubenshuis, this scene may suggest the possibility of household performance in Antwerp. The characterisation of the General, his sound military strategy and the specific references to horses and horsemanship in the opening scenes all seem to be compliments to William; intriguingly the figure of the General disappears completely from the play after Act 1. In the final scene, allegory is fused with reality as the women's military victories are reformulated into a set of specific realistic domestic rights validated by the king, a figurehead who only appears at the end of the play, confirming political and social gains, reminiscent of Lord Calsindow's appearance at the end of *The Concealed Fancies* (*see* Chapter 3). The play may indeed critique the relatively passive role of the besieged sisters in *The Concealed Fancies*, through Lady Victoria's active engagement in warfare.

The Civil War is also the topic of *The Sociable Companions* or *The Female Wits* (1668). This is Cavendish's most 'Restoration' comedy, addressing the realistic aftermath of war, specifically the economic and personal losses experienced by cashiered soldiers. The play foregrounds money, constructing all relationships as financial. The two-dimensional sub-plot depicts a stream of suitors to a daughter who pragmatically chooses a rich old man as her husband. As the play's subtitle indicates, women are staged as the energetic agents who can ingeniously remedy the financial losses of the war. Structured in two discrete halves, the action deals at first with the ineffectual efforts of three redundant Civil War soldiers to seek any reparation they can. The profiteering cashiered soldiers are drunk, debauched, immoral, full of relentless bawdy innuendo, apparently even open to prostitute their own sisters. In a tavern scene they indicate their willingness to

---

7.   I wish to thank Paulina Kewes for this observation.

commodify any women available: 'But what the Devil makes these Women come hither? / 'Tis but changing of Sisters, and they will serve us for Wenches' (2.2).

Cavendish's sophisticated dramatic structure is indicated by the turning point created at the end of Act 2, midway through the play. From this point onwards, the play focuses on the inventive sisters, Jane Fullwit, Anne Sencible, Peg Valourosa 'busie about some Female-design', since they recognise that 'we may live by our Wits' (2.4). Madam Informer is a pivotal character, stigmatised as a bawd by the men, but valuable to the clear-sighted women in targetting rich husbands. The ostensibly powerless and financially invalid women demonstrate their highly pragmatic ability to reverse the economic relations of prostitution and get fortunes through marriage, drawing lots for husbands. Jane Fullwit cross-dresses to perform the part of a lawyer's clerk, while the women direct their brothers as brokers, go-betweens and supporting actors in their ingenious and fraudulent charades. One of the most theatrically extravagant and enjoyable scenes is set in a mock spiritual court, as the play evolves into a fantastic, surreal sexual comedy about platonic conception. The extended contemporary philosophical joke about the platonic versus the real is another reference to Henrietta Maria's court culture of platonic love. Gender reversals and comedy multiply when Harry Sencible cross-dresses, to pass as a chambermaid to old Lady Riches, to gain her as a wife for Dick. Multiple-layered tricks and staged events lead to satisfactory marriages for all three women and Usurer, the richest husband, donates funds to the men at the end, demonstrating that the sisters' wit has made the brothers' fortunes, as the women have exploited men sexually and financially. The play characterises women as competent, creative, resourceful and well able to mitigate and deflect the consequences of war.

Loves Adventures I and II (1662) also utilises a war scenario; the play is a fast-paced highly stageable comedy about the power of female agency. The heiress Lady Orphant is obsessed with the scrupulous Lord Singularity, who has rejected their arranged marriage on principle. Cross-dressed as a soldier named Affectionata, she becomes his page, progresses ably through the military ranks and in echoes of the Viola/Orsino plot from *Twelfth Night*, wins his friendship, admiration, and declared love in a highly suggestive 'Ganimed' relationship. The sensational denouement, which is replete with dramatic irony, includes the revelation of Affectionata's true sex and identity at the murder trial resulting from Orphant's mysterious disappearance, revealed by Singularity's plan to defuse the sexual tension by marrying Affectionata to Orphant!

The play is partly based on contemporary romance motifs in newsbook reports from the Civil War such as: 'a rare example of the powerful effects of love . . . the story of a Female souldier' whose 'love to her comerade was such, that in the habite of a young man she had followed him through all the dangers of the War' (*The Weekly Intelligencer of the Commonwealth* 17–24 July 1655 in Raymond 1993: 167). Romance was a key royalist form (*see* Chapter 3); this plot emphasises women's agency, courage, persistence and good sense, in a rewriting of *All's Well that Ends Well*. Orphant, Cavendish's aristocratic version of Helena, imitates Shakespeare's orphaned heroine by travelling to the war in Italy disguised as a pilgrim to find her rejecting lover. Like Bertram, Singularity can only desire his mistress when he is ignorant of her identity. Orphant is significantly more empowered and active than Helena, who retains her female identity throughout Shakespeare's play. It is also possible that Orphant's active and heroic military activities once again function as a critique of the passive behaviour of the besieged women in *The Concealed Fancies*.

Loves Adventures contrasts three couples' marriage negotiations. The second plot is a comic social satire, Cavendish's fullest reworking of *Epicoene* through the courtship of a 'Silent Man' the enigmatic anti-hero, Sir Serious Dumb, and a 'Silent Woman' the non-conformist and socially inept heiress, Lady Bashful, who bears some resemblance to Cavendish. Society, represented by Lady Wagtaile, a satiric target for her 'endless tongue' (II.1.5), is dismissive of both: 'for by my troth, all those that are dumb are meer fools; for who can be witty or wise that cannot speak, or will not speak, which is as bad' (II.1.18). 'Bashful' is a very significant term for Cavendish, in terms of her own autobiography and as a starting point for her protofeminist reappropriation of a particular gender value of her age. Her recognition that bashfulness is an enigmatic performance quality is indicated in *The Female Academy* (1662) 'extreme anger and extreme bashfulness have often one and the same effects to outward appearance' (4.24).

The inclusion of silent characters in a play is a crucial performance issue. While there are obvious limitations to reading such characters aloud, in performance a silent character can command a powerful stage presence: strong, interrogative, enigmatic in motivation, requiring commentary or interpretation by other characters. Cavendish exploits this performance dimension effectively by using Sir Serious Dumb to expose empty social mores, as a speechless moral inversion of the free-talking and aptly named rogue Parolles in *All's Well that Ends Well*. When Sir Serious Dumb is unjustly mocked, a carefully-crafted moment of decisive action occurs, as the scene abruptly explodes into a highly dramatic extended sword-fight in which Lady Bashful plays a major and energetic part. The stage directions choreograph the several stages of the fight precisely, suggesting that performance is envisaged.

Lady Bashful. What, are you not ashamed to assault an unarmed man.

. . . Sir Humphry Bold runs, and catcheth Sir Timothy Compliments sword, and offers to make a thrust at Sir Serious Dumb, who puts the sword by, and beats it down with one hand, and with the other strikes it aside, then closes with him, and being skillful at Wrestling, trips up his heels, then gets upon him, and having both his hands at liberty, wrings out Sir Humphrey Bold's sword out of his hand, then ariseth and gives the sword to the right owner, who all the time trembled for fear, and never durst strive to part them. The women in the mean time squeeks.

(II.1.8)

This heroic action and emphatic gender reversal bring Lady Bashful the confidence to propose to Sir Serious Dumb. Love brings him fluency, too; in a surprising denouement, he finds his voice and speaks for the first time in the play (3.20). The compliments of Cavendish's faithful and worthy 'Silent Man' reveal him as the reverse of Jonson's mocking dissimulating Epicoene. The play concludes by celebrating marital harmony. Bashful characteristically rejects the performance dimensions of a public wedding 'so I will not be drest for a Pageant show'(II.4.27) and disappears, leaving the stage clear for the magnificent public wedding festivities of Orphant and Singularity and the introduction of an intriguing meta-theatrical performance dimension, which strongly indicates the possibility of production within the Newcastle household.

The final scene of *Loves Adventures* assumes the form of a dramatic epilogue. Lord Singularity, who, like many of Cavendish's heroic male protagonists, resembles William Cavendish, is metatheatrically accosted at his wedding by musicians who: 'desire your Excellence will give us leave to present you with a Song written by my lord Marquiss of Newcastle'. William Cavendish was a knowledgeable and well-known music enthusiast (Chalmers 1997; Hulse 1996), yet comically and uncharacteristically Lord Singularity, his fictional counterpart, responds with ennui. He is rude and inattentive to the music, mistaking the song itself for discordant tuning up. The offer of one more song for the bride, an 'Eppilanian' (*sic*) enrages him; his response is simultaneously a joke about his own sexual desire and a compliment to his wife. 'O! it will be my funeral song, you rogues, know all delays doth kill me; and at this time your best Musick sounds out of tune.' '. . . quick, quick . . .' (II.5.39). The songs, which are actually by William, are lyrical and beautiful; the concluding epithalamium in particular is a lingering celebration of the bridal couple's erotic and spiritual harmony (II.5.39). Such an unlikely inversion of William Cavendish's musical judgement, composition skills, and courtly manners would have been very funny to a household or coterie audience, such as the Newcastles' Antwerp neighbours, the musical Duarte family.

The scene publicises Cavendish's teasing and confident intimacy with William. Its prominent position in the first play in Cavendish's 'first Folio', a volume advertised and sold commercially, which includes numerous collaborative contributions and a complimentary dedication by him, must indicate close consultation and literary confidence between them. It may also reveal Cavendish's competitive attitude to the literary family coterie into which she had married. Cavendish and Brackley's plays and poems envisage the absent William Cavendish as their key intended auditor (Ezell 1988: 253–7); a manuscript is likely to have been sent to him in exile, since literary texts were extensively used as a means of dialogue and communication within the Cavendish family (Ezell 1988; Randall 1997). Jane Cavendish and Elizabeth Brackley used their collaborative dramatic works to affirm their relationship with their father, their writings refer frequently and longingly to their father's absence in exile. *The Concealed Fancies* also seems to contain scenes mocking their stepmother-to-be. The satiric comedy of Lady Tranquillity's ridiculous courtship manoeuvres may well have been intended, given the number of other family jokes in the text, to represent a hearsay version of Margaret Lucas while courting William Cavendish (Findlay 1998: 268; Starr 1931: 837–8). It also seems to have been the impetus for Margaret Cavendish to redirect her dramatic energies to rewrite a motif from a female-authored play in the household tradition.

This scene seems to be Margaret Cavendish's direct literary response to Jane Cavendish and Elizabeth Brackley, her play speaking authoritatively to theirs. Her multiple metatheatrical and confidently disrespectful jokes in the wedding scene are a marked contrast to Jane and Elizabeth's dramatisation of their deferential grief at personal separation from their father and dutiful longing for his return. Father figures in *The Concealed Fancies* and *A Pastorall* are never rendered comically. This comic finale by contrast dramatises Cavendish's intimate relationship with William and their literary collaboration eulogised in a 1662 Preface: 'thus our Wits join as in Matrimony, my Lords the Masculine, mine the Feminine Wit, which is no small glory to me, that we are Married, Souls, Bodies, and Brains, which is a treble marriage . . .' (A6).[8]

The Presence (1668) is the most apparently autobiographical of all Cavendish's plays, tracing the courtship of another Lady Bashful, a new maid of honour to the Princess, and Lord Loyalty. This play is crucial to the debate about the performance status of Cavendish's plays, offering hitherto overlooked evidence about her thoughtful editing practices and informed

8. One of Margaret Cavendish's explications of the 'household salon' illustration commissioned in Antwerp interprets it as an idealised image of Cavendish children and spouses positioned as a domestic audience to the united figures of Margaret and William (Fitzmaurice 1997b: 356–9).

attitude to dramatic structure. *The Presence* announces its performance status with a dramatic introduction spoken by discriminating male theatre-goers, and appears in the 1668 folio immediately followed by a dramatic text labelled 'Scenes' and with the explanatory heading 'These Scenes were design'd to be put into the *Presence* but reason I found they would make that Play too long, I thought it requisite to Print them by themselves' (1668: 93). There are no two-part plays in the 1668 collection, but Cavendish's publishing strategy here functions to offer two possible performance texts of *The Presence*, cut or complete, indicating a flexible and opportunistic approach to performance length. The play is set at a fictional court, and acutely satirises details of court manners, mode fashions and values. The title refers to the presence-chamber and is also a verbal joke about the stage absence of the Emperor, which leaves his daughter the Princess as court authority.

Lady Bashful is caricatured as a fool by her female counterparts, yet ultimately vindicated. The 'cuts' or reconsiderations revealed by the material included in 'Scenes' significantly reduce this plot, omitting all of Lord Loyalty's original lines and appearances, reducing him to an invisible and silent character. Lady Bashful's lines are also heavily reduced, giving her self-vindication additional impact as her longest speech: 'I had rather be thought a Fool for saying nothing than be proved a Fool for speaking Nonsense; and of the two evils, it were better to be a silent Fool, than a prating Fool' (2.5). Bashfulness was an intensely significant quality to Cavendish personally, with a distinctively gendered performance dimension. *The Presence* is not simply autobiographical, but an attempt to stage this gender position within the claustrophobic confines of a court setting. 'Scenes' reveals that an entire sub-plot has been removed from *The Presence*, an economic plot about the corrupt management and vicissitudes of wardship, in which virtue finally triumphs. Anna Battigelli has called *The Presence* Cavendish's 'most aesthetically-flawed play' (1998: 34), yet the explicit editing strategy reveals an informed awareness of performance aesthetics. The final link between the excised sub-plot and the aristocratic main plot, in which the Ward's servant courts the 'Mother of the maids' is further evidence that these two texts were originally conceived as one.

The formal lengthy declamatory speeches given to many of Cavendish's female protagonists should be read as microcosmic dramas where women stage themselves authoritatively. The enclosed separatist settings of some plays are revealed as spaces where women are staged as creative, oppositional, empowered and unlike the material theatre of the day can hold centre stage before an appreciative audience, a rare position in reality for women, and one denied by marriage. Two 1662 plays, *Youths Glory and Deaths Banquet* and *Lady Contemplation*, investigate the extent to which intellectual freedom and creative imagination might prove a realistic alternative to marriage for women.

Lady Contemplation I and *II* (1662) stages the idea of a woman dramatist. Lady Contemplation's intellectual and imaginative life is much more vivid and exciting than reality. She imagines and engages intellectually with a series of sensational 'Airy Fictions', dramatic and erotic scenarios, which improve on reality, offering different alternatives to marriage. Comically, all are broken off dramatically just before the climax by the intervention of characters from the play. For example, she imagines a passionate lover who attempts suicide due to her indifference: 'he got secretly neer my chamber-door, and hung himself just where I must go out, which when I saw, I started back in a great fright, but at last running forth for help to cut him down, in came Monsieur Amorous, which hinderance made me leave him hanging there, as being ashamed to own my cruelty; and he hath been talking, or rather prating here so long, as by this time my kind Love is dead'. The skilful and pleasureable dramatic achievement of these passages is the equal immediacy of both the imaginary and the real scenarios. Lady Contemplation requests her auditor, 'Pray leave me alone, that I may cut him down and give him Cordials to restore life' (I.3.27).

Youths Glory and Deaths Banquet I and *II* (1662) also constantly invokes the idea of women taking centre-stage to perform to an audience. The double plot concerns the intellectual Lady Sanspareille who devotes herself to education, becoming a public orator instead of marrying, and the love triangle household of Lord L'Amour, his wife Lady Innocence and his mistress Lady Incontinent. The play opens with an impassioned conflict between Sanspareille's parents about education and gender. While their aptronyms suggest equal commitment to her well-being, Mother Love advocates a conventional domestic education to make her receptive and passive, to learn 'to fashion herself to all companies, times and places' (I.1.1) and accuses her of becoming the moral opposite 'transformed from what you should be, from a sober young maid, to a Stage-player, to act Parts, speak Speeches, rehearse Verses, sing Sonets and the like' (I.1.3). Father Love has implemented a masculine programme of rigorous intellectual study which Sanspareille prefers. She rejects marriage and private relationships to become almost a university in her own right, an accomplished and successful public orator, who also publishes her ideas, extending the treatment of elite education for women in *The Female Academy*.

Theatrical imagery distinguishes Sanspareille's intellectual career; she can 'act parts and speak speeches on the Stage' (II.1.3) and her orations resemble stage performances as she stands on a raised platform, symbolically costumed, to address her audience, who compliment her father, 'Sir, you have adorned her Theater to inthrone her wit' (I.3.9). The style of each performance matches the topic; she wears a symbolic wedding costume to address an entire audience of prospective husbands on marriage. *Enter the*

Lady Sanspareille, all in white Satin, like as a bride, and her Father and her audience, which are all Lovers; these stand gazing upon her (II.2.5). Her intensely negative analysis and rejection of marriage abruptly proves to be her last oration, for she falls suddenly ill and dies. Throughout the play Father Love's close and impassioned relationship with her has incestuous overtones, doubly implied in the slipped syntax which includes him in her audience of lovers. Incest is a significant sub-textual motif in a number of Cavendish's plays and may in part be a response to the intensity of Jane Cavendish's manuscript poems to William Cavendish. For example, the poem 'Passions Sire is my Lord my Father' contains the lines:

> For without you, I am dull peece of earth,
> And so continues nothinge, till you make my birth
> For want of you, I can too truely tell
> The severall ways of grief, that makes a hell
> Soe in the middest of passions greife 'twas such,
> As I did thinke my life was much too much.
> (Cavendish and Brackley *c.* 1645: 1)[9]

In Cavendish's play such imagery and sentiment emanates from the father not the daughter, however. He responds to Sanspareille's death by articulating an astonishing gender reversal, requesting the burial convention for the mother of a still-born child: 'I will have you rip my body open, and make it as a Coffin to lay her in' (II.4.17).[10] He uses further gynaecological imagery 'then cover us with a Dark, Black, Pitchy, Spongy cloud, made of thick Vapour, drawn from bleeding Hearts'. His sole oration of the play, at her funeral, fuses imitation and commemoration of his 'own Flesh and Blood'; he dies at her graveside and is buried with her.

In *Youths Glory and Deaths Banquet* the death scenes have marked similarities with the stylised deaths of the female protagonists in two public theatre plays: Thomas Kyd's *The Spanish Tragedy* (1592) and John Ford's *The Broken Heart* (1629). As in *Bell in Campo*, Cavendish pays detailed attention to the physical and visual staging of death, giving complex stage directions for the mechanics of these scenes: *Her Father starts up from her Bed-side, and stares about the Bed, and the dead Lady is drawn off the stage* (II.3.14) and *The whilst her Father is carryed in sick in a Chair, the Chair covered with black, and born black by Mourners, he himself also in close Mourning; when they have gone about the Stage, the Herse is set neer to the Grave, there being one made. Then the Father is placed in his Chair, upon a*

---

9. I wish to thank Alison Findlay for this point.
10. I wish to thank my student Sharon Lythgoe for this insight.

raised place for that purpose, the raised place also covered with Black; he being placed, speaks her Funeral Sermon (I.5.22).

The contest between Lady Incontinent and Lady Innocence for Lord l'Amour's affections in the sub-plot also ends in multiple deaths. With tragic irony, l'Amour forms the secret audience for the wronged Innocence's ritualised suicide performance without recognising it as real:

> De l'Amour.   What are you acting a melancholy Play by yourself alone?
> Innocence.   My part is almost done.
> De l'Amour.   By Heaven, she hath stabb'd herself.
>
> (II.4.19)

Generically *Youths Glory and Deaths Banquet* symbolically dramatises and intercuts funeral, wedding and childbirth motifs in a moving and shocking manner. While the play ends as tragedy, it is also possible to interpret Sanspareille's affirmative self-staging as a provisional triumph. Generally, Cavendish shows particular skill in dramatising solemn formal death scenes. *The Unnatural Tragedy* (1662) reworks the brother–sister incest plot from John Ford's *'Tis Pity She's A Whore* (1632). Significantly, however, the sister in Cavendish's play is raped, and never consents to the incest. This is a further example of Cavendish's refusal to create female characters who are commodified as whores.

Whatever the genre, Cavendish's overriding dramatic interest is in women claiming an alternative space to marriage. *The Convent of Pleasure* (1668) is the play which has so far attracted the most critical and production attention (Williams 1998; Roberts 1997; Rosenthal 1996: 92–101) due to its metatheatrical investigations of economic and erotic alternatives to heterosexual marriage. In general, the 1668 plays appear more dramatically sophisticated and confident, published with only a brief Preface to the volume. *The Convent of Pleasure* (1668) is the most economical and confident in its dramatisation of Cavendish's central concerns, exploring the construction of gender, with particular reference to cross-dressing and same-sex love. Aristocratic women are dramatised engaging in a series of intersecting theatrical performances before an audience, in different genres. The play constitutes Cavendish's most explicit claim to theatrical space for women, though it has a conservative conclusion which dissolves the Convent as performance space, silences Lady Happy, the play's protagonist, and confirms heterosexual values.

Cavendish particularly concentrates on dramatising the major themes of courtship and marriage, defined by T. E. in 1632 as the central and defining female experience in early modern society: 'All women are understood married or to be married' (Aughterson 1995: 153). Sara Mendelson and Patricia Crawford argue, however, that 'women were likely to experience wedlock as a violent discontinuity'. 'The (momentous) metamorphosis from 'maid' to 'wife' transformed every aspect of their existence.' Women's experience of marriage was contradictory, simultaneously bringing enhanced social status and legal non-existence. They also point out that 'seventeenth century writers produced an enormous literature purporting to describe married life. Nearly all of it was written by men . . .' (1998: 124–34).

Cavendish contributes to redressing this balance by devoting the majority of her plays to dramatising and redramatising an oppositional female perspective on marriage. It would be hard to improve on her first Lady Bashful's incisive critique of the bad bargain marriage offers women:

Lady Bashfull.	No, not marry.
Mistress Reformer.	Why so?
Lady Bashfull.	Because I am now Mistriss of my self, and fortunes, and have a free liberty; and who that is free, if they be wise, will make themselves slaves, subjecting themselves to anothers humour, unless they were fools, or mad, and knew not how to choose the best and happiest life.

(Loves Adventures I.4.17)

Such sentiments are echoed at length by Lady Happy in *The Convent of Pleasure*.

Cavendish's plays present a series of empowered female protagonists who attempt to renegotiate or reinvent courtship and marriage. The choices made by these eligible aristocratic heiresses are often provocative and extreme, at odds with social convention and audience expectation. Society criticises their unconventional choices, which often triumph in the end. Cavendish's plays do not reject the institution of marriage, indeed most of her comedies conclude conventionally with the staging of wedding scenes or 'Pageant show[s]' (*Love's Adventures II* 4.27); a sustainable alternative is rarely offered. She does create dramatic space for a protofeminist reassessment of the universal female condition. Some plays teasingly raise the possibility of same-sex love but suggest satisfaction is most likely to be found in successfully negotiated heterosexual relationships. The plays provide an affirmative view of female potential and ingenuity as married women characters are also shown using various strategies to renegotiate the conditions of marriage itself.

Despite the strong evidence for household performance in *Loves Adventures* and the numerous theatrical indications in Cavendish's plays, questions about the original performance status of her plays remain. Publication evidence suggests that contradictions in Cavendish's statements about performance may have been generated by adverse criticism. A close examination of gaps and inconsistencies in page numbering and differences in the design of page headings of the numerous 1662 Prefaces suggest that they actually comprise a mixture of original material and later additions.[11] The 'original' Prefaces (3, 6, 9, 10) seem to be conventional rhetorical disclaimers, tentative about performance and adverse critical response. The inserted Prefaces (1, 2, 4, 5, 7, 8) are more forceful in rejecting any expectation of performance, suggesting the interesting possibility that Cavendish amended her material at a late stage prior to publication in response to particular criticism. The most emphatic denials: 'the printing of my playes spoils them forever to be acted ... I shall never desire they should be acted ...' appear in the second inserted Preface, which reads remarkably like the response to a question. The intricacies of the argument repay detailed attention:

> The reason why I put out my Playes in print, before they are acted, is first
> that I know not when they will be acted, by reason they are in English,
> and England doth not admit, I will not say of wit, yet not of Playes ... but
> the Printing of my plays spoils them forever to be Acted: for what men are
> acquainted with is despised, at lest neglected; for the newness of Playes,
> most commonly, takes the Spectators, more than the Wit, Scenes, or Plot,
> so that my Playes would seem lame or tired in action, and dull to hearing
> on the stage, for which reason, I shall never desire they should be acted;
> but if they delight or please the readers, I shall have as much satisfaction as
> if I had the hands of applause from the Spectators.
>
> (1662: sig. A[1+1]v)

Cavendish is both defiant and anxious about criticism.

This passage has been read as a blanket rejection of performance (Tomlinson 1992b: 134), whereas Cavendish is actually referring specifically to the public theatres of England and their closure (confirming an earlier composition date). The perceived tension between wit and newness is highly significant, emphasising her consistent valorisation of wit as the crucial element of a successful play; the 1662 volume is dedicated to 'those that do delight in Scenes and wit' (A1). Her express cynicism about the poor and superficial judgement of audiences who value 'newness' above all is developed further in her Utopian prose fiction *The Blazing World* (1666),

---

11. After printing and prior to publication. This is not an unusual practice for Cavendish. I
    am most grateful to Shirley Stacey and Dr Oliver Pickering for advice on the pagination
    and binding of *Playes* (1662).

where she features as a character in her own text, consulted by the fictional Empress about the writing of plays 'after the mode'. Cavendish's response is both modest and sarcastic about the judgement of her unidentified critics, 'the wits of these present times'. 'The Duchess answered, that she had as little skill to form a play after the mode, as she had to paint or make a scene for show. 'But you have made plays,' replied the Empress: 'yes', answered the Duchess, 'I intended them for plays; but the wits of these present times condemned them as incapable of being represented or acted, because they were not made up according to the rules of art; though I dare say the descriptions are as good as any they have writ' (1994: 220). Indeed the vapidity of 'mode' values is frequently strongly satirised in her plays, for example, in the characterisation of Monsieur Mode in *The Presence* or the animal courtiers in *A Piece of a Play*.

Cavendish's manner of addressing her intended audience in her prefatory texts varies; the Prefaces to the volume/s are addressed to 'Readers' (plural), whereas many individual plays have dramatic Prologues and/or Epilogues addressed to 'Spectators'. She may have flexibly and expediently compiled a collection of potential performance texts which could also function as a volume to be read, at a time when production possibilities were limited by the closure of the public theatres, compounded by possible indefinite exile, and adverse critical reaction. Interestingly, the Prologue to *The Publick Wooing* juxtaposes reading and performance as alternatives: 'if you do take delight / To read her Play or acted to your sight' (1662: 369). Straznicky assumes that reading is a solitary activity (1995: 359), for Cavendish, however, reading carries the specific meaning of reading aloud, itself a kind of communal performance; Cavendish gives detailed instructions about tone of voice, vocalisation 'for Scenes must be read as if they were spoke or Acted . . .' (1662: 10). Her opinions about the reading aloud of plays are further developed in *Sociable Letter* 173, which once more invokes Jonson's ubiquitous ghost (Fitzmaurice *et al.* 1997a: 172–3).

Cavendish established herself as a literary dramatist; the incomplete texts included in the 1668 volume are clear evidence of her editing strategies and practice. Her plays are certainly stageable, though their publication in monumental folio collections rather than as actors' quartos may indicate that she prioritised their literary above their theatrical status. Another possibility is that publication was a safer substitute for performance, given the closure of the theatres, her own exile and the political uncertainties of the age. Historically, her critical reputation has undeservedly foregrounded eccentricity at the expense of a close analysis of the achievement of her plays. Many more deserve sustained analysis and exploration as performance texts. They are entertaining, subversive about gender and explore ways in which women might stage themselves in public.

Just as *The Presence* (1668) illustrates her sensitivity to dramatic structure, the 1668 volume concludes by resisting closure, with an intriguing partial text, often ignored by critics, which stages Cavendish's satirical view of contemporary theatre values. The unfinished drama *A Piece of a Play* consists of just four scenes, prefaced by an 'Advertisement to the Reader' explaining: 'The Reader is desir'd to take notice, That the following Fragments are part of a Play which I did intend for my Blazing-World, and had been printed with it, if I had finish'd it; but before I had ended the second Act, finding that my Genius did not tend that way, I left that design; and now putting some other Comedies to the Press, I suffer this piece of One to be publish'd with them' (1668: 1).[12]

The play offers a satiric view of an empty 'Mode-world' peopled with self-important animal-like characters full of false pretensions. *Volpone* is clearly the model for this incisive critique of the follies of fashionable society, although it is not clear whether Cavendish's characters are humans with animal characteristics or animal-creatures as in *The Blazing World* (Sanders 1998: 295). The sole action of the play is talk; the fashionable and empty-headed characters are intensely preoccupied with anticipating Lady Phoenix's projected arrival. Rumours multiply into a fantastic description: '. . . she is clothed all with light, and the beams issuing from that light, make her train many miles long, which is held up by the Planets; also, she is perfumed with all the Spices in the East-Indies; her Chariot is made of air, in the fashion of a Ship, and that airy Ship is gilded with the Sun; she hath numerous attendants, those that usher her, are Blazing-Stars, and those that follow her, are fiery Meteors' (I.1). Cavendish is obviously satirising the unbounded capacities of social gossip and rumour here, but it is also possible that this is a description of a projected future masque scene in the play; the companion text, *The Blazing World*, has been characterised as science fiction due to its numerous fantastic elements (Lilley 1994: xxiii).

Why was this fragmentary text published? It forms an intriguing final note to Cavendish's publishing career as a dramatist, since she notably did not publish new editions of her plays, unlike her other works.[13] The play, the volume and Cavendish's career as a dramatist end with a self-reflexive theatrical joke. Monsieur Ass, a libel-maker, invites the ladies to 'a Mode-Play', denigrated by another character as 'all Rhime, and no reason, or all Action and no Wit' (2.2). In response, and to general embarrassment, Ass reveals that he is the author of the play in question. This demonstrates Cavendish's sharp satiric sense of humour. Her first collection of plays

---

12. The 1668 plays are individually rather than consecutively paginated.
13. I am grateful to Paul Salzman for raising this point in on-line discussion.

began with a dramatic introduction in which audience members discussed the factors that might impede a woman dramatist; this last play concludes her publishing career on an ironic note as her society characters leave the stage 'content' to go and see a male-authored play 'of Monsieur Ass's making' (2.2).

Cavendish did look beyond the contemporary stage and 'the Wits of these present times' for validation as a dramatist, however. Her male play-goers in the 1662 introduction express her often repeated hope in the critical judgement of her future audiences that 'the future Ages may be more wise, and better natur'd as to applaud what the others have condemned' (1662: 15). She claimed a cultural space for her plays at a moment of political and cultural transition, and valorised posterity by constructing herself as a literary dramatist who published her 'Works' in folio, the most enduring and privileged form drama could take. 'A General Prologue to all my Playes' concludes by antithetically prioritising literary 'remains' over any physical or even religious memorial:

> I care not where my dust, or bones remain,
> So my Works live, the labour of my brain.
> I covet not a stately, cut, carv'd Tomb,
> But that my Works, in Fames house may have room.
>
> (1662: A8)

CHAPTER 5

Licensed to Thrill:
Early Restoration Drama

ALISON FINDLAY

In 1660, women were recruited to the King's Company and the Duke's Company who, between them, had the exclusive right to stage plays in commercial theatres. A patent granted to Thomas Killigrew specified that 'all the women's parts to be acted in either of the said two companies for the time to come may be performed by women, so long as their recreations . . . be esteemed not only harmless delight, but useful and instructive representations of human life' (Howe 1992: 25–6). The entry of women into this form of dramatic production was an important innovation. Elizabeth Howe (1992) has demonstrated the significant contribution of actresses to the dynamics of Restoration theatre and their presence played a key part in the development of female-authored drama.

The first public appearance by an actress was probably on 8 December 1660, when a female Desdemona in *Othello* was announced in a special prologue, with the words 'A woman playes today, mistake me not, / No man in Gown, or Page in Petty-Coat'. The Prologue (written by Thomas Jordan) took pains to explain that the boy actors who had been trained to perform female roles had now grown too old and large to be convincing. It appealed to the male spectators' gallantry, reminding them that acting was an honourable profession for women in France and that 'a vertuous woman' could remain unsullied even while playing on a stage 'where all eyes are upon her' (Jordan 1664 cited in Howe 1992: 19). The casual association between acting, seduction and prostitution had a long cultural history, to which Jordan indirectly alludes in addressing a potentially lascivious male audience. As far as female spectators were concerned, the actress was an especially remarkable figure because of her anomalous public presence. In fact, public roles for women declined in later seventeenth-century England (Maus 1979: 600), so for women confined to the domestic sphere, the actress may have been a focus of possibility. The epilogue to this innovative performance addressed the female audience thus:

> But Ladies what think you, for if you tax
> Her freedom with dishonour to your Sex,
> She means to act no more, and this shall be
> No other Play but her own tragedy; ·
> She will submit to none but your Commands,
> And take Commission onely from your hands.
>
> (Wilson 1958: 6)

Would the actress open up new opportunities or become an index of anti-feminist prejudice, an icon to reinforce rather than break down stereotypes? The Epilogue is optimistic, assuring women that their representative on stage would be their instrument (not that of men), a mouthpiece for their ideas.

Given this invitation, it is telling that more women did not hurry to script material for the actresses. We have records of only seven plays by women written for public theatres between 1663 and 1671. The cultural pressures against trying to insert one's work into a previously all-male arena must have been enormous for a female dramatist. Perhaps it is not surprising, then, that Katherine Philips's *Pompey* (1663), the first play to be performed in the professional theatre, followed in a female tradition of translation, begun by figures like Jane Lumley, Mary Sidney and Elizabeth I. Katherine Philips (1632–64) expressed doubts about her translation of Corneille, 'my Incapacity to perform it, as that so many others have undertaken it' (Philips 1992: 48–9). However, her letters to Sir Charles Cotterell show a keen desire to complete her piece before a male-authored translation, *Pompey The Great*, 'which will otherwise appear first and throw this into everlasting Obscurity' (Philips 1992: 62). Philips seems excited by the prospect of public exposure, whatever her modest claims to the contrary. When her mentor the Earl of Orrery plans to stage her text, her protestations therefore ring a little hollow in comparison to her anticipation about the production:

> notwithstanding all my Intreaties to the contrary, he is going on with [it], and has advanc'd a hundred Pounds towards the Expence of buying *Roman* and *Egyptian* Habits. All the other Persons of Quality here are also very earnest to bring it upon the Stage, and seem resolv'd to endure the Penance of seeing it play'd on *Tuesday* come sevennight, which day is appointed for the first time of acting it. My Lord ROSCOMON has made a Prologue for it, and Sir EDWARD DERING an Epilogue.... The Songs are set by several Hands; the first and fifth admirably well by PHILASTER [John Jeffreys], the third by Doctor PETT, one by *Le GRAND* a *Frenchman*, belonging to the Dutchess of ORMOND, had, by

her Order, set the fourth, and a *Frenchman* of my **LORD ORRERY**'s the second; so that all is ready, and poor I condemn'd to be expos'd, unless some Accident, which I heartily wish, but cannot forsee, kindly intervene to my Relief.

(Philips 1992: 74–5)

The performance, on 10 February 1663 at the Smock Alley Playhouse in Dublin, elicited many commendatory letters and verses. Philips' success was certainly due in part to the 'wide network of male allies' who encouraged her (Mulvilhill 1991: 87). Nevertheless, her dramatic translation was also seen as feminist. An anonymous female admirer, 'Philo-Philippa', hailed Philips as the 'glory of our Sex' (Greer 1988: 204, ll.13–16), seeing her pioneering work as the dawn of a campaign in which women would demand 'Tribunals for our Persons, and Command' (Greer 1988: 205, l.58). Philo-Philippa notes the creative power of translation, especially in Philips' representation of the character of Cornelia: 'In the French Rock *Cornelia* first did shine / But shin'd not like herself till she was thine' (Greer 1988: 207, ll.131–2). It is in the translator's power to refashion, and perhaps to write in a more politically explicit way than the original author.

Philips' choice of text carries local and national political meanings. As Andrew Shifflet (1997) has pointed out, *Pompey* dramatises the notion of royal clemency, interrogating this virtue in relation to the Act of Indemnity and Oblivion, by which the behaviour of parliamentary and royalist supporters was judged after the Restoration. The celebration of royalism in certain elements of the text may also be an attempt to counteract the prevailing image of Katherine's husband. On 27 June 1661, James Philips was suspended from the House of Commons (where he sat as MP for Cardiganshire) for allegedly being a member of the High Court who had passed the death sentence on the royalist John Gerard in 1654. James claimed that he had left the court before the prisoners were brought in and the House formally recognised his innocence on 25 February 1662. Katherine's translation (begun in August 1662) may have been designed to advertise respect for royalty in the Restoration court, to help restore his good name (Philips 1992: 14). In particular, songs between the acts 'which were added' to the play by Philips (The Printer to the Reader, p. 2), are blatantly royalist in tone. The first song recommends the proper duty of each subject:

> To our Monarch we owe, whatsoe're we enjoy:
> And no grateful Subjects were those,
> Who would not the safety, he gives them, employ
> To contribute to his repose.
>
> (1.4.139–42)

As self-contained performance pieces, Philips's songs popularised her political message. She noted that the first song proved so popular that 'Almost all that can sing here have learnt it already' (1992: 72). More than a political manifesto, it forms a graceful compliment to the theatre-loving Charles II since its chorus points out the need for hardworking kings to '*slacken . . . their Mind*' with entertainments. The Restoration audience see their king's addiction to '*Intervals . . . soft*' (1.4.137) justified as they watch the actors playing Ptolemy and his advisor being entertained by Katherine Philips' song and the following 'Antick dance of Gypsies' (1.4.44). Indeed, Katherine Philips may well have imagined Charles II in the spectator's role since she presented him with a copy of the play (1992: 90).

Philips does not simply return to principles of absolutism held by the earlier Stuart monarchy as though the Civil War had never happened. Corneille's text offers her a vehicle to present a complex analysis of power through the depiction of Ptolemy, Caesar and Cleopatra. The protagonists are not mouthpieces for clear-cut royalist or republican positions, but this would hardly have been appropriate to the complicated political arena of 1662–3 where different combinations of republican and royalist sympathies were at play. Shifflet argues that *Pompey* is designed to 'criticize the notion of royal clemency itself' and to rethink 'the stoic rhetoric that could support it as an instrument of royal absolutism' (1997: 107). He reads a distinctly republican sub-text in the play, especially in the figure of Cornelia, Pompey's widow, who is celebrated for criticising the magnanimous (royal) clemency of conquering Caesar and looking forward to a republican Elysium with Pompey. While this reading usefully illuminates Philips' critical perspective on the monarchy, it is also important to recognise her own royalist sympathies as part of a circle of Cavalier supporters in Wales (Philips 1990: 5–6). The play's representation of Caesar, Pompey and Ptolemy allows Philips to offer a non-partisan commentary on government.

Conquering (republican) Caesar is condemned for bringing '*Rivers of Blood*' (2.4.87) on to the land, recalling the horrors of the Civil War (2.4.103–4), yet Philips also presents a critical view of monarchy in the figure of Ptolemy. Striving for absolute power, especially over his sister Cleopatra, Ptolemy is essentially weak. He vacillates with his counsellors, betrays his ideal image, in the person of Pompey, and only redeems himself in his courageous death. Until the end of the play, Ptolemy is like a ghost of the negative aspects of Charles I. Dead Pompey, a Roman (republican) and yet also a kingmaker, becomes a model of absent good government, an ideal to which Charles II should aspire. His ghost appears to his widow Cornelia at the end of Act 3 in an extended musical scene of Philips' own invention. Here, her use of song to carry the action forward as an integral part of the plot was a theatrical innovation (Price 1979: 64). The royal ghost's lines '*By*

Death my Glory I resume' (3.4.103) encapsulate the renewal of monarchy enacted through the traumatic process of Civil War and the Restoration.

Cornelia, a faithful and high-principled widow, is presented as an idealised figure, the matchless model on which Philips styled herself. Although Cornelia knows she must physically submit to Caesar, she warns him 'think not to subject my Will' (3.4.46). Refusing to be tempted to cowardly vengeance, Cornelia reveals to Caesar that Ptolemy is plotting his murder. Her courage and constancy are her most striking qualities, so much so that she is seen as the incarnation of her husband, 'a part' of Pompey (4.4.10).

In contrast to Cornelia stands Cleopatra: simultaneously alluring, faithful, self-sacrificing and ambitious. The play makes clear that she has a right to the throne; she accuses Ptolemy 'You in the Throne usurp'd my equal seat' (1.3.93) and the plot traces her path to power. Unlike the Cleopatra of Mary Sidney's translation *The Tragedie of Antonie* (*see* Chapter 1), this queen is very worldly. She claims to put the interests of her country before her emotional ties by silently accepting Pompey's murder. Far from declaring that her beloved 'is my self' (Sidney 1996: 2.1.352) and killing herself, this Cleopatra ends *Pompey* by ascending the throne alone. She is celebrated in the Epilogue as

> One who ambition could withstand,
> Subdue revenge, and Love command,
> On Honours single score.
>
> (5.5.62–4)

Cleopatra is not as blameless as the first line of the song states. Ptolemy believes her 'Ambition is become so vain' (1.2.9) that she sees Pompey's murder as a stepping stone to the throne. The text remains carefully obscure about her real motives. She admits 'I have Ambition, and bee't good or ill, / It is the only Sovereign of my will' and believes it is a 'Noble passion' that a 'Princess may without a Blemish own' (2.1.77–80). However, even to be 'Mistress of the World' (2.1.76), she says she would not 'buy greatness with the loss of Fame' (2.1.82).

In the complex characterisation, it is possible to see a projection and displacement of Philips' own literary ambitions. Her technique of self-promotion is encapsulated in Ptolemy's accusation to Cleopatra: 'Through your false zeal, flashes of Pride escape; / And interest does act in Virtue's shape' (1.3.44–5). When Philips's writings were published in January 1664, she zealously constructed herself as a virtuous, retiring lady '*that can not so much as think in private, that it must have my imaginations rifled and exposed to play the Mountebanks, and dance upon the Ropes to entertain all the Rabble*' (Philips 1992: 129). The horror at having the fruits of her wit exposed as public entertainments is contradicted by Philips' activities in Dublin and London, where she actively set herself on the public stage through her translation of *Pompey*. Her attitudes to the production reveal 'a woman vitally interested in the public life of a professional writer', as Lucy Brashear remarks (1979: 70). Philips had an acute sense of the spectacle she had created. As if aware of Davenant's attempt to burlesque her play in Act 5 of his *The Play House To Be Let* (1663), she wrote to Cotterell echoing the words of Shakespeare's Cleopatra (5.2.212–17):

> you will shortly see a Farce, or a Puppet-show at LONDON, call'd IRELAND *in ridicule*; wherein all the Plays will be repeated, and the Actors themselves acted in Burlesque. Then POMPEY will be squeak'd out in a Tone as lamentable as the Language; and, unless you prevent it, the very Puppets will take Example by the Printers, and fall out among themselves whether CAESAR or PTOLEMY shall have the best Hobby-Horse.
>
> (Philips 1992: 97)

Philips' appetite for literary fame made her authorise a reprinting of *Pompey* and begin another translation, of Corneille's play *Horace* (Philips 1992: 124).

She started this in the winter of 1663–4, but contracted smallpox when she came to London in the spring, and was buried on 23 June. Philips had translated four acts of *Horace* by her death, Sir John Denham completing the text. *Horace* finally reached the stage on 4 February 1668, when it was produced at court with Lady Castlemaine, Charles II's long-standing royal mistress, as a performer (Magalotti 1980: 144). Thomas Killigrew then staged it at the King's Theatre throughout January and February 1669. Sadly, in production, the addition of songs, masques and music 'seriously muddled and unbalanced' the tragic ethos of Philips' text (Mulvihill 1991: 98). It is a much freer translation which clearly shows 'the complex appeal of Corneille's *Horatius*' (Randall 1995: 227).

Horace traces a national conflict between Rome and Alba by focusing on the ruling families of the Roman Horace and the Alban Curiace. These rivals are bound in more than friendship and honour since Curiace's sister Sabina is married to Horace and Horace's sister Camilla is in love with Curiace. The audience view the tragic conflict from the viewpoint of the two women, whose loyalties are torn between their blood kin and their lovers. Their passions reflect each other like tragic mirrors of suffering in which each is trapped, helpless to prevent the pattern of self-destruction to which their men are committed by high principles of 'honour'. The play is beautifully structured around this mirror-like model of opposition and sameness. Through the two female protagonists, it illuminates the impossible position a bride occupied when relationships between the families of her birth and marriage were not friendly:

> For Blood as well as Marriage, is a knot,
> We quit our Kindred, but forget them not.
> Never does Hymen Nature undermine,
> Who loves her Husband does not hate her Line.
>
> (3.4.27–30)

The conflict between romantic love and family love, especially acute for women, had been explored by Elizabeth Cary in *The Tragedy of Mariam* (*see* Chapter 2). By choosing to translate a text which foregrounds this issue, Philips refocused attention on the difficulties faced by women who had to pass from one family to another (Findlay 1999a: 139–40). Since many families had been estranged as a result of conflicts in the recent Civil War, the play's focus on marriage as a crisis of loyalty may have been especially pertinent.

Curiace and Horace are blamed as 'ambitious souls' whose vaunting sense of honour makes them 'as obstinate as brave' in wishing to determine the national quarrel by single fight (3.1.34–5). The women, by contrast, are drawn together by their futile attempts to prevent the conflict. Sabina challenges the primacy of male and national bonds by interposing herself as a sacrifice to, and cause of, their hatred (implicitly pointing out that they have no logical reason to hate each other at present) (2.6.20–1). It is a family quarrel, she insists, stressing the equal value of the private realm in which she will have to face a murderous brother or husband 'Reaking with blood that is to me so dear' (2.6.40–1). Such a challenge destabilises male ideas of honour far too dangerously and the women are confined at home so that 'no femall tears, & clamours may / Disturb the manly business of the day' (2.8.2–4). Behind the manly physical combat in which Horace kills Curiace lies the unnerving power of womanish passions to dissolve a fragile masculine, military identity.

Old Horace gives voice to the prevailing order in which 'Domestick losses we may well excuse / When they doe publick victorys produce' (4.3.3–4). Camilla openly defies this Roman ideology (4.4.42–4). Recognising that she must be 'Barbarous' to be 'noble' (4.2.42), she confronts young Horace with the naked passion of her grief for Curiace (4.5) and inverts the imperialistic model which his victory over the Alban lord has supposedly secured. It is Rome and its values which are barbaric, she declares:

> May all her Neighbours in one Knot Combine.
> Her yet unsure foundations t'undermine;
> And if *Italian* forces seem to[o] small;
> May East & West conspire to make her fall;
> And all the Nations of the barbarous World,
> To ruine her.
>
> (4.5.54–9)

Once loosed from her domestic prison, Camilla single-handedly deconstructs the colonialist policies of Roman state, its values of stoicism and public citizenship. Her passionate expression of grief stresses the disruptive presence of emotion, which a patrician state may wish to demonise as a barbaric 'other', but which is inevitably within. Horace's impulsive, brutal reaction – to murder Camilla – is testimony to that fact.

By translating Corneille, Philips found a way to put forward some daring ideas about women's confinement within masculine value systems and the weakness of those systems. Her admirer Philo-Philippa saw translation as only a stepping stone to greater things 'But if your fetter'd Muse thus praised be, / What great things do you write when it is free?' (Greer 208, ll.165–6), but perhaps translation was the ideal genre for the Matchless Orinda. Christopher Wheatley suggests that her muse was 'deliberately fettered' to show her feminine modesty, and that the enthusiastic praise she received 'is partially a consequence of those fetters' (1992: 24). In the early 1660s, when the public stage was still new territory for women, translation allowed her to speak to feminist issues with a masculine authority, or, as Philo-Philippa remarked 'thy more than masculine Pen hath rear'd / Our Sex: first to be Prased, nex't to be feard' (Greer 205: ll.35–6).

It was not until 1669 that an original composition by a woman was performed in the public theatre. In a letter of 1669, Elizabeth Cottington remarked 'there is a bowld woman hath oferd one: . . . Some verses I have seen that ar not ill: that is commendation enouf: she will think so too, I believe, when it comes upon the stage. I shall tremble for the poor wooman exposed among the critticks' (Greer 1988: 233). The play is probably *Marcelia* or *The Treacherous Friend*, performed by Killigrew's King's Company at the Theatre Royal in 1669. It is Frances Boothby's only known work and nothing is known of the author beyond the dedication of the published text to Lady Yate of Harvington in Worcestershire (1610–96), whom Boothby addresses as 'Kinswoman' (Boothby 1670: A2v). Boothby asks her patron to *'oppose the Censuring world upon this uncommon action in my Sex'* and to generously protect the play like *'Heavens Bounty'*. The Prologue says the author expects the audience to desert the house when presented with a play from *'A Woman's Pen'* (A3), but hopes the women spectators *'out of Pride / And Honor, will not quit their sexes side'* (A3v).

Marcelia examines the culture of visibility in the court and the theatre, and begins to explore women's new position on the Restoration stage as the focus of the audience's gaze. Feminist criticism has discussed the ways in which women are objectified by the male gaze and how this process is often extended in visual entertainments (Mulvey 1975; de Lauretis 1984). The main plot of *Marcelia* compares men and women as desiring subjects in order to highlight the biased cultural conditioning that objectifies women.

The villain Melynet poisons the love between the eponymous heroine and the hero, Lotharicus, in order to win Marcelia for King Sigismund, who has fallen in love with her despite his betrothal to Calinda. Boothby contrasts the King's faithlessness (a topical subject in the court of Charles II), with an image of female loyalty, as Calinda is comforted by her devoted companion Ericina.

The objectification of woman is clear when Melynet takes Marcelia to the court, to 'see the Mask' in order to lessen her grief at the loss of Lotharicus's love (F1v). In Act 3 Scene 6, which is highly reminiscent of Margaret Cavendish's short story 'The Contract' (1656), she becomes the focus of all eyes, an object of desire, even though she is supposedly there to watch (Cavendish 1994: 14). The metatheatrical dimensions of the situation are emphasised by its representation on stage. The theatrical framing of the gaze confuses subject/object positions, although men still have more power to make active interventions. The King is both spectacle and spectator throughout. Like Charles II in the court and the playhouse, he is the observed of all observers whose purview constructs those around him. His bow to the ladies of the court, 'so many Beauties', fixes them like butterflies, even though he says they have power to entrap the hearts of courtiers and King (F2v).

The foolish Moriphanus upstages the ladies with his 'incomparable dress' and his ridiculous train of attendants. He relishes the chance for self-advertisement and functions as an antemasque, which is 'more divertisement to the King and Ladies, then the Masque' (E1). The climactic entrance of Marcelia, 'so great a wonder to the Court to night, so daz'ling a Sun at mid-night' (F3v), completes the court's off-stage masque. The King's 'publick Address' (E3v) to Marcelia's 'Conquering Beauty' actively frames them both as the spectacle for court and theatre audiences (F4). The playhouse audience's interpretation of what they have seen is magnified and masculinised through the lens of Lotharicus's jealous viewpoint as he comments 'Woman, what art thou but mans tempting shame' (F4v), bringing the pattern of objectification back full circle to the king's opening comments on the ladies.

The play's comic resolution depends on Marcelia's constancy. When her brother reveals Melynet's plot she determines to refuse the king 'To shew that greatness dazles not [her] sight' (K3). In spite of her power to remain clear-sighted, in line with her own desires, she has little agency. When Lotharicus miraculously reappears, recovered from an attempt on his life, Marcelia is placed in the powerful position of being able to choose her lover but Boothby does not follow this promising moment through. Marcelia says she has no choice and relinquishes agency to the King, who overcomes his passion, mercifully giving her back to Lotharicus. By raising the possibility of female independence and then rejecting it, Boothby may be commenting on the limitations as well as the possibilities offered to women in the new arena of theatre. While the stage seems to give them a voice, the Duke's and the King's Companies are male-dominated institutions, still under a king's licence.

The sub-plot of *Marcelia* uses metatheatrical devices to denaturalise conventional subject–object relations and the materialisation of women. The rake Lucidore promises to display his mistress to the other courtiers for the price of 100 pistols. Woman is one entertainment among many: they argue 'you hold the sight too costly; you forget that we can see the Creation of the World for 18 pence, where there are twenty fine sights besides woman' (C3v). Lucidore defers the spectacle to increase their appetites, 'the sight will come too cheap else' (E4) and in an overtly theatrical 'discovery' scene, he exposes the gross materiality behind courtly protestations of love:

> *The Scene opens, and there lies heaps of money up and down; and there stands five persons about the Table with bags in their hands, dress'd in Antick habit: (as others at the door) They come out and dance, and keep time with their Bags and Pockets.*
> Luc. What think you Gentlemen of her? There she is; and her
> Attendants . . . You see this is the Mistress of my heart and pleasure.
>
> (G3)

When Lucidore courts the widow Perilla, his protestations of love are inevitably coloured by the audience's awareness of his strong financial motives. By association, Perilla becomes an extension of his piles of gold.

Perilla obviously enjoys her status as an independent widow so is unlikely to welcome such a role. It is therefore surprising when she accepts Lucidore's offer of marriage, even though she knows he is interested in her money. She observes 'you are very sharp set to my Estate; if you possest that, I believe you would easily bequeath my person for a Legacy to my next Heir' (L3). Possibly she is attracted by his candid approach, shown in the unconventional wooing entertainment he presents. The interlude appeals to Perilla's status as a desiring subject by representing Lucidore as an object on display. It mocks the devoted and self-sacrificing lover by blatantly exposing Lucidore's own changing affections in comic form. A group of boys bring in a huge serving dish, supposedly containing Lucidore's heart, which absurdly changes 'hot and cold, cold and hot' as the boys leave it to cool and Mercury uses coals and then bellows to reheat it (L1v). A heart with wings then commends Lucidore's love to Perilla, proclaiming his faults, but saying that his sins will be open unlike those of other men (L2). The man's willingness to make a spectacle of himself, and offer himself openly to her judgement, marks a striking contrast to the secretive world of the court, where deception and desire so nearly ruin the lives of Marcelia, Lotharicus and Calinda. The women in *Marcelia* are not allowed to escape objectification (even Perilla remains a rich catch in spite of Lucidore's attempt to place himself in the object position). While working within those conventional cultural and dramatic structures, however, Frances Boothby subtly suggests the need for reform in romantic relations between men and women.

Another female dramatist who wrote for professional theatre in these years is Elizabeth Polwhele (*c.* 1651–91), who composed at least three plays in the years up to 1671. In the dedication of her racy comedy *The Frolicks* (1671) to Prince Rupert, she suspects 'I shall be taxed for writing a play so comical, but those that have ever seen my *Faithfull Virgins* and my *Elysium* will justify me a little for writing this' (Polwhele 1977: 57–8). No record of the *Elysium* has been found, but the tragedy *The Faithfull Virgins* does exist in manuscript, the hand matching that of *The Frolicks* and concluding with the initials E. P. (Polwhele *c.* 1670). Nothing about the identity of 'E. Polewheele' is known beyond what she reveals in the dedication of *The Frolicks*, where she writes: 'I am young, no scholar, and what I write I write by nature, not by art' (Polwhele 1977: 58). Her modern editors, Milhous and Hume, propose an Elizabeth Polwhele born *c.* 1651, daughter of the nonconformist vicar of Tiverton, Devonshire. This Elizabeth married another prominent clergyman, Stephen Lobb, some time well before 1678 (when she bore him a son), her marriage perhaps accounting for the absence of any further dramatic writing after 1671 (Polwhele 1977: 44–6).

Whoever she was, Polwhele was a skilled dramatist with at least some experience of theatre practice. In the dedication to Prince Rupert, she describes herself as 'a virgin' who is 'haunted with poetic devils' and the ghosts of Jacobean tragedy certainly haunt her play *The Faithfull Virgins*. Her protestation 'I write by nature, not art' seems artfully innocent (Polwhele 1977: 57–8). She borrows from Davenant's *Albovine, King of the Lombards* (1628) in Act V of her own tragedy (Summers 1935: 340) and obviously knows Shakespeare's plays well since both her texts echo Shakespearean lines and scenes. In *The Faithfull Virgins*, for example, Polwhele models the plot of the cross-dressed page on Viola in *Twelfth Night* and presents a witches' prophecy scene which recalls Davenant's spectacular adaptation of *Macbeth*, performed by the Duke's Company in 1664–8 and November 1670 (Brooke 1994: 36–8).[1]

By the time Polwhele came to write *The Frolicks*, she certainly had working experience of the theatre since *The Faithfull Virgins* (*c.* 1669–70) had been produced professionally. The manuscript reads 'This Tragedy apoynted to be acted by the dukes Company of Actors' (Polwhele *c.* 1670: 49). We do

---

1. *See The Faithfull Virgins* (58v) for the rewriting of *Macbeth*. In the triangular love plot *see*, for example, (69) and 3.1.114 of *Twelfth Night*.

not know exactly when it was performed, although it must have been some time before March 1671/2 and *The Frolicks* (and presumably before *Elysium* too); Milhous and Hume suggest *c.* 1670, a significant time for the Duke's Company. From Davenant's death in 1668 until 1673, the Duke's was managed by Lady Davenant in the interests of her infant son. She took an active role in controlling the company so Polwhele's initiation into the world of professional theatre probably happened under the aegis of another woman (Pearson 1988: 32). The company's decision to stage such an old-fashioned tragedy as *The Faithfull Virgins* at this time is bound up with its personnel and history.

In 1668 competition between the Duke's and King's companies had been focused on the comic female leads, Moll Davis and Nell Gwyn. As Bax notes, the two actresses 'had been pitted against each other by their managements and by the public' (1932: 124). At the end of May 1668, however, the Duke's company lost Moll Davis, who retired from the stage when she became Charles II's mistress. Without their leading comic actress, the Duke's turned to staging tragedies. Polwhele's *The Faithfull Virgins* was a suitable piece for the company, having four fairly equal female roles.[2] Although it is not a vehicle for a single star, the play 'gives women a high visibility and allows them to speak almost half the lines' as Jacqueline Pearson notes (1988: 138).

Tableaux effects are especially important in the presentation of the female characters. The final act presents juxtaposed images of femininity, one to be condemned and one to be celebrated. The Duchess Isabella functions as a pictorial index of the lustful slaughter in which the protagonists perish. She is discovered 'on a couch in a rich night dress, soft musique and a songe within' (Polwhele *c.* 1670: 76v). Her voluptuousness is demonised; once she discovers that the Duke is infatuated with Umira, she exploits her own sexuality to blackmail a lustful suitor and persuade him to murder the innocent virgin. The bedchamber scene shows the Duchess waiting to reward her suitor. Immediately after this, the audience are presented with the ideal of sacrificial female chastity in the faithful virgins: 'The scene Opens discovering, Umira, Merantha; and Erasila like a woman in white – with sparckling wreaths or coronetts upon their heads dead on a couch' (77r). Umira and Merantha have remained true to their love for the dead Philamon

---

2. Since Winifred Gosnell took over from Moll Davies as female lead, it is possible that she, Mary Betterton, Jane Long (who specialised in breeches roles) and Mary Lee, whose strength was in romantic and tragic roles, or Anne Shadwell (née Gibbs) (who had played Olivia in *Twelfth Night* in 1661), performed in the production (Wilson 1958: 117–20, 145–6, 159–60, 165–6, 186–7). Possibly Mrs Johnson, famous for her dancing, could have played one of the spirits (Wilson 1958: 152–3).

throughout the play while Erasila has killed herself to follow her beloved Statenor, murdered by the Duke in the final debacle. It is such self-sacrifice, crystallised in the beautiful female corpses, which is to be lauded with 'sparckling wreaths or coronetts'. The Duchess, by contrast, becomes the play's scapegoat for the vices of inconstancy and jealousy. She is blamed for abandoning her beloved Cleophon in favour of a loveless marriage to the Duke and then yielding to jealousy and to her suitor's lust. Cleophon tells her:

> goe wash your blemish't soule in contrite tears
> till it grows white, as now it black apears,
> may you a pentitentiall Convert dye
> though you must still survive to infamy
> but fame to this and after ages shall
> the faythfull virgins, ever more extoll.
>
> (78r)

Far from using theatre to promote a feminist ideal, the play's finale seems to reinforce the crude stereotyping of virgin and whore. However, Polwhele does not simply reproduce old-fashioned types; she modifies them and employs them in combination with a highly critical perspective on male desire. A performance of *The Faithfull Virgins* at Lincoln's Inn in *c.* 1669 or 1670 must have raised some very disturbing questions about the destructive nature of lust.

The script was, in fact, cut by the censor; the manuscript records that it was played 'leaving out what was Cross'd by Henry Herbert MR' (49). The cuts (only seven lines in all) did not expunge the critical commentary on Charles II's behaviour which audiences cannot fail to have noticed. As Milhous and Hume remark, the very unattractive picture of the Duke of Tuscany seems nothing less than 'an unsubtle hit at Charles II' (Polwhele 1977: 43). Even before he appears, the Duke is criticised by Cleophon for stealing his beloved. Here (unlike at the end of the play), Isabella appears as a victim of the Duke's lust and her father's authority to marry her advantageously. She is unable to do anything but weep as she is handed over (54). Cleophon warns her what to expect:

> go shackle with the duke and be Admir'd
> till he is with som new sprung beauty fyr'd
> which will be swiftly Isabella[,] hee;
> should have been woman for unconstancy
> he must have mistreses and often change
> And when a does you must not think it strange
> Such shall the soule of Tuscany comand

> Whilst a scorn'd wife Must as a Cypher stand
> too soone you will the plauge of greatness know
> when you shal be a princess scarce in show.
>
> (52v–3)

Sir Henry Herbert, The Master of the Revels, excised the first five lines, but even so the speech's immediate relevance to the English royal household can hardly have been missed. This early characterisation of Isabella as a poor painted queen attracts sympathetic attention to Catherine of Braganza's situation, trapped in an arranged marriage and surrounded by Charles II's mistresses from the court and the theatre. Even though Charles II had spoken highly of his queen after their wedding night (Hutton 1989: 187), he continued his affair with the ambitious Lady Castlemaine and lusted openly after Frances Stuart, Duchess of Richmond (Miller 1991: 96–7, 105).

By the time *The Faithfull Virgins* was performed, the queen had miscarried in May 1668 and again in 1669 and there were discussions of divorce (Miller 1991: 149–50). Catherine of Braganza knew all too well the 'plauge of greatness'; the bleak picture of marriage given to Isabella must have sounded poignantly accurate to any spectator with the least sympathy for Catherine, the 'scorn'd wife' forced to stand as 'a Cypher'. Charles had recently established the actress Moll Davis as another royal mistress (Bax 1932: 123), and Pepys's diary records the strained atmosphere at court: 'At the play at Court the other night, Mrs Davis was there and when she was come to dance her Jigg, the Queene would not stay to see it; which people do think it was out of displeasure at her being the King's whore, that she could not bear it' (Pepys IX: 214). Given the context of the failed royal marriage, it is hardly surprising that Herbert would not allow a ruler who 'must have mistreses' (52v) to be libelled as a 'woman for unconstancy'. The script as played recommends patient sufferance ('you must not think it strange'), but not without reminding spectators of the cost of Charles's lust: the sufferings of their queen.

A moral masque within the play is introduced by two gentlemen who remark that virtue is an 'out of fashion thing / Scorn'd now as much by Beggar as by –' (59v). In the years 1668–70, Charles 'took to manoeuvring between a number of mistresses', as Ronald Hutton delicately puts it, so the characterisation of Lechery, who claims 'one will not satisfie; I must have more' (60), would have appeared as a thinly disguised attack on the monarch's behaviour (1992: 262). Only if Polwhele had written in total ignorance of the affairs of the court (which seems unlikely) could the masque be deemed innocent. I believe *The Faithfull Virgins* makes deliberate use of the old-fashioned forms of Jacobean tragedy and, within that, Tudor morality, to broadcast an indirect yet obvious condemnation of the

King's licentiousness. More than this, the masque also implies his lack of political control. Ambition is the ruler to whom the mistress Pride kneels; Lechery is a minor figure, absent in bed, while the real exchanges of power are made.

In the Vices of Pride, Flattery and Ambition, the sins associated with Charles's mistresses, especially Lady Castlemaine, are roundly condemned. When Avarice complains that his brother Lechery 'misspend's the Treasure' on his whore (61v), spectators may well have recalled the growing complaints about the public cost of Charles's mistresses. Lorenzo Magalotti, an Italian visitor to the court in 1668, noted that the King's 'shameless adultery' with Castlemaine brought his subjects 'to consider him as an abyss into which are poured those riches that the people bear so great a burden to contribute for the safety and security of the realm' (Magalotti 1980: 72). Pepys scornfully reported of Moll Davis 'The King it seems hath given her a ring of 700*l*, which she shows to everybody' (IX: 24). Ambition's promise to deck Flattery 'with jems more rich than er'e adorned the neck / of the Admir'd and famous Cyprian queen' (61) would have carried added resonance in the theatre where Moll Davis herself had played.

At the end of the play, the Duke falls 'a sacrifice to his owne lust' and the play judges 'the gods are mercifull – but they are just' (75r). Polwhele's attempt to push home this message to a courtly audience was thwarted since her lines 'for it is fitt / all that so sinn, should punisht be for itt' (76), were cut by Herbert. Nevertheless, the play's moral outrage at what was being flaunted so openly at court cannot fail to have created a controversial and disturbing atmosphere in the theatre.

Given these explicit condemnations of the Duke, the scapegoating of the Duchess at the end of the play is patently ridiculous. In the morality interlude, Chastity enters 'with her hayre dishelved with a wreath of lylies upon her Head' and is placed at the feet of the Duchess 'whose vertue allwaye will propitious bee / To that unsullied glory shines in thee' (60v). This idealisation may be another tribute to the isolated Catherine of Braganza. In structural terms, it demonstrates the folly of the angel/whore dichotomy. At the end of the play, the Duchess is driven to despair, having had to face the shame of public rejection by her husband. Polwhele seems to reintroduce the stereotype of whore only to show spectators its inadequacy as a definition of woman in a society dominated by male lust.

The treatment of the eponymous heroines also moves beyond stereotypes because Polwhele celebrates their passivity as a positive strength. Indeed, Jacqueline Pearson remarks that conventional sexual roles are reversed; the women 'display "manly" heroism while its men are dead, ineffective' or 'unmanly' like the lustful Duke (1988: 92). Although they are relatively static figures and rivals in love, Umira and Merantha develop a deep sisterly relationship that allows them to maintain their independence from other men. They set up a sisterhood of mourning where they can 'faythfully divide [their] greife' (51r), keeping a joint vigil by Philamon's hearse, and looking forward to an afterlife in which both their loves can be gratified. Merantha confidently believes 'wee'le smile at all that jealousie can doe / he there shall still be yours, and yet mine too' (54v). By infinitely deferring the consummation of the virgins' desires, Polwhele creates a space in which women's love for each other has a rare opportunity to grow. Philamon's absence is gradually replaced by female presence. When Umira is murdered, Merantha kills herself to follow 'my umira in the other world' Philamon having disappeared from her thoughts. She pledges herself to her soul mate: 'dear virgin, as thy love was great to mee / thus I express myne was no less to thee' (74v).

The third faithful virgin of the title, Erasila, offers another example of quiet female strength in adversity. Disguised as the page Floradine until the final scene, she is caught in a love triangle with her beloved Statenor and Merantha. The play firmly rejects the image of woman as weak, for in the play's first soliloquy Floradine complains 'my brest's inflexible' (54) and her heart too strong to break. She is a stoic survivor like Katherine Philips's heroines Cornelia and Cleopatra. Polwhele makes extensive use of soliloquy and aside to develop Erasila's emotional character, foregrounding once again a remarkable female resistance to jealousy. After a tormenting dialogue with Statenor, modelled on Act 2 Scene 4 of *Twelfth Night*, she is left on stage to contemplate the task of wooing Merantha:

> oh how perverse, and rigid is the fate
> which rules me – must I be an Advocate
> agaynst my self; for him I love and sue
> in's Cause to her that is my rivall too
> both love and fate my ruin sure Conspire
> and I must envy her I doe admire
> the kind and just merantha to whose ey's
> my Statenor will only sacrifice.
> but why at her should I malicious bee
> that is a miracle of Constantcy
> or Let my passion rage to jealousie
> Love's frenzie and the torture of each soule
> it does invade. I must betymes controule
> The power it usurpeth in my brest
> whilst it by reasons force m[ay] be suprest
> Yet all that are by love inspir'd like mee
> Must know and feele the paine of jealousie.
> (66)

Her sense of paralysis is increased by the particular restrictions placed on women's expressions of desire. She is certain that Statenor will despise her if she dares to 'disclose my flame' and believes ''tis given to men / to hate and slight those which most doat on them' (66v). By giving Erasila opportunity to reproduce these thoughts in the private and yet public form of stage soliloquy, Polwhele questions the prejudices which hinder open communication of emotion between the sexes. Failure to deal honestly with feelings is a direct cause of tragedy in this sub-plot. Statenor finally realises in the death scene that his pursuit of the unattainable Merantha has been a waste of time because his true feelings are for Erasila. He asks her 'why; would you conceale / this truth which much to[o] late you now reaveale' (75v). Erasila's soliloquies have already provided an answer. A courtly love model, which encourages male pursuit of an impossible object and the silencing of female romantic interest, inevitably leads to the tragedy of missed opportunity. At the end of the play, Statenor and Erasila can do nothing but kiss in death and dedicate themselves to each other in the world beyond the grave (78v).

Polwhele's comedy *The Frolicks* is so different from *The Faithfull Virgins* that it is difficult to believe they are from the same pen, although of course other dramatists such as Dryden did write successfully in both genres. While *The Faithfull Virgins* had exposed the destructive power of lust and jealousy from a distant, high moral viewpoint, in *The Frolicks*, Polwhele turns the telescope round to magnify erotic exchange and sexual dynamics in an atmosphere of gaming, enjoyment and fun. She also seems to have changed theatre companies. The dedication to Prince Rupert, a close friend of Killigrew, suggests that she conceived this comedy to be performed by the King's Company, although no record of a production survives (the Duke's did not act it as Hobby states (1988: 113)). Polwhele's shift of genre and company are, I would argue, informed by a wish to anatomise the power of the actress, possibly in response to what she had learned during the production of *The Faithfull Virgins*. While the Duke's Company had lost their lead actress and were concentrating on tragedy, the King's were celebrated for producing 'gay couple' comedies starring Nell Gwyn, whose charms had already won Charles II's attentions (Holland 1979: 82–6). *The Frolicks*, with its sharp-witted heroine Clarabell (a breeches role), could have been written for Nell Gwyn.

In this play, Polwhele examines the operations of desire from the perspective of the actress–mistress rather than that of the Queen. Its dedication to Prince Rupert is therefore doubly appropriate since his mistress, Margaret Hughes, had made a success of both the newest and oldest professions for women. She was an active member of the King's Company and, from 1670, she was established as a royal mistress (Wilson 1958: 149–51). *The Frolicks* explores the position of woman as actress, demonstrating the close relationship between performance and erotic desire. The theatre, with its tightly packed auditorium and intimate relationship between performers and spectators, was, as Peter Womack observes, a sexy place: 'the social and sociable network of gazes, linking boxes, pit, stage and galleries, is eroticized; the dialects of playgoing, seeing and being seen, spectatorship and sartorial display – are specified as exchanges of sexual energy' (Shepherd and Womack 1996: 127). The place of the actress within this network is automatically assumed to be that of an eroticised object. Presenting her body on stage, for the delight of all paying spectators, was a rarefied form of prostitution. However, Deborah Payne has rightly pointed out that although women who appeared on stage were necessarily objectified, their positioning in the public arena of theatre simultaneously 'amplified' the actress, giving her remarkable authority in a culture whose nexus of power was located in the visual (Payne 1995: 16, 31). Polwhele's play dramatises the opportunities for movement, expression and influence which the actress's special positioning gave her.

The cultural territory of *The Frolicks* is governed by the provocation and satisfaction of male sexual pleasure. As in the fashionable, theatre-going world of Restoration London, male promiscuity has become a national institution:

> He that one woman can satisfy
> Is an enemy to his nation,
> Since he with a score may multiply,
> For its service, his generation.
> (2.509–12)

It is within this arena that the female characters have to function. The leading figures are all performers of one type or another and use their acting skills to manipulate their status as eroticised objects and advance their interests as subjects. The crudest exploitation of the status quo is made by the bawd Procreate. She dedicates her house and her energies to promoting opportunities for Francis Makelove to seduce Lady Meanwell, and Lord Courtall to seduce her sister Faith Meanwell. Procreate tells Courtall 'I'm of a soft and melting nature, which does encourage you to use me any how' (2.244). She can be bought and sold, so does little to escape the subjugated feminine position. Nevertheless, she succeeds in winning herself a rich match and her overriding motives strike an important note in the play: reminding spectators that they and the actresses they watch are part of an economic transaction in which the pleasure of playing or watching has its price.

A much more appealing character is Clarabell, the heroine of the main plot whose manipulation of the sexually charged environment is subtle and deft. Far from being an object of the male gaze, Clarabell is a desiring gazer herself. At the beginning of Act 2, she has the opportunity to assess Rightwit, 'a handsome fellow' (2.5), from a privileged viewpoint where he cannot see her. This reversal of the usual type of voyeurism draws attention to the privileged position of the actress on the Restoration stage, who, at times, could see the spectators better than they could see her because lighting was often better in the auditorium. Barbara Freedman has pointed out that in the theatre, an actress's power to actively return the audience's look deconstructs the male gaze and enables women 'not only to reflect how they have been perceived but to look back and forward' to different ways of constructing a self. Unlike film, the theatre is characterised by a maternal gaze, a positive and disruptive presence which denies any fixed subject position because it is always ambivalent, displacing one view with another. For the actress to return the look in this context is to break up the performance space and restructure herself (Freedman 1996: 95–6).

Clarabell's role exploits the actress's presence – physically and in terms of her personality – as a way of actively responding to the audience's gaze. Martin Esslin rightly reminds us that in the theatre the actor performs in 'cubed semiosis' (1987: 59), in which the audience perceive simultaneously the character (Clarabell), the type (witty heroine in 'gay couple' relationship) and the actor (the public persona of the actress herself – such as that of Nell Gwyn). *The Frolicks* frequently exploits the overlap and discrepancies between these different identities for the pleasure of spectators with a sophisticated, intimate knowledge of the theatre and its emergent 'star' personalities. For example, when Rightwit and Speak cast aspersions on Clarabell's virginity, their remarks carry additional comic effect for spectators who recognise the actress–mistress behind the role:

Speak [To Clarabell].	You do so fleer and gibber [laugh and chatter] that I dare swear you are not so honest as you should be. Besides you look no more like a maid than I look like an emparoll [emperor] – [*They laugh*].
Rightwit.	I hope he touch'd your copyhold there . . . I lost my bachelorship so long ago that I defy the name of one. But if all bachelors must lead bears and all maids apes in Hell, thou and I shall both go to Heaven, since thou art sure no more a maid than I a bachelor.

(2.99–101, 118–21)

In her first meeting with Rightwit, it is clear that Clarabell is 'a maid' (2.14), so these lines from Act 2 are not about the character. Instead they play out a sub-text about the performers for whom Polwhele seems to have been writing, very probably Charles Hart as Rightwit, and Nell Gwyn as Clarabell.

Hart knew full well that Gwyn was no maid since he had been her lover before Charles Sackville and Charles II (Howe 1992: 67). Rightwit's confident words 'thou art sure no more a maid than I a bachelor', tease actress and audience with an in-house joke.

The sexual appeal of the actress was emphasised by breeches roles (in which Nell Gwyn was very successful). Clarabell's 'frolic', to 'turn boy for an hour or two' (2.543–5), explores this aspect of female performance. It is not a complete disguise; the servant Mark observes 'you may serve for a girl in boy's habit. The trick is common' (2.547). The identities of character and actress blur in a 'trick', which is common to them and to other characters and actresses. Clarabell and the female performer will always be visible so the disguise is not like that of Renaissance comedies, an opaque shield behind which woman enjoys freedom to behave as a man and escape gender constraints. Instead, cross-dressing becomes a half-mask, a licensed freedom from gender restrictions, rather like a fool's cap and bauble. Cross-dressing in *The Frolicks* gives the character and the actress licence to play. For Clarabell, it is a means of escaping her identity as her father Swallow's possession, his 'only Clarabell' (3.67). It allows her to put this dutiful daughter to bed at home while she goes to the tavern with Rightwit (3.68–9). At the same time, the disguise constructs her and the actress as a spectacle of pleasure. Rightwit finds her 'prettily metamorphos'd' (3.48), her legs and thighs a source of delight to him – and to some spectators in the theatre no doubt. Pepys said that Nell Gwyn's performance in *The Maiden Queen* was 'best of all, when she comes like a young gallant . . . It makes me, I confess, admire her' (Pepys VIII: 91).

Polwhele's play takes cross-dressing further, into the realm of farce, to interrogate the position of the actress as object of desire and the assumptions which surround her. In the tavern, Clarabell sets up a dance in which both sexes are cross-dressed, calling fiddlers to play 'The Frolics' (3.136) and inviting her suitors Zany and Sir Gregory to 'disguise and act' the parts of women (3.139). The height of artifice is reached in a jig where Clarabell dances the male part to Sir Gregory's lady (3.167). As the foolish suitors strive to leave Clarabell with the tavern bill, they are caught '*as making unready*' (SD 3.193). The play stages in reverse the common practice of surprising the actresses backstage in a state of undress, such as that described by Pepys: 'up into the tireing-rooms; and to the women's shift where Nell was dressing herself, and was all unready, and is very pretty, prettier than I thought' (VIII: 463). In a comic scene that plays out the new supremacy of the actress, Zany and Gregory are surprised and arrested in their women's clothes. The shortcomings of male transvestite performers is made patently clear when the Constable remarks 'these lewd beasts in petticoats' are 'not worthy to be styl'd "women"' (4.44). At the same time, the sin of lewdness, with which actresses were so often charged, is cleverly displaced onto the male impersonators. The comic moment shows how the actress as whore is a male creation. By reversing the normal cross-dressing pattern, the play produces an alienation effect to ridicule the assumption that all actresses are 'ladies of pleasure.' Seeing the men, Swallow declares 'There is but little pleasure in them, sure' (4.38–9).

The Frolicks also explores how the actress can use her sexual appeal to assert herself as a controlling authority. The potential violence of desire is suggested early in the play when, having only just met Clarabell, Rightwit grasps and kisses her without leave (SD 2.41). While acknowledging the dangers, the role gives character and actress ample opportunity to exploit the powerful current of sexual energy in the theatre. Excited by Rightwit, Clarabell gives an amazingly seductive performance. She responds to his line 'I have much ado to forbear kissing thee' in song:

> Thou shalt not touch my lips,
> Nor anything else that is warm.
> I know thou wilt do me no good,
> And, by God, thou shalt do me no harm.
>
> (3.112–15)

This song is a refusal and at the same time provocative. It relies upon the actress's unique position, a spectacle available to every paying customer, highly visible and yet untouchable for the spectators and for Rightwit. Character and actress tease the audiences on and off stage with the display of a pleasure, which will be infinitely deferred, and yet prolonged until the end of Act 5.

The functions of character and actress overlap very closely in moments like this. As Peter Womack remarks 'Doing a play appears, like sex, as an act whose meaning is not derived from some external referent which it is to denote, but develops through the vigour and inventiveness with which the connection itself is made.' With an actress like Nell Gwyn, a live performance enacts in the real world of the theatre the same erotic energies it is staging in the fictional world represented. It is a form of flirting which 'claims no general validity, but merely reflects with provocative amorality, the immediate life of the show' (Shepherd and Womack 1996: 135–6). Because flirting is always a tentative play of sexual energy it is impossible to define or contain, thus extremely dangerous for a possessive male and potentially useful to a woman caught in an arranged marriage. The sub-plot to *The Frolicks* explores its covert, subversive power. Lady Meanwell tells her husband that her flirting with Makelove is counterfeited in order to win a husband for her sister (whom he does marry), but Makelove certainly doesn't trust Mistress Meanwell, vowing 'Yet will I watch my wife if I can, for having a trick of the sister' (5.170–1).

In Clarabell, Polwhele creates a heroine who is passionate about Rightwit, yet determined to control her destiny. 'I fear I shall be fool enough, and madwoman together to fall in love with him. But I will resist it with an Amazonian courage. . . . If 'twill not be, I'll study how to get him' (2.204–10). She succeeds in her 'quest to curb Rightwit's promiscuous energies, chastising him when his bastard babies are bound to his back (4.188–93) and literally holding him under her control during a prison scene (4.346–55). The rake's sexual magnetism is made to look ridiculous as Rightwit arrogantly offers to seduce her, apparently forgetting that he is behind bars. Clarabell even has the strength to reject his condescending proposal of marriage, setting him a final challenge to test his theatrical wit before she agrees to marry him and thus establishing her authority as mistress of the play. Hobby misses the point by complaining that 'there is nothing to celebrate' at the end (1988: 114). In both the main plot and the sub-plot, *The Frolicks* suggests that, by drawing on the resources of performance, women can negotiate their way through the sexual minefield of Restoration London to their own pleasure and advantage. The play is, in some ways, a celebration of the power of the actress to control the scene.

Women's entry into the professional theatre was extremely important, but it was not the only arena for female practitioners. Women continued to perform and to produce drama in the country house and the court, for which they had developed distinctive styles. The female tradition of masque and pastoral, practised by Henrietta Maria and the Cavendish sisters in the Civil War, was perpetuated by Lady Elizabeth Delavel (1649–1716), who directed and starred in a production of Guarini's *Il Pastor Fido*, translated by Sir Richard Fanshawe (1648). The production took place at the house of Lady Elizabeth's aunt, Lady Stanhope, at Nocton in Lincolnshire. In her meditations of 1662–71, Elizabeth writes that she has 'been labouring now for above 7 weeks together' night and day:

> to teach some of my aunt's servent's and a sort of unlearn'd contry people how to act the refined pastorall of Pastor Fido, which they understoode for a long time no more how to pronounce then they wou'd now be able to speake Hebrew.
>
> Yet I boldly undertoke to make them do this against my father and his lady came downe to visit us.
>
> I grudg'd neither my time nor pain's but thirsted after praise, which at length I got to the height of my expectation, not only from my father and my aunt (whose passion's I moved so much in acting the part of Amorillis

that I drew tear's from there eyes) but I had also much praise for my troup as well as my selfe from the cheifest of all our neighbour's and from above 300 people more that fill'd the place where we acted. I for my part was transported with delight that I had so well gone through the hard tasque that I had set my selfe.

(Delavel 1978: 40)

The account is revealing, first, because it gives unequivocal evidence of a woman directing a production and, second, because details about the audience of 300 neighbours so clearly explodes the myth of country house drama as a 'private' or 'closet' activity. The production was not a unique event. Delavel remarked '*there was severall play's acted at Nocton in which I commonly acted a part*' (Delavel 1978: 217) and confessed 'my time was waisted in dressing, in danceing, in seing and acting of plays' (123). Part of her theatrical experience was gained in London since she lived there with her grandmother for some time, and from 1663–6 was one of the Queen's Maids of the Privy Chamber (123). At court, she would have been able to see masques, French comedians, as well as plays that transferred from the professional theatres (Boswell 1932: 280–1).

In Delavel's account of her production of *Il Pastor Fido*, the discrepancy between the sophisticated world of the court and the local 'contry people' is sharply pointed up. Ironically, the Arcadian idyll is like Hebrew to the rural performers, and in trying to direct it, Lady Elizabeth Delavel finds work rather than *otium* or leisure. Nevertheless, her choice of play is highly appropriate in that the female lead, Amyrillis, allows her to play out aspects of her own situation before her father, stepmother and aunt. Delavel recognises that she has often sinned by discussing 'of severall way's how I wou'd be revenged when I thought my selfe injured, and off severall contrivances how to steal away and mary without the consent of my parents' (Delavel 1978: 126–7). Like the heroine, she vehemently opposed arranged marriage and followed her heart by pursuing secret relationships with the romantic, but poor, Comte Dohna, cousin to William III of Orange, and then with James, Lord Annesley.

Playing the tragicomic part of Amaryllis gave Elizabeth a chance to speak her mind about the evils of arranged matches behind the guise of a character and to play out the fantasy of a romantic attachment. At her first appearance, Amaryllis dreams of having 'the command / Over my self' even if this means being a poor shepherdess (Fanshawe 1964: 2.5.1655–6). She is promised to Silvio to pacify the goddess Diana, who demands the sacrifice of a virgin every year in Arcadia. In love with Mirtillo, Amaryllis bitterly resents her metaphorical imprisonment, longing to live like the shepherdess:

Not such as men or Gods to chuse her hand,
But such as Love did to her choice commend;
And in some favour'd shady Mirtle grove
Desires, and is desir'd.

(2.5.1694–7)

The effect of these lines, addressed by Elizabeth to her father, aunt and
stepmother in the audience, must have been somewhat provocative. The
criticism of Amaryllis's 'unbridled will' (2.5.1856) may have vocalised their
thoughts about the actress.

Amaryllis is accused of losing her honour to Mirtillo after meeting him
in a cave in the woods, but when her name is cleared, she is still to be
sacrificed to Diana. The role of female sacrifice is willingly accepted, but
as in Jane Lumley's translation *Iphigenia at Aulis*, or Mary Wroth's *Love's
Victory*, it becomes a form of agency for the heroine when she has the
chance to save her beloved (5.2.4500–1). The comic resolution releases
the lovers from 'horrid Sacrifices' to unite them in 'times of grace and
love; glad nuptiall bands' (5.6.5189–90), yet the play carefully balances the
two options as if to show their connection as much as their opposition.
Perhaps, as the Earl of Newburgh's daughter, Lady Elizabeth Delavel knew
only too well that her happiness would be sacrificed to an advantageous
match. When her father married her to the wealthy Robert Delavel, she
felt he wanted to 'ty me up in bonds I never wou'd have chose' (Delavel
1978: 69). Perhaps her father remembered seeing and hearing his daughter
in the role of Amaryllis, challenging her father with the words 'Thy belov'd
Daughter's *Wedding* callst thou this? / To day a bride; to day a Sacrifice'
(4.5.3700–1).

At the Restoration Court as well as in the country house, dramatic
productions perpetuated a female theatrical tradition. Lavish entertainments featuring the Princesses Mary and Anne, daughters of the Duke and
Duchess of York, and other aristocratic performers looked back to the courtly
entertainments promoted in England by Queens Anna of Denmark and
Henrietta Maria. Especially spectacular was John Crowne's *Calisto* (1675)
in which court ladies and gentlemen performed alongside professional
actors. Princesses Mary and Anne took the starring roles as Calisto and
Nyphe, playing alongside Moll Davis as the personified Thames and the
Shepherdess Sylvia, and Charles Hart, of the King's Company, as Europe
(Boswell 1932: 130, 198–9).

Rare en Tout (1677), a political romance interspersed with masque-like
entr'actes, interrogates the powers of performance in a courtly context. The
play was presented before royalty at Whitehall on 29 May 1677. The only
script we have is a French text by Madame La Roche-Guilhen, published

in Covent Garden in 1677. It seems likely that this is the text performed at court and that the writer was involved as a director since the Lord Chamberlain's records for 22 May 1677 include an order for the musicians attached to the royal household to attend 'at such tymes as Madam Le Roch & Mr Paisible [master of musicians] shall appoynt' to rehearse for *Rare en Tout* (Boswell 1932: 99). In the printed text there are also traces of English, however, suggesting that English writers and/or performers may have been involved. For example, the servant Latreille describes how he is inflamed with an unsettling passion 'qui de ma vigeur viendra bien tost about' (4).

French was certainly the appropriate language for the printed edition, since it is dedicated to the Duchess of Grafton, daughter-in-law to the Frenchwoman Louise de Querouaille, Duchess of Portsmouth and Charles II's most powerful concubine in 1677.[3] The play is admirably suited to its Whitehall context, interweaving, as it does, international politics and those of the star personalities of the court. Indeed, the romantic plot of *Rare en Tout* is explicitly drawn in and within an international context. Charles II's connections to Europe and his relations with France, after signing the Treaty of Dover in 1670, are played out through the text. The situation in Europe had reached crisis point when Louis XIV launched a massive offensive against the Dutch and their Spanish and Austrian allies in March 1677. Some prominent Members of Parliament, including Shaftesbury and Buckingham, led a campaign to wage war on France. Enraged by their presumption in guiding his own foreign policy, Charles imprisoned Shaftesbury and Buckingham in the Tower and on 28 May adjourned Parliament. The following night *Rare en Tout* was presented (Hutton 1989: 342–3).

The play opens with a masque-style prologue that echoes *Calisto* by featuring the personified figure of Europe appealing to the spirit of the Thames for royal intervention to settle disputes between the European princes. *Rare en Tout* makes an explicit bid for the King's commitment to peace rather than a war with France. Such a policy would have been firmly advocated by Louise de Querouaille and her entourage of course. Charles II, celebrating his birthday at this Whitehall performance, is flattered by Thames's fantastic description of England as living in harmony under the virtuous authority of the King. Only this 'Grand Roy' can arbitrate between the warring European princes and bring peace to the people: 'sa Vertue doit charmer tout le monde' the Prologue obsequiously concludes (Roche-Guilhen 1677: Prologue).

---

3. Louise had succeeded in getting her bastard sons titled as Dukes of Southampton and Grafton in 1675 (Hutton 1989: 337).

Such conservative attitudes are not duplicated in sexual politics of the romantic plot. The hero 'Rare en Tout' is set up as a typical rake, eccentric, flamboyant and highly individual. Far from being celebrated, however, Rare en Tout is shown as selfish in his desertion of a French mistress, Climène, in favour of an English beauty, Isabelle. His attempts to win Isabelle's affections are thwarted when Climène appears at the musical concert at which he had hoped to win his new mistress's heart. He dismisses Climène, vowing 'Q'un homme comme moy, libre en ses actions / Doit pour son plaisir seul suivre ses passions.'[4] He then admits that his changing preferences may also lead him to desert Isabelle in the future (31–2). Such candid self-interest is punished rather than rewarded; having overheard this, Isabelle goes off to marry someone else. Finette, her maid, likewise rejects the hero's valet in favour of another husband, so instead of ending with a triumphant double wedding, this play ends with a pointed double rejection.

The political resonances of the romantic plot persuade Charles II to remain faithful to his promises to France rather than redirecting his attention inwards to English interests and the wishes of Parliament. The stage directions indicate that the romance is played on exactly the same set as the Prologue, 'un Paysage ou l'on decouvre le Palais de Whitehall' (Prologue).[5] This is, of course, the very palace in which *Rare en Tout* is being performed. The play self-consciously registers its own political influence, more specifically, its power to sway royal policy through romantic interest in the royal mistresses. The figures of Climène and Isabelle are probably dramatic representations of Louise de Querouaille and Nell Gwyn, arch rivals for the King's attentions. In 1676, the French ambassador reported that Charles II had 'to face the fury of the Duchess of Portsmouth for drinking twice within twenty-four hours to the health of Nell Gwyn, with whom he frequently sups and who still makes the Duchess a butt for her irritating sarcasms' (Bax 1932: 170). In the parliamentary conflict, they took opposite sides: Louise supporting the Lord Treasurer's arrest of Shaftesbury and Buckingham, while Nell Gwyn intervened to secure Buckingham's release (Hutton 1989: 335, 343). Climène's grief plays out the fears of Louise de Querouaille that she would be deserted and her interests neglected.

The romantic plot simultaneously questions the positioning of women within operatic entertainments. The coarse objectification of the female performer is criticised through Rare en Tout's responses to Climène and Isabelle. His passion for Isabelle is inflamed when she appears refusing a lover in a short operatic interlude:

---

4. A man like me, free in his actions / Should follow his passions purely for his own pleasure.
5. A landscape setting showing the Palace of Whitehall.

Cessez coeurs languissans de pretendre à me plaire,
J'ayme l'heureuse liberté
Et si l'amour est un mal necessaire,
Je ne me soûmets point à sa necessité.

(8)[6]

Ironically, as she declares her freedom from love's influence, she is inescapably defined on stage (and probably off stage as well) as the object of male desire. The playwright manipulates the figure of the singer to demonstrate how women in the new dramatic tradition are being misinterpreted, that their own voices or words are being ignored in favour of the spectacle they present to an erotic male gaze.

It seems as though Isabelle, like other actresses, is trapped, yet women's appropriation of romance for their own purposes is signalled in the play. Finette says that she has been serving a young countess who presides over a salon of authors and admirers, reads avidly, and knows everything (11). This oblique reference to Madeleine de Scudery registers women's expertise in affairs of the heart and seems to promise a self-directed route through romance. Climène's role is that of a victim, but her heartfelt complaints that men are a faithless sex make it difficult to respond positively to Rare en Tout, and so challenge conventionally indulgent responses to the rake figure in Restoration comedy. In its courtly context the play probably offers a veiled criticism of Charles II's behaviour too. Isabelle's decision to reject the hero and so frustrate the comic resolution seems reasonable. Indeed, Finette implies that both she and her mistress will find happy marriages outside the play (35). The pastoral Epilogue begins with Cupid pointedly promising more deserving objects of love to the women spectators (39–40), while shepherds and shepherdesses chorus that sincerity and faith are of paramount importance in romance (40–1). The play thus spells out a challenging riposte to the celebration of male indifference which characterises Restoration comedies of the public stage, concluding with a more refined courtly celebration of love and loyalty.

Such an opposition between court and public playhouse is artificial. What all the plays discussed here show is a mutual fascination: the king and his court visiting the theatres to be regularly entertained by plays in which their own spectacular behaviour was enacted. The close relationship between court and playhouse made dramatic production a powerful cultural agency

---

6. Cease, languishing hearts, from trying to please me
    I love the happiness of freedom
    And if love is a necessary evil
    I will not submit to that necessity at all.

for female performers and writers. Productions such as Delavel's *Il Pastor Fido* or Roche-Guilhen's *Rare en Tout* testify to women's continued use of non-commercial theatre as a potent form of self-promotion. Actresses such as Moll Davis and Nell Gwyn exploited the play of their own personalities on stage, entering the margins of the court as royal mistresses. However, any form of dramatic production by a woman on the public stage was open to male censure, not just that of the audience or the Master of the Revels, but the traditionally male-dominated institution of the commercial theatre. Working within those constraints required women to exercise their wits. They had to stretch the conventions and to seize on existing tastes or fashions, manipulating these to further their own interests in the highly visual culture of the early Restoration.

CHAPTER 6

Undress, Cross-dress, Redress: Aphra Behn and the Manipulation of Genre

STEPHANIE HODGSON-WRIGHT

When Aphra Behn (1640–89) arrived in London in 1667, the precedent for women writing for the public stage had already been set. As Sarah Heller Mendelson notes, Aphra had the 'impressive example of feminine theatrical success to inspire her' (1987: 127) in the shape of Katherine Philips' *Horace* (*see* above). However, the circumstance of a longer life, plagued by a constant need to make money from her writing meant that Aphra Behn would become the second most prolific playwright of her age. In her seminal work *The First English Actresses*, Elizabeth Howe asserts that:

> The overall impact of the female playwrights was . . . necessarily limited by the fact that they created only a fraction of the drama performed between 1660 and 1700 . . . While the changes wrought by professional women writers were not insignificant, the most powerful female influence on drama in the period came not from them but from the actresses.
>
> (Howe 1992: 17–18)

While the point has a certain validity, in making it, Howe overlooks this crucial fact of Behn's prolificacy and that the scarcity of new plays in the later part of Behn's career (Hume 1976: 340) increases the relative significance of Behn's dramatic *oeuvre*. Rather than evaluating the relative impact of the actress on the one hand, and Behn on the other, this chapter will consider the extent to which Behn's plays make positive use of the female performer to rehearse feminist and anti-patriarchal arguments.

Such an evaluation necessitates investigation of Behn's use of the material conditions of production, and here one immediately uncovers a striking feature of Behn's work. Her preferred genre was comedy. Of her 17[1] surviving plays only one, *Abdelazar*, or *The Moor's Revenge* (1677) is a tragedy. Among the remaining 16, nine are referred to as comedies on their respective title pages,[2] two as farces,[3] and two as tragicomedies.[4] The remaining three have title pages that make no generic claims, although they have comic and rather than tragi-comic or tragic resolutions.[5] Behn's staging techniques often contravened the conventions of her preferred genre. She tended to use the upstage 'discovery' areas, mainly used for tragedies, rather than using the forestage area, conventionally the playing space for comedy. Peter Holland counts 31 discoveries in ten comedies (1979: 41). In fact there are 57 in the 16 non-tragic plays being dealt with here. Elin Diamond considers that it is 'a fascinating contradiction of all feminist expectation to discover that Aphra Behn, more than any of her Restoration colleagues, contributed to that visual pleasure by choosing, in play after play, to exploit the fetish/commodity status of the female performer' and she wonders if this contradiction is not a 'deliberate use of fetishistic display [which] dramatizes and displaces the particular assault Behn herself endured as "Poetess/Punk" in the theatre apparatus' (1999: 47–8). Here, Diamond draws upon the theories of the feminist film critic, Laura Mulvey, without fully considering the differences between the gaze as constructed by the camera and that which operated within the theatre. The shortcoming of using feminist film theory for investigating plays is that the gaze in the theatre is not controlled in the way that the cinematic gaze is controlled. This is especially true of Restoration theatre, where the auditorium was as brightly lit as the stage, and the presence of royalty or high nobility meant that there were other things to attract the attention of the audience. Behn frequently used the discovery scene as a means of framing the action in particular scenes. One could argue that the use of the discovery scene, which was upstage, was a deliberate means whereby the audience's attention was drawn away

---

1. This does not include *The Debauchee*; or, *The Credulous Cuckold* (1677) and *The Revenge*; or, *A Match in Newgate* (1680), which have been attributed to her, though her authorship is not absolutely certain.

2. *The Amorous Prince*; or, *The Curious Husband* (1671), *The Dutch Lover* (1673), *The Town-Fopp*; or, *Sir Timothy Tawdrey* (1676), *Sir Patient Fancy* (1678), *The Feign'd Curtizans*; or, *A Nights Intrigue* (1679), *The Roundheads*; or, *The Good Old Cause* (1682), *The City Heiress*; or, *Sir Timothy Treatall* (1682), *The Luckey Chance*; or, *An Alderman's Bargain* (1687) and *The Younger Brother*; or, *The Amorous Jilt* (1696).

3. *The False Count*; or, *A New Way to Play an Old Game* (1682) and *The Emperor of the Moon* (1687).

4. *The Forc'd Marriage*; or, *The Jealous Bridegroom* (1671) and *The Widdow Ranter*; or, *The History of Bacon in Virginia* (1690).

5. *The Rover*; or, *The Banish't Cavaliers* (1677), *The Second Part of The Rover* (1681), *The Young King*; or, *The Mistake* (1683). All quotations are taken from Behn (1996a, 1996b and 1996c).

from the forestage and the auditorium, to focus on the intimate scene within. Therefore, while we might consider the problems concerning the gaze raised by Mulvey (1975: 6–18 and 1988: 69–79) in relation to such scenes in Behn's drama, we should also be aware that Behn as a playwright is exercising considerable control. Behn uses discovery scenes throughout her dramas variously to reveal male characters, female characters, single sex and mixed groups. A positive alternative to Diamond's interpretation is that when Behn uses the most objectificatory means of staging her women characters, by placing such objectification within the context of comedy rather than tragedy, the characters are not confined by the generic conventions of the latter. They are not reduced to the polarised objects of speculation, e.g. the wronged paragon of chastity or the spectre of female evil, typical of the tragic genre. Indeed, as Deborah C. Payne has argued, the 'technology amplified the actress by framing her against the most powerful site within the spectacle' (Payne 1995: 27).

In *The Forc'd Marriage*, Behn offers a revision of the final scene of *Othello*, the first play performed on the post-Restoration stage in which the female roles were played by women. The role of Desdemona was therefore the first in which the erotic spectacle of the semi-dressed, supine and passive actress was exploited. In Behn's play, Erminia is involved in four discovery scenes, each one progressively according her more power and agency. In 4.4 she is discovered '*sitting in a dishabit*' (4.4.s.d.) and her lover, the prince Phillander, enters to her, falls at her feet, and declares his love. She invites him into her bedchamber, where they are both discovered sitting on a bed in 4.6. Erminia's husband, Alcippus, arrives and threatens to kill Phillander. However, rather than allowing the men to fight over her, Erminia instructs Phillander to go, and leave her to deal with Alcippus. A few lines later he '*strangles her with a Garter, which he snatches from his Leg, or smothers her with a Pillow*' after which he '*throws her on a bed*' (4.6.s.d.) where she remains for the rest of the scene. Unlike Desdemona, Erminia really is in love with another man; also, unlike Desdemona, Erminia is not really dead. The next two scenes in which she appears are also discovery scenes, but she is not the object discovered. In 5.2, Alcippus is discovered '*rising from the Couch*' (5.2.s.d.), weeping and pondering his deed. He is then subjected to a masque-like vision in which Erminia appears '*drest like an Angel with wings*' (5.2.s.d.) and in which several of the other main characters also perform. Alcippus is instructed to sit down and observe, and after the vision is over '*he remains immoveable for a while*' (5.2.s.d.). This scene is part of the necessary process of re-educating Alcippus to effect comic resolution. It also demonstrates the power that performers have over their audience. Alcippus does not operate a gaze that constructs and objectifies Erminia; rather, he is re-constructed by her performance. In the final scene, Alcippus is discovered weeping at what he supposes is Erminia's hearse; when she appears alive, he successively shows the fear, contrition and complicity which are required for the play to resolve adequately. Significantly, the process of empowering Erminia does not involve compromising her virtue. As if to render her virtue indubitable, she was played by Mary Betterton, who was, according to Cibber, 'a woman of an unblemished and sober life' (cited Wilson 1958: 120).

In many instances, when women characters are 'discovered', they are not merely offered as objects of desire for the audience's consumption. Lady Fancy and Isabella in *Sir Patient Fancy*, Ariadne in *The Second Part of the Rover*, Lady Lambert and Lady Desbro in *The Roundheads* and Lady Fulbank and Leticia in *The Lucky Chance* are all 'discovered', yet the scenes involve the articulation of their own desires and their plans to pursue them. As Julie Nash argues in relation to *The Rover*, 'Behn introduces women who resist the passive realm to which they would seem to be destined; in doing so, she provides other possibilities for the female spectator and subverts the limited binary opposition of active/male and passive/female' (1994: 82). Furthermore, the extent to which men, rather than women, are 'discovered' in Behn's plays suggests a deliberate problematising of this theatrical device. For example, in *The Young King*, Behn's first play, possibly composed while she was still in Surinam, although not performed until 1683, stages the female gaze. Act 1 Scene 2 is set in '*A Grove of Trees / Within the scene lies* Thersander *sleeping*' (1.2.s.d.). Cleomena and her maid Semiris enter, dressed like Amazons. At first they do not see him, and Cleomena's words reveal that she is already predisposed towards love. She stands like the melancholy man '*with her Arms across*' (1.2.s.d.) while Semiris finds Thersander's cap and feathers. This leads Cleomena to see Thersander:

Cleomena.	'Tis a fine Plume, and well adorn'd,
	And must belong to no uncommon man:
	– And look, *Semiris*, where its Owner lies –
	– Ha! he sleeps, tread softly lest you wake him:
	– Oh Gods! who's this with so divine a Shape?
Semiris.	His Shape is very well.
Cleomena.	Gently remove the Hair from off his Face, [*Semiris puts back his hair*]
	And see if that will answer to the rest:
	– All lovely! all surprizing! oh my Heart,
	How thou betrayst the weakness of our Sex!
	– Look on that Face where Love and Beauty dwells –
	And though his Eyes be shut, tell me, *Semiris*,
	Has he not wonderous Charms?

(1.2.88–100)

The audience therefore sees and constructs Thersander via Cleomena's and Semiris's combined gaze; this is the first time he appears in the play. Furthermore, it is Thersander who carries the burden of fear about loss of honour if he reciprocates Cleomena's love: she is a Dacian and therefore the 'mortal Enemy' (1.2.145) of the Scythian Thersander. A rather more threatening use of the discovery scene occurs in 3.3 of *The Dutch Lover*, which '*discovers* Antonio *sleeping on the ground*; Hippolyta *sitting by*' (3.3.s.d.). In this instance, the characters are known to the audience. Hippolyta is in a highly compromised position, as she has eloped with Antonio, who has refused to marry her and instead paraded her as a courtesan. Hippolyta sings a song of betrayed love, and then speaks 22 lines in quasi-soliloquy, while holding a dagger and contemplating murdering Antonio. Hippolyta's story, articulated by other characters earlier in the play, is now retold directly to the audience by Hippolyta herself. When Antonio awakes, his construction of Hippolyta as 'false woman' (3.3.71) is therefore rendered void. Although Antonio gets the dagger from her and subjects her to verbal abuse, this disarming is temporary. Later in the play, she pursues her revenge in masculine dress, armed with a sword (*see* below).

Furthermore, Behn's cross-generic use of the scenes is both significant as a theatrical phenomenon in itself and is also a metonym for greater cross-generic activity. Arguably, by using such a technique, Behn was indicating to her audience a more serious agenda than the genre and subject matter might otherwise imply. As Peter Holland says:

> the peculiarities of staging comedy on the Restoration stage allowed the audience to read the scenery, not just absorb it. . . . The scenery is . . . opaque, its opacity defined by the fullness of the specific information that it offers to the audience.
>
> (Holland 1979: 19)

The subject matter within many of Behn's comedies is also often out of keeping with the genre. While the trajectories of most of her plays head towards the traditional comedic ending of multiple marriages, certain moments within the plays push hard at the boundaries of the comic genre. More than one of her comedies involves an inordinate amount of physical fighting and blood-letting. Off-stage deaths occur, and the threat of death or serious injury is presented on several occasions. As John Franceschina has argued in relation to *The Rover*:

> Based on theatre craft alone, Behn's comedy is comparable to *The Fatal Jealousy*, *The Empress of Morocco*, *Love and Revenge*, *Alcibiades*, and *The Libertine*, plays which were all considered tragedies . . . This clearly infers (*sic*) that, in terms of stage production, Behn was consciously fitting her play with

serious resonances that would both contrast and reinscribe the essence of her comedy and that would produce a work whose genre was purposefully ambiguous.

(Franceschina 1995: 32)

The rape scene, a popular feature of Restoration tragic drama, is not employed by Behn in her transgression of comic generic boundaries; rather, she introduces the threat of rape only to question the theatrical and cultural politics surrounding the issue. The rape scene offered an opportunity to display the actress's body and also give a sexual dimension to an otherwise virtuous female character. Howe (1992: 43–5) notes that in such scenes, the rape takes place off-stage, and the unfortunate victim is revealed in an alluringly dishevelled state post-rape. Behn's heroines, however, ultimately avoid the rapacious intentions of their attackers. In 3.2 of *The Rover*, the drunken rake hero Willmore subjects the virtuous heroine Florinda to an attack, while she is waiting in the garden '*in an undress*' (3.2.s.d.) for her lover, and Willmore's friend, Belvile. Florinda rebuffs him verbally, calling him 'filthy beast' (3.2.139) and 'wicked man' (3.2.148) before resisting him physically '*She struggles with him*' (3.2.s.d.). Crucially, Willmore has not recognised that she is a 'woman of quality' – someone whose sexual property is at a premium – and assumes that her resistance is the bargaining tactic of a prostitute. His ridiculous and paltry offer of a pistole for sexual intercourse underscores the violent sexual affront with a highly embarrassing social *faux pas*, thereby discomfiting the male viewer, as the highly class-conscious audience is obliged to identify with Florinda rather than Willmore. Fortunately, Belvile and Frederick arrive in time to save Florinda, and Willmore is reduced to the status of a buffoon as he tries to excuse his behaviour in a manner which only angers Belvile further: 'By this Light I took her for an Errant Harlot' (3.2.216).

Florinda's next encounter with a would-be rapist is rather more sinister. In 4.1, having run away from home, Florinda steps into Blunt's chambers to avoid being seen by her brother. Blunt is not feeling well disposed towards women, having been robbed, stripped and dumped in the street by Lucetta 'a Jilting Wench' (*dramatis personae*). His decision to rape Florinda is motivated entirely by revenge and he is overt about being driven by violent, rather than sexual desires:

I will kiss and beat thee all over; kiss, and see thee all over; thou shalt lye with me too, not that I care for the injoyment, but to let thee see I have tain deliberated Malice to thee, and will be reveng'd on one Whore for the sins of another.

(4.1.611–15)

When Frederick arrives, and prepares to join in, he encourages Blunt's vengefulness, rather than his lust: 'she is inamour'd with thy Shirt and Drawers, she'l strip thee even of that' (4.1.644–5). The text deliberately makes reference to the convention of off-stage rape, as Blunt says Florinda is 'condemn'd by publick Vote to the Bed within' (4.1.665–6), that 'publick' clearly encompassing the audience. Such expectations are frustrated, however, as Florinda buys herself some time with Belvile's diamond ring. Florinda is, indeed, sent off to the bedroom, but with Frederick as her protector, rather than ravisher. When Belvile, Willmore and Don Pedro arrive at Blunt's lodgings in 5.1, Florinda is again put under the threat of rape. However, as she is off-stage, it is the would-be rapists, including, rather uncomfortably, her own brother Don Pedro, who are offered up for the scrutiny of the audience. Florinda comes on-stage to face her attackers, but is saved within a matter of a few lines by Valeria's arrival.

The meaning of the word 'rape' is twofold. On the one hand it refers to the unlawful taking of the woman's sexual property from the father, guardian or husband who owns it; on the other it means the unlawful taking of sexual intercourse from the woman herself. Behn's presentation of attempted rape in *The Rover* foregrounds the latter by throwing it into relief against the attitudes of all the male characters involved, that rape can only be perpetrated upon a woman whose sexual property is owned exclusively by one man. Frederick's words sum up the view: ''twould anger us vilely to be trust up for a rape upon a Maid of quality, when we only believe we ruffle a Harlot' (4.1.682–3). By leaving Florinda on stage and depicting her personal distress, Behn forces the audience to see rape as a violation of one human subject by another, over and above any socio-economic considerations of sexual property and female chastity. Furthermore, Blunt's use of rape as a means of revenge reveals the crime as one of violence rather than passion. Behn explores this idea further in two other plays. In *The Amorous Prince*, the threat of rape is dealt with briefly, but in a similarly graphic fashion. When Frederick threatens Laura with rape in 3.1, '*She draws a Dagger*' (3.1.s.d.) to defend herself, and he reciprocates by drawing his own, taunting her thus: 'Pretty *Virago*, how you raise my Love? / I have a dagger too; What will you do?' (3.2.71–2). Laura is put out of danger by the arrival of her lover, Curtius, whose first words emphasise the violence, rather than the passion of Frederick's behaviour: 'How! the Prince! arm'd against *Laura* too!' (3.1.73). With Curtius's entrance, the audience is invited to refocus its gaze upon Frederick and Laura, and see them as two individuals engaged in an armed struggle rather than as desiring subject overwhelming the desired object with his passion.

In 5.1 of Behn's sole tragedy, *Abdelazar*, the point at which Abdelazar's discourse with Leonora turns from that of lover into that of rapist is crucially

at the point when she has insulted him. He may desire her, but his motivation
to rape is anger caused by the threat she poses to his sense of masculinity.

> Abdelazar.   ... How tame Love renders every feeble sense!
>   – Gods! I shall turn Woman, and my Eyes inform me
>   The Transformation's near: – death! I'le not endure it,
>   I'le fly before sh'as quite undone my soul. –   [*Offers to go*]
>   But 'tis not in my power, – she holds it fast, –
>   And I can now command no single part. –   [*Returns*]
>   Tell me, bright Maid, – if I were amiable,
>   And you were uningag'd, cou'd you then love me?
> Leonora.   No! I cou'd dye first.
> Abdelazar.   Hah! – awake my could from out this drowsie fit,
>   And with thy wonted Bravery, scorn thy Fetters.
>   – By Heaven 'tis gone! and I am now my self: –
>   Be gone, my dull submission! my lazie flame
>   Grows sensible! and knows for what 'twas kindled.
>   – Coy Mistress, you must yield, and quickly too:
>   Were you devout as Vestals, pure as their Fire,
>   Yet I wou'd wanton in the rifled spoils
>   Of all that sacred Innocence and Beauty.
>   – Oh my desires grow high!
>   Raging as Midnight flames let loose in Cities,
>   And like that too, will ruine where it lights.
>
>   (5.1.538–58)

Here again Behn equates rape with violence. Whereas her male characters
might demand the satisfaction of a duel from another male character who
had affronted them and challenged their masculinity (and such duels happen frequently in Behn's dramatic *oeuvre*), the response to such an affront or
challenge from a female character is rape.

As well as questioning the theatrical use of the rape scene, Behn is also
questioning the genre which gives rise to such scenes. The genre demands
that Leonora acts like a heroine, disdainfully rejecting Abdelazar while in a
situation of utmost vulnerability. Duplicitous playing for time, or wielding a
weapon against her attacker, would diminish her moral stature, these being
tactics typical of the villainous queen in the play. So the character of Leonora
is forced into responding in the most unintelligent and least believable
fashion, leaving it to the playwright to get her out of the situation, which is
exactly what Behn does. Leonora cries out that she has 'nought but Heaven'
(5.1.564) to defend her and begs help of the 'Powers that favour Innocence'
(5.1.567). Having given herself the cue, Behn responds by sending in
Leonora's women and Osmin, Abdelazar's officer, with a message '*Just as
the Moor is going to force in Leonora*' (5.1.s.d.). The rape scene is stopped short,

frustrating the expectations of the audience by preventing both the rape of Leonora within the play and the spectacle of the semi-naked and dishevelled actress upon the stage. Ironically, although Leonora says she prefers Abdelazar's anger to his love, it is the former that is the real threat. This is apparent when comparing Abdelazar's behaviour with the King's towards Abdelazar's wife Florella, with whom he is in love. In 3.3 the King visits Florella's lodgings to declare his love. However, Abdelazar, knowing of the King's intentions, has armed Florella with a dagger and instructed her to kill the King in defence of her honour. Florella's fears that he comes 'like a Ravisher . . . / With love and fierceness' (3.3.21–2) are soon allayed by the King:

> Ah do not fear me, as the fair *Lucretia*
> Did the fierce *Roman* Youth; I mean no Rapes,
> Thou canst not think that I wou'd force those joys,
> Which cease to be so, when compell'd.
>
> (3.3.24–7)

Here, Behn places a chasm between the lover and the rapist, between the fulfilment of sexual desire prompted by love and the violent satisfaction afforded by rape. Furthermore, the idea of rape is used here to explore the problematic ways in which a woman relates to her own sexual desires. Florella fears the King's sexual advances not because she does not desire him, for she patently does, but because of what her internalised notions of honour, manipulated by Abdelazar (and constrained by the tragic genre) will force her to do, that is either kill him or kill herself.

In comedy, where the necessity for heroic behaviour is less urgent, such exploration of this aspect of rape is more feasible. Robert Markley has argued, in relation to Lady Galliard in *The City Heiress*, that 'resisting women are constructed as alienated from their own desires, as suffering from a self-imposed repression that must be challenged by "a kind of Rape" in order to enable the possibility of "mutual Love"' (1995: 132). Indeed, when Lady Galliard eventually gives in to her own and Wilding's desires, she constructs it as a defeat, with herself as victim:

> Turn your face away, and give me leave
> To hide my rising Blushes: I cannot look on you,
> [*As this last Speech is speaking she sinks into his Arms by degrees*]
> But you must undo me if you will. –
> Since I no other way my truth can prove,
> – You shall see I love.
> Pity my Weakness, and admire my Love.
>
> (4.1.274–9)

This is the closest Behn comes to presenting a passive woman as the object of a man's desire. Yet Behn has been careful to delineate the precise extent to which Lady Galliard is in fact a desiring subject alienated from her desires, rather than merely a passive object:

> . . . I love you more than ere my Tongue,
> Or all the Actions of my Life can tell you – so well –
> Your very faults, how gross so e'er, to me
> Have something pleasing in 'em. To me you're all
> That Man can praise, or Woman can desire;
> All Charm without, and all Desert within:
> But yet my Vertue is more lovely still;
> That is a price too high to pay for you.
>
> (4.1.187–94)

The mercantile image at the end of this speech, which casts Lady Galliard as purchaser and Wilding as the purchased, is contradicted by Lady Galliard's fear of what she will become if she follows her desires:

> . . . A Whore! Oh let me think of that!
> A man's Convenience, his leisure hours, his Bed of Ease,
> To loll and tumble on at idle times;
> The Slave, the Hackney of his lawless Lust!
> A loath'd Extinguisher of filthy flames,
> Made use of, and thrown by. – Oh infamous!
>
> (4.1.228–33)

Lady Galliard's image of herself as a whore is entirely paradoxical; as an economically independent widow, she need never place herself in such a position. The possibility that Lady Galliard might enjoy the encounters which she describes is sublimated (perhaps what she really fears is being 'thrown by') and she can only access her sexual self by playing the imagined roles of rape victim or whore.

By the Restoration, the term 'whore' was demonstrably impoverished as a means of classifying and castigating women. While the actresses were conventionally put in the class of 'whore', they were simultaneously legitimated in their trade by both Act of Parliament, the frequent presence of the King at the theatre and their own presence in the beds of the most powerful men in the country. When Nell Gwyn referred to herself as the 'Protestant whore' she effectively undermined the power of others to dismiss her as a mere 'whore', knowing that she was closer to the King than the vast majority of those who would attempt such a dismissal. Furthermore, whereas before the Restoration the term had been used to define any women who was sexually active outside of the marriage bed, now such activity was called by various different names. Behn presents us with the courtesan, the kept woman, the mistress and the woman who indulges in adulterous liaisons for money, who are separate from each other and from those who operate on the streets or in brothels.[6] In *The Amorous Prince*, Antonio declares that 'uncertainty disturbs me more, / Than if I knew Clarina *were* a – Whore' (1.4.229–30). He hatches a plot not dissimilar to that in *Cymbeline*, whereby another man is set to test the chastity of Clarina, Antonio's wife. But unlike Posthumus in *Cymbeline*, for whom the only acceptable outcome is proof of his wife Imogen's chastity, Antonio seeks the knowledge whereby he can categorise his wife. In *The Rover*, Belvile reproves Blunt for being taken in by Lucetta, whom he thinks is a woman of quality:

> *Frederick.* Pox, 'tis some common Whore upon my life.
> *Blunt.* A Whore! – yes with such Cloths! such Jewels! such a House! such Furniture, and so Attended! a Whore!
> *Belvile.* Why yes Sir, they are Whores, tho' they'll neither entertain you with Drinking, Swearing, or Bawdry; are Whores in all those gay Cloths, and right Jewels, are Whores with those great houses richly furnisht with Velvet Beds, Store of Plate, handsome Attendance, and fine Coaches, are Whores and Errant ones.
>
> (2.1.64–71)

This masculine uncertainty about whether or not a particular woman is a whore and indeed what constitutes a whore – as can be seen from the two very different meanings used above – is exploited throughout Behn's drama.

Behn also logically extends the sex-for-money exchange to include marriage itself. More than one of her female characters understands marriage as a selling of self. For example, Olivia in *The Younger Brother* objects to her arranged marriage purely on principle:

> to be sold unseen, and unsigh'd for in the Flower of my Youth and Beauty, gives me a strange aversion to the Match. . . . what, come a stranger to my Husbands Bed? 'Tis Prostitution in the lewdest manner, without the Satisfaction; the Pleasure of Variety, and the Bait of Profit, may make a lame Excuse for Whores, who change their Cullies, and quit their Nauseous Fools.
>
> (1.1.37–45)

---

6.   Behn herself, as a professional writer who necessarily exposed part of her self in the theatre, also had her trade metaphorically associated with prostitution, as Catherine Gallagher has convincingly demonstrated (1999: 12–31).

Olivia is fortunate, as she unwittingly falls in love with the man to whom she has been contracted. However, the consequences are serious for those who have no such luck, as detailed by Hellena, in the opening scene of *The Rover*:

> being a Frugal and a Jealus Coxcomb, instead of a Valet to uncase his
> feeble Carcass, he desires you to do that Office. . . . That Honour being
> past, the Gyant stretches it self; yawns and sighs a Belch or two, loud as
> a Musket, throws himself into Bed, and expects you in his foul sheets, and
> e're you can get yourself undrest, call's you with a snore or Two. . . . And
> this man you must kiss, nay you must kiss none but him too – and nuzel
> through his Beard to find his Lips. – And this you must submit to for
> Threescore years, and all for a Joynture.
>
> (1.1.102–15)

In *The Second Part of the Rover*, Behn represents in graphic form what women become when they are treated as property to be ensnared in marriage. The giantess and the dwarf lady in *The Second Part of the Rover* are each pursued by two men (as many as the romantic heroine, Ariadne) who are simply after their fortunes. Arguably this might merely be a cynical use of female deformity to show the lengths to which the men will go to get a fortune, thereby drawing the audience into a cruel, judgemental male gaze upon these two female characters. However, the use of two differently sized creatures (as opposed to any other means of deformity) might be seen as a deliberate strategy to expose that the woman of fortune is simultaneously more than a woman (hence the giantess) and less of a woman (hence the dwarf) as the property she brings at once exceeds and diminishes her.

Most radically, however, Behn also demonstrates the way in which marriage itself is a means to perpetuate the trade of sex-for-money outside of marriage. In *The Town-Fopp*, the eponymous character Sir Timothy Tawdrey explains that his reason for marrying is 'to be Master of my self, and with part of her Portion to set up my Miss, *Betty Flauntit*, which, by the way, is the main end of my Marrying' (1.1.25–7). His reasons are neither unknown, nor uncommon, as the Nurse to Celinda (Sir Timothy's intended bride) points out:

> to patch up your broken Fortune, you wou'd fain Marry my sweet Mistriss
> Celinda here – but faith Sir, you're mistaken, her Fortune shall not go to
> the maintenance of your Misses, which being once sure of, she, poor soul,
> is sent down to the Countrey house, to learn Housewifery, and live without
> Mankind, unless she can serve her self with the handsom Steward, or so
> – whil'st you tear it away in Town, and live like Man and Wife with your

Jilt, and are every day seen in the Glass Coach, whil'st your own natural Lady is hardly worth the hire of a Hack.

(1.2.152–60)

While Celinda is beloved by Bellmour and their eventual union forms the main romantic comedy plot line, Sir Timothy does get married and ends the play exactly where he began, asserting '*Marriage but a larger Licence is / For every Fopp of Mode to keep a Miss*' (5.1.617–18). The play offers no regenerative effect upon him. Sir Timothy does not have to be laughed out of his folly, for the legitimate and illegitimate exchanges of sex for money are not anathema to each other, but part of the same economic system, which forces women into competition with each other to sell to men. Needless to say, it is a buyer's market.

The other type of female behaviour which could potentially elicit the term 'whore', i.e. the woman who acts upon her own sexual desires, seeking sexual pleasure without any form of economic exchange, had become a stock characteristic of Restoration comedy. The adulterous wife, trapped in an unhappy marriage, was given licence by many playwrights to seek satisfaction elsewhere.[7] However, for Behn, the prospect of snatched liaisons was not necessarily a solution to the problem. While she was prepared to use it for comic effect in *Sir Patient Fancy*, the central scenes of which are a positive mêlée of interchangeable bodies and unwitting liaisons, in this play, and also in *The False Count* and *The Luckey Chance*, she employs the legally improbable but theatrically satisfying device of divorce to effect resolution. In *The Luckey Chance*, Lady Fulbank, having unwittingly participated in an illicit liaison with Gayman, the man she loves, expresses a total crisis of identity, suggestive of a rape victim:

> *Gayman.*   Can you be angry *Julia*!
>   Because I only seiz'd my Right of Love.
> *Lady Fulbank.* And must my Honour be the Price of it?
>   Cou'd nothing but my Fame reward your Passion?
>   – What make me a base Prostitute, a foul Adulteress?
>   Oh – be gone, be gone – dear Robber of my Quiet.
>   (5.2.229–34)

Clearly, Lady Fulbank is guilty of neither prostitution nor adultery, as she was deceived. However, her use of largely contradictory terms – a prostitute's sexual pleasure is incidental to her job, whereas an adulteress is

---

7. *See*, for example, William Wycherley's *The Country Wife* (1675) and Edward Ravenscroft's *The London Cuckolds* (1681).

motivated purely by sexual pleasure – is a tellingly paradoxical interpretation of her situation. Lord Fulbank, in lieu of the £300 that he owes him,
has agreed to let Gayman spend a night with Lady Fulbank. To effect this
he has arranged to deceive her into thinking that she is spending the night
with himself. Lady Fulbank's ignorance has robbed her of the opportunity
to give consent to a pleasurable sexual experience that would have rendered her an adulteress. In one sense, she has been raped, in that sexual
congress has been taken from her without her consent; however, it is the
enjoyment that has been taken from her, rather than the sex itself. Logically,
as she was denied sexual pleasure because she thought she was having
sex with her husband, the prostitution to which she refers is the non-
pleasurable sex of the marriage bed. By employing the solution of a divorce,
Behn allows Lady Fulbank to honour her prior vows to Gayman, thereby
regaining her sense of identity.

As a contrast to the women who exchange sex for money, Behn has male
characters who do the same thing. Gayman himself, for example, is equally
forced to prostitute himself by exchanging his sexual favours for money. He
is preyed upon by his lustful and unattractive landlady, who uses her ability
to lend him money as a means to furthering her desires. He also resigns
himself to an assignation with a woman he assumes is unattractive because
she has sent him a bag of gold to lure him to her. Wittmore occupies the
position of kept man in *Sir Patient Fancy*, explaining to Sir Patient that he
and Lady Fancy 'have long been Lovers, but want of Fortune made us
contrive how to marry her to your good Worship. Many a wealthy Citizen
Sir, has contributed to the maintenance of a younger Brother's Mistress'
(5.1.709–12). Similarly, in *The Rover*, Willmore benefits from Angellica
Bianca's love, and, as her servant Moretta points out, this is all part of the
economy of desire:

> is all our Project fallen to this? to love the only Enemy of our Trade? nay,
> to love such a Shameroone, a very Beggar, nay a Pyrate Beggar, whose
> business is to rifle, and be gone . . . *Trophies, which from believing Fops we*
> *win / Are Spoils to those who couzen us agen.*
>
> (2.1.423–31)

But for the men this is only one means of getting money among many, and
this particular means does not define them. Willmore has his sword, which
will allow him to earn his living as a mercenary, as he explains in *The Second
Part of the Rover*: 'I know no danger worse than fighting for my Living, and
I have done't this dozen years for Bread' (3.1.309–10). The woman who
earns her money by selling sex is defined by it, either legitimately, as wife,
or as kept woman, courtesan, mistress, whore. Sex, and nothing else, is her

trade. Yet, in performance, Behn's women characters show us complexities well beyond such a formula. Moreover, they were represented by women who professed a skill other than sex. The categorisation of women as exclusively *sexual* traders is inevitably challenged at the very moment of performance, which testifies to the accomplishments of the actresses who play them and the woman playwright who has written their parts.

In *The Rover* Angellica Bianca states:

> Nice reputation, though it leave behind
> More virtues than inhabit where that dwells,
> Yet once gone, those virtues shine no more.
> (4.1.78–80)

Peggy Thompson has argued that here, while Angellica

> admits that only one plot is available to the sexually experienced woman, no matter what other qualities she may have. . . . Angellica's recognition of this principle, which denies her full humanity, is ironically part of the powerful and moving characterization that will not let us dismiss her as a whore.
>
> (Thompson 1996: 79)

One could extend Thompson's argument to the entire play, in which the character demonstrates a depth and dignity (signified among other things by her almost exclusive use of iambic pentameter) not apparent in her male counterpart, Willmore. Olivia and Tereisa in *The Younger Brother* appropriate and rewrite discourse which similarly makes only one plot available to them, by itemising the talents and abilities, which, rather than defining their price in the marriage market, are considered as tools which will allow them to transcend such commodification:

Tereisa. 'Tis as you said, *Olivia*, I am destin'd to your Father.
Olivia. What, the Sentence is past then?
Tereisa. Ay, but the Devil is in us, if we stay till Execution Day: Why this is worse than being mew'd up at *Hackney-School* – My Fortune's my own, without my Grandmother, and with that Stock, I'll set up for my self, and see what Traffick this wide World affords a young beginner.
Olivia. That's well resolv'd; I am of the same mind, rather than Marry Mr. *Welborn*, whom I never saw. – But prethee let's see what we have in Stock, besides Ready Mony – What Toys and Knick-nacks to invite.
Tereisa. Faith my Inventory is but small – Let me see – First, one Pretty well made Machine, call'd a Body, of a very good Motion, fit for

several uses – one Pretty Conceited Head-Peice, that will fit
any bodies Coxcomb, – when 'tis Grave and Dull, will fit an
Alderman, when Politick and busy, a States-man; turn it to
intreigue, will fit a City Wife, and to Invention, it will set up
an Evidence.

Olivia.   Very well!

Tereisa.   *Item*, one Tongue that will prattle Love, if you put the Heart in
time (for they are Commodities I resolve shall go together) I have
Youth enough to Please a Lover, and Wit enough to please
myself.

Olivia.   Most Excellent Trifles all! As for my out-side, I leave to the
Discretion of the Chafferer; but I have a rare Devise, call'd an
Invention, that can do many Feats; a Courage that wou'd stock a
Coward; and a pretty Implyment, call'd a Heart, that will strike
Fire with any convenient force; I have Eight thousand Pounds
to let out on any able Security, but not a Groat, unless I like
the Man.

(2.1.41–65)

By giving such inventories, both Olivia and Tereisa define and claim
ownership of themselves. The crucial economic independence that allows
them to do so is not glossed over, but made overt. For Behn's heroines,
self-determination is contingent upon self-sufficiency.

Behn also exposes the paucity of a society which privileges homosocial
bonding over heterosexual attraction in the making of marriages by dramatising the relationships created by antagonism between men. In *The Town
Fopp*, Sir Timothy Tawdrey plans to debauch Bellmour's sister Phillis rather
than fight him for Celinda. Sir Timothy's plot to subject Phillis to a sham
marriage is, however, successfully countered and in Act 5 he discovers
that the ceremony was legitimate. But although the marriage between Sir
Timothy and Phillis fits the generic convention of comedy, it is clearly not
destined for happiness. Phillis is a marginal character in the play, a position
that she also holds within the world of the play itself. Her last lines ring
dissonance throughout the happy ending, perhaps all the more powerfully
having come from such an unlikely source: 'Sir, you deny'd me in my
Portion, and my Uncle design'd to turn me out of doors, and in my de-
spairs, I accepted of him' (5.1.586–7). In *The Dutch Lover*, Antonio pretends
to set up Hippolyta as a courtesan in revenge against Marcel:

> 'twas not love to thee,
> But hatred to thy Brother *Don Marcel*,
> Who made addresses to the fair *Clarinda*,
> And by his quality destroy'd my hopes.
>
> (3.3.81–4)

Antonio is not motivated by desire; the action is about theft of property and honour as inscribed upon the body of Hippolyta. Taken to its logical conclusion, such apparent sexual transgressions make actual sex redundant. As Thompson argues:

> By foregrounding the nonsexual dynamics of this relationship, Behn questions the assumption that such men are acting on natural libidinous energy, which women are responsible for controlling, and thus further critiques the simplistic illusion that the stories of comic heroines should be determined exclusively by their sexual innocence or experience and by the relative 'generosity' of male response.
>
> (Thompson 1996: 77)

To adapt Thompson's phrase, where mutual 'libidinous energy' is not the controlling dynamic of heterosexual partnerships (legitimate or otherwise), the very factor that defines heterosexual partnerships, i.e. sex itself, becomes a pointless irrelevance. Fortunately for Hippolyta and Antonio, Behn does allow the regenerative force of the comic genre to take effect, though not without pushing that genre to its very limits. For Hippolyta, her position as 'feigned' courtesan has near-tragic consequences. This generic juggling allows Behn to give her an interiority and dramatic stature similar to that of Angellica Bianca. Just as we cannot simply dismiss Angellica as 'whore', no more can we simply dismiss Hippolyta as 'victim'.

Apart from Mary Betterton and the infamously chaste Anne Bracegirdle, the actresses who performed the roles of virgins and chaste women were palpably not so. Indeed, Anne Bracegirdle never played anything other than chaste roles, which suggests the strongly iconic nature of actresses' trade: the unchaste feigning chastity was theatrically convincing, whereas the chaste feigning lack of chastity was not. This is something which is obliquely questioned in *The City Heiress*. Charlot has disguised herself as a Northern (i.e. Scottish) woman in order to pursue Wilding and wrest him from his other mistresses. She flirts with him, and performs a song for him, but soon lets her disguise slip. Anxious to reassert the supremacy of his gaze, Wilding uses this opportunity to claim that he knew her all along:

> This 'tis to practise Art in spight of Nature.
> Alas, thy Vertue, Youth, and Innocence,
> Were never made for Cunning,
> I found ye out through all your forc'd Disguise.
> (3.1.499–502)

However, the audience knows from his earlier asides that this is a blatant lie. This erroneous self-assertion of the supremacy of the male gaze may

WOMEN AND DRAMATIC PRODUCTION 1550-1700

function to undermine the status of the male theatre audience. The 'feigned courtesans' of Behn's plays were possible because the actresses who pretended to be virtuous were not, and those who were virtuous did not pretend to be otherwise. A temporary pretence to courtesanship is therefore made safe, because the audience are operating within a paradigm in which such a pretence was perceived only to happen within the fiction of a play and not within the reality of the theatre proper. The security of that paradigm is, however, subtly challenged in Behn's presentation of Wilding's faulty perceptions.

Arguably, the feature that sets the courtesan apart from the wife is the fact that she sells herself, rather than is sold or bartered by her male relations. In two plays, Behn's heroines seek to evade the power of their male relatives and claim the economic autonomy enjoyed by the courtesan. Euphemia, in *The Dutch Lover*, leads Alonzo to think that she is a courtesan in order to effect a meeting with him. During this meeting, Euphemia negotiates her own marriage to Alonzo: 'Now do I find, you hope I am a Curtizan that come to bargain for a night or two; but if I possess you it must be for ever' (1.3.41–2). Behn utilises this plot line more fully in *The Feigned Courtesans*, in which Marcella and Cornelia disguise themselves in order to find husbands. However, their perilous proximity to actual prostitution is made clear and Cornelia's serious consideration of the courtesan's life poses a radical threat to the distinction between the courtesan and the woman of quality:[8]

> Marcella. A too forward Maid *Cornelia*, hurts her own fame, and that of all her sex.
>
> Cornelia. Her Sex, a pretty consideration by my youth, an Oath I shall not violate this dozen year, my sex shou'd excuse me, if to preserve their fame, they expected I shou'd ruin my own quiet: in chusing an ill favoured Husband, such as *Octavio* before a young handsome Lover, such as you say *Fillamour* is.
>
> Marcella. I wou'd fain perswade my self to be of thy minde, – but the World *Cornelia*. –
>
> Cornelia. Hang the malicious World –
>
> Marcella. And there's such charms, in wealth and Honour too!
>
> Cornelia. None half so powerfull as Love, in my opinion, life Sister thou are beautifull, and hast a Fortune too, which before I wou'd lay out upon so shamefull a purchase as such a Bedfellow for life as

---

8. This exchange might well have brought to mind the sexually catholic tastes of Charles II, which extended far across the social spectrum, to include Lady Castlemaine, the Duchess of Portsmouth, Nell Gwyn and Margaret Hughes.

> *Octavio*; I wou'd turn errant keeping Curtizan, and buy my
> better fortune. . . . Faith Sister, if twere but as easy to satisfy
> the nice scruples of Religion, and Honour, I shoud finde no
> great difficulty in the rest – besides another argument I have,
> our money's all gone, and without a Miracle can hold out no
> longer honestly.
>
> (2.1.49–63 and 99–102)

Marcella and Cornelia henceforth rely upon the wits of their servant, Petro, to fleece two Englishmen, Sir Signal Buffoon and Mr Tickletext of their money. Although they are women 'of quality' their economic position is little different from that of Lucetta in *The Rover*, who promises sexual favours to Blunt and then robs him without fulfilling that promise. Although the comedic ending promises repayment of the cullies' money, the class of the women, the attractive cunning of their general factotum, and the hypocrisy of Sir Signall Buffoon and Tickletext are invoked to provide a fig leaf to cover what is, outside of the theatrical fiction, the culpable behaviour of the 'jilting wench'.

Perhaps the most troublesome of all Behn's female characters is Mirtilla in *The Younger Brother*, the last of Behn's plays to reach the stage, having been premiered in 1696, seven years after her death. As a woman who fetishises both the riches which adulterous liaisons can bring, and also the status of the man with whom she is having such a liaison, Mirtilla successfully sublimates her desire for the man whom she first loved. At the beginning of the play, Mirtilla, having been in love with an impoverished suitor, George Marteen, the 'younger brother' of the title, has married a rich fool in his absence and has developed a desire for her page, who happens to be George's sister Olivia in disguise. Unlike the heroines in *Sir Patient Fancy*, *The False Count* and *The Lucky Chance*, who find happiness as their unsatisfactory marriages are dissolved in favour of previous love matches, Mirtilla refuses to be confined to this dramatic trajectory. Instead of seeking the fulfilment of her original attachment, she receives the attentions of Prince Frederick. She submits herself wholly to his gaze, and then joyfully embraces her identity as the beloved of a prince, while still toying with her page. In Act 5, once her deceptions have been discovered, Frederick tries, and fails to create a comedic resolution:

> *Prince.*   . . . Didst thou not take this Woman for a Man?
> *Mirtilla.* I did – and were she so, I wou'd with Pride own all the Vows
>   I've broke.
> *Prince.*   Why this is fair – and tho' I buy this Knowledge at the vast
>   Price of all my Repose; yet I must own, 'tis a better Bargain than
>   chaff'ring of a Heart for feign'd Embraces – Thou hast undone

me – yet must have my Friendship; and 'twill be still some Ease
in this Extream, to see thee yet repent, and love *Lejere* [*Marteen's
assumed name*]

Mirtilla. No, Sir, this Beauty must be first declining, to make me take up
with a former Lover.

(5.2.168–77)

George also refuses Mirtilla, as he in love with, and ultimately marries,
Tereisa, one of the play's romantic heroines. The exchange is cut short by
other events and the last we see of Mirtilla, she is still apparently beloved by
Frederick, who disputes her husband's 'right' to her. Sir Morgan Blunder
proposes an arrangement whereby Frederick is given leave to visit her.
Throughout this exchange, Mirtilla says nothing, and we could interpret
her as disempowered, the object of a civilised arrangement between her
husband and her lover. But, having asserted herself to her lover in the
previous scene, she still retains his love, and having cuckolded her husband,
she is not to be punished. There seems little more for Mirtilla to say; her
silence merely gives the impression that the male characters are coming to
an arrangement, which suits them, when in fact it is precisely the resolution
she seeks. Unlike Angellica Bianca and La Nuche, she operates from within
the sanctioned position of wife. Unlike Lady Fancy, Lady Fulbank or Leticia
she has not internalised those notions of honour, which oblige her to return
to her first love. She goes forward to liaise with a politically and economically powerful man, to whom she had made no apology for her sexual desires
for another. Both wife and courtesan, desiring subject and desired object
Mirtilla is arguably more subversive than any of Behn's female characters,
because she evades definition.

Of course, the pleasurable sight of the female body on the Restoration stage was not confined to the costume of the courtesan or the 'undress'
of the woman engaged in a shady liaison. The breeches part had a
popular appeal because it necessitated the display of the actresses' legs.
Elizabeth Howe takes a rather pessimistic view of the breeches part, claiming that it

became little more than yet another means of displaying the actress as
a sexual object. Even in those plays where the device does not blatantly
exploit the actress's physical attractions, transvestite roles rarely seem to
have been written in a way which might disturb male spectators. In most
cases a woman dons male disguise as an unnatural action caused by some
obstacle to her marrying her lover or otherwise getting her own way. Once
her wishes are met she almost invariably returns, like her Renaissance
predecessor, to a conventional female role at the end of the play.

(Howe 1992: 59)

Behn uses the breeches part to varying degrees in nine of her plays.[9] While it would be difficult to argue for a consistently feminist agenda under-pinning each occasion on which Behn puts an actress in cross-dress, on more than one occasion Behn's use of the breeches part both disturbs the male spectator and transcends the objectification of the actress. In *The Amorous Prince*, Cloris cross-dresses for a theatrically conventional reason – to pursue her faithless lover. She serves him as a page named Phillibert, and thereby gains his esteem. However, Phillibert also arouses the interest of another male character, Lorenzo 'a rich extravagant Lord' (*dramatis personae*) and self-proclaimed womaniser, who '*gazes on Phillibert*' (4.3.s.d.) whom he con-siders out loud to be a rival, and privately to be a potential lover:

> This stripling may chance to mar my market of women now –
> 'Tis a fine lad, how plump and white he is;   [*Aside*]
> Would I could meet him somewhere i'th dark,
> I'de have a fling at him and try whether I
> Were I right *Florentine*.
>
> (4.3.84–8)

In 5.1 Lorenzo seeks to buy Phillibert's sexual favours, warning him that congress with women may lead to loss of his features, and therefore make him unattractive to men, who are the 'better market of the two' (5.1.154). Of course, Lorenzo is mortified at the prospect of his desires being made public, which is threatened in 5.3, and is relieved when the truth is revealed. Lorenzo's desire for Phillibert arguably functions precisely to disturb the gaze of the male spectator upon the body of the cross-dressed actress. Although they know she is female, the erotic charge created by masculine dress and the audience's reaction to it is both reflected and problematised by an on-stage spectator whose desires are avowedly homosexual. There-fore, the relief which Lorenzo feels once Phillibert's true sex is revealed cannot be shared by the audience, who have known her sex all along, for the question of how they should look at a cross-dressed actress still remains.

In *The Town Fopp* a female character, Diana, is attracted to the cross-dressed Celinda, who deliberately encourages her affections in order to oust Bellmour, the man she herself loves. Bellmour has been forced to marry Diana but refuses to consummate their marriage. The devastated and vengeful Diana quits the house, only to see the transvestised Celinda engaged in a sword-fight. Diana asks her for protection and 4.1 '*Discovers* Celinda *as before sitting in a Chair*, Diana *by her in another, who sings*' (4.1.s.d.). The

---

9. i.e. *The Amorous Prince*, *The Dutch Lover*, *The Town-Fopp*, *The Rover*, *The Second Part of the Rover*, *The Feigned Courtesans*, *The Young King*, *The Widdow Ranter* and *The Younger Brother*.

audience's view of the alluringly performing Diana is refracted through that of Celinda, whose words 'Oh how numerous are her Charms' (4.1.19) are motivated by feelings far removed from those of sexual desire. Indeed, Celinda manipulates the erotic potential of this encounter, to supplant Bellmour in Diana's affections and to ascertain that consummation has not taken place:

> *Celinda.* Oh blessed Man!
> *Diana.* How Sir?
> *Celinda.* To leave thee free, to leave thee yet a Virgin.
> *Diana.* Yes, I have vow'd he never shall possess me.
> *Celinda.* Oh how you bless me – but you still are Married,
>   And whil'st you are so – I must languish.
> (4.1.96–101)

Such rhetoric from Celinda prompts an offer of sexual congress from Diana. This necessitates a comically hasty retreat and the tactics Celinda chooses are telling. She affects disdain of Diana after she has given voice to her own desires: ''Tis Sin enough to yield – but thus to sue / Heaven – 'tis my bus'ness – and not meant for you' (5.1.123–4). Such sentiments are therefore disingenuously, if comically, employed as a means to escape discovery by a woman who both is (with Bellmour) and is playing (with Diana) the desiring subject herself. Diana's riposte, because of its comic double entendre, also undermines the conventionally masculine attitudes assumed by Celinda:

> How little Love is understood by thee,
> 'Tis Custom, and not Passion, you pursue . . .
> Dull Youth farewell
> For since 'tis my Revenge that I pursue
> Less Beauty, and more Man, as well may do.
> (4.1.125–6 and 139–40)

At this point, a 'real' man does arrive, in the shape of Celinda's brother, Friendlove, to respond to Diana's wishes. In this instance, the cross-dressed actress is not simply set up as an object to excite the pleasure of the audience, but as a critique of the male desiring subject/female desired object dichotomy.

Celinda's venture into the masculine activity of sword-fighting is shared by a number of Behn's cross-dressed female characters. For example, Marcella in *The Feigned Courtesans*, like Celinda, comes to the aid of her lover in a street brawl. Hippolyta in *The Dutch Lover* performs the duty which none of her male relations has undertaken, in demanding the satisfaction of a formal duel with Antonio, the man who has betrayed and debauched her. Assuming the name of Alonzo (the man to whom she was promised in marriage), she seeks out Antonio, but during their duel, the real Alonzo arrives and becomes involved in the fight:

> *Alonzo.* Stand by, I shall be angry with thee else,
> And that will be unsafe –
> *As Alonzo fights with one hand, he keeps her off with t'other; she presses still forward on Antonio with her sword indeavouring to keep back Alonzo*
> *Enter to them Marcel*
>
> *Marcel.* Sure I heard the noise of swords this way!   [*Draws*]
> Hah, two against one? courage, Sir.   [*To Antonio*]
> *They fight all four, Marcel with Hippolyta whom he wounds and Alonzo with Antonio, who is disarm'd*
>
> *Hippolyta.* Good Heaven! how just thou art!
> *Marcel.* What, dost thou faint already? – Hah, the pretty talking youth I saw but now! [*Runs to her, and holds her up*]
> Alas, how dost thou?
> *Hippolyta.* Well, since thy hand has wounded me.
> *Antonio.* My life is yours, nor would I ask the gift,
> But to repair my injuries to *Hippolyta*.
> *Alonzo.* I give it thee –   [*Gives him his sword*]
> (4.3.205–16)

Hippolyta's appropriation of masculine dress and behaviour thereby engenders homosocial exchange between the male characters, out of which her situation can be resolved. The character is named for (and therefore invites comparison with) the Amazon queen who also gains a husband by fighting him. However, the Amazon queen is defeated into marriage by Theseus, Duke of Athens, whereas Hippolyta actively seeks Antonio in order to avenge herself upon him and it is her heroic actions in 4.3 that ultimately reform him. In many senses, she is a 'better man' than her husband or her brother. Her heroism here and in other instances in the text (*see* above) transcends the comic genre into which her character has been written and disturbs the comedic ending in which she is married to a man demonstrably unworthy of her.

However, Behn does not always make her female characters resort to cross-dressing in order to display masculine characteristics and qualities. In her earliest play, *The Young King*, and one of her latest, *The Widdow Ranter*, she creates two very different masculine women, whose eventual resort to masculine attire is the catalyst for their respective marriages. Cleomena in *The Young King* has been overtly fitted for the role of monarch, in place of her brother Orsames, who has been kept away from the world because of a prophecy that he will be a tyrant. Her country, Dacia, is at war with Scythia, and she unwittingly falls in love with the Scythian prince, Thersander, disguised as Clemanthis (*see* above). To prevent continual bloodshed, the two countries agree to settle their differences via single combat and after a series of bloody mistaken identities, in 4.2 Cleomena, disguised as Clemanthis, fights Thersander. She is both wounded by him and also recognised by him. Cleomena's next scene shows her reaction to the proposal from the Scythians that she marry Thersander to secure peace; still not realising who Thersander is, Cleomena resorts to cross-dress again, this time as a shepherd. She gains entrance to Thersander's tent and tries to murder him. After being imprisoned, Cleomena is brought to face the wounded Thersander, significantly effeminised '*in a Night-gown sitting on a Couch*' (5.4.s.d.). The marriage between the two is the crucial factor in the peace between the Scythians and the Dacians, yet it is the woman, rather than the man, who is reformed by love, away from a bloody continuation of the hostilities and into this peaceful solution.

The Widdow Ranter, or, The History of Bacon in Virginia is also set against a background of armed hostilities, although these take place in the recently colonised seventeenth-century Virginia. Behn's eponymous heroine does not appear in cross-dress until she enters the theatre of war in search of her beloved, Dareing. However, her demeanour and speech patterns echo masculine conventions:

> . . . go ye Dog, go tell your Lady, the Widdow *Ranter* is come to dine with her
> [*Exit Boy*]
> – I hope I shall not find that Rogue *Dareing* here, Sniveling after Mrs.
> *Chrisante*: if I do, by the Lord, I'le Lay him thick, Pox on him why should I love the Dog, unless it be a Judgment upon me.
>
> (1.3.13–17)

She is strikingly self-aware, stating that 'we rich Widdows are the best Commodity this Country affords' (1.3.83–4) yet behaves like anything but a commodity. While cross-dressed, in 4.1 she puts herself into competition with Dareing for Chrisante and then has the joke backfire on her as Dareing insults her to her face. However, Dareing ultimately accepts her as his soul mate, and the bargain is struck in libidinously ambiguous terms:

> *Dareing.* Give me thy hand Widow, I am thine – and so intirely, I will never – be drunk out of thy Company . . . prithee let's in and bind the bargain.
> *Ranter.* Nay, faith, let's see the Wars at an end first.

Dareing.   Nay, prithee, take me in the humour, while thy Breeches are on
          – for I never lik'd thee half so well in Petticoats.

                                                        (4.2.277–82)

Ranter's gender ambiguity continues, as she fights in the battle, even though her true sex has been exposed. Dareing tries *'putting her back'* but *'in vain'* (5.1.s.d.) and concludes that 'now I find you can bear the brunt of a Campaign you are a fit Wife for a Souldier' (5.1.360–2). The eponymous widow's cross-dressing in the theatre of war is mirrored and then inverted by that of the Indian Queen, beloved by the eponymous male character, Bacon. As Janet Todd has noted, Bacon self-consciously and theatrically styles himself as an heroic figure (1999: 74). Indeed, he and the Indian Queen occupy a tragic trajectory which contrasts sharply with the comic ending experienced by Ranter and her associates. In 5.1 the cross-dressed Indian Queen superflously identifies herself as female, stating that her 'fears and blushes' (5.1.164–5) will betray her. Ironically (or perhaps deliberately) they do not and she is slain, unrecognised, by her lover. Her experience of cross-dressing is therefore diametrically opposed to Ranter's. The fate of the Indian Queen perhaps indicates that tragedy is a genre in which women are permanently the colonised other, without a discourse by which to enunciate themselves and their desires, and any attempts to imitate the discourse of the coloniser inevitably leads to a literal deathly silence.

   The Indian Queen aside, however, Behn's cross-dressed heroines are feisty creatures when compared with their equivalents in Shakespeare's plays. At the prospect of duelling with a man (or indeed getting into a full-scale skirmish with a group of men) they do not remind the audience how much they 'lack of a man', as Viola does in *Twelfth Night* (3.4.69), but throw off their coats and get on with it. When Hippolyta faints at the sight of blood, unlike Rosalind, it is not that of her lover's on a handkerchief, but her own, flowing out a wound she sustained while fighting. Ironically, the very fact that the performer in cross-dress 'really is' a woman means that culturally-inscribed references to femininity, such as those written into the dialogue of Shakespeare's transvestite female characters, are no longer obligatory to remind the audience of the gender of the character. The range of activities for the female character in the Restoration was opened up precisely because of the presence of the actress: the legitimating gaze of the King upon the actresses in the theatre challenged the proscription upon women appearing to be something they were not. Behn exploits both the presence of the actress and the licence allowed by the comic mode to create powerfully vocal, mobile and resourceful women characters. In the preface to *The Dutch Lover*, she overtly expresses her contempt for the academic rules governing drama: 'for their musty rules of Unity, and God knows what besides, if they meant any thing, they are enough intelligible, and as practible by a woman' (Behn 1996a: 163). She also argues that women can write drama as well as men because a playwright does not need education to create convincing characters and situations. In her own dramatic writing Behn goes further, to create a vision of, perhaps even set a precedent for, women acting beyond the culturally imposed limitations upon their sex and to offer the disturbing vision that every woman in the audience could potentially be something other than she appeared.

CHAPTER 7

A Woman's Place is in the Play/House

ALISON FINDLAY AND STEPHANIE HODGSON-WRIGHT

It would be tempting to make this final chapter an affirmation of the ways in which women writers made an unequivocal response to the legacy of Aphra Behn. It would also be wrong. From the premiere of *The Forc'd Marriage* to the posthumous premiere of *The Widdow Ranter* in 1689, Behn was the only woman known to be writing for the public stage. Marta Straznicky describes the period as an age 'when women established themselves permanently in the professional theater' (1997: 703). Yet this view benefits from hindsight, whereby we see Behn standing at the beginning of a long tradition, about which no woman dramatist in the 1680s could possibly have known. Throughout her career, Behn was obliged to defend her drama against the prejudices of those who condemned her writing on the grounds of her gender, epitomised in the frustrated observation 'a Devel on't the Woman damns the Poet' (Behn 1996c: 217) made in her Preface to *The Luckey Chance*. Straznicky also argues that the playwright was both exposed and invisible upon the public stage, managing only 'to wrest a kind of marginal presence' (Straznicky 1997: 708). Yet women playwrights were both more present and further marginalised by virtue of their gender. This chapter will examine the strategies employed to circumvent the double bind of exposure and marginalisation.

Ephelia (*fl.* 1679), Anne Wharton (neé Lee, 1660–86) and Anne Finch, (neé Kingsmill), Countess of Winchilsea (*d.* 1720), wrote their plays in a cultural milieu that had either no woman writing for the public stage, or Behn as sole exemplar. Ephelia's *Pair-royal of Coxcombs* (>1679) was performed privately 'At a Dancing School' (Ephelia 1679: 16). Anne Wharton asserts that *Love's Martyr* or *Witt above Crowns* (1679/81)[1] was not 'ever designed to

---

1. Date suggested by Greer & Hastings (1997: 327).

177

be publick' (Wharton 1997: 195). Anne Finch expressly stated that 'a more terrible injury cannot be offer'd me' (Finch 1903: 271) than to have *The Triumphs of Love and Innocence* (*c.* 1682–8) and *Aristomenes* or *The Royal Shepherd* (*c.* 1690)[2] staged in the public theatre. Ironically, despite the express wishes of Wharton and Finch, their plays have benefited retrospectively from the legacy of Behn; critics are less willing to deny that the plays are performance texts.[3] There were various sites and occasions other than the public theatre to which aristocratic and genteel women writers could address themselves. Performances at court were still regular occurrences, and several records survive of amateur performances at private houses and at boarding schools between 1670 and 1690.[4] The song and the pastoral dialogue were genres particularly popular among women writers, both implying different kinds of performance from the plays written for the public stage. For example, Ephelia dramatises her troubled relationship with 'Strephon' via a series of songs, and Anne Finch's pastoral dialogues in the Wellesley manuscript are replete with scenery and *dramatis personae* (Finch 1998: 114, 118).[5] The very number of songs and pastoral dialogues featuring as entertainment performed within the fictional worlds of stage-plays throughout the period, indicates the extent to which the domestic domain of the upper classes was adeptly and regularly configured as a theatrical space.

Despite the private auspices of *The Pair-royal of Coxcombs* (of which only the Prologue, Epilogue and two songs survive), Ephelia comments on the prejudice that a woman playwright might experience in any arena. The Prologue is mix of special pleading for her own play and a feminist call for positive discrimination towards women playwrights, asking the gallants in the audience to be kind. Exploiting her pseudonym, which renders her any woman rather than a particular woman, she demands that the play be approved because 'A Woman wrote it; though it be not rare, / It is not common' (1679: 16–17). In other words, women playwrights in general, rather than this woman playwright in particular, need encouragement. The fact that this statement ends in a caesura emphasises the point;

---

2. Both dates suggested by Barbara McGovern (1992: 53–4 and 61).
3. Greer and Hastings state that *Love's Martyr* is actable (1997: 59) and Pearson describes it as 'a competent but undistinguished tragedy' (1988: 123). Finch's two plays are described as 'perfectly actable' (Pearson 1988: 123) and 'well-suited to stage performance' (Straznicky 1997: 704).
4. *See*, for example, Danchin (1981: 554, 632, 640, 652, 682 and 1984: 42, 491, 568, 630, 633) and Van Lennep (1965: 263, 300, 301, 378).
5. Approximately one-quarter of the material in Anne Killigrew (1686) *Poems* and one-sixth of the material in Elizabeth (Singer) Rowe (1696) *Poems on several occasions, Written by Philomela*, is in dialogue form.

the performer stops mid-line before continuing. Ephelia uses humility as a weapon, hoping that the wits who 'Censure the Poets, and undo the Stage, / Won't undervalue so their mighty Wit, / To criticize on what a Woman writ' (17). The auspices of the play are a further defence: she does not care for their censure, because the play was not written for critics' approval, but 'to divert her Friends' (17). Furthermore, she equates the right to criticise with the cost of a seat: 'you should Censure only when you Pay' (17). The private performance is a site of artistic liberation, where the playwright is freed from the need to seek commercial success: 'they must fawn, that write for a Third day. / She scorns such Baseness, therefore will not sue' (17). The ladies, however, are the truly valued audience and in addressing them, Ephelia asserts the quality of the play, noting their judgement is too fine to be inveigled into praising an inferior piece: '[I know] no Reason why / You may not Pardon all the faults you spy' (17). When her wit is more developed, it is to the ladies that she will present the fruits of her mature mind, but 'till It come, / This, Ladies, humbly begs a gentle Doom' (17). While the men may make the most noise, it is the women for whom Ephelia is really writing, and whose approval she most keenly seeks.

The Epilogue begins by anticipating the adverse reaction of the men: 'The Play is damned; well, That we looked to hear' (21). However, she entreats them to be kind, not for her sake but for their own. All who venture to put their theatrical efforts before an audience, she warns, should be wary of criticising the attempts of others to do the same. If they are unkind to her play now, and focus too closely on what she significantly identifies as 'small Errors' (21), she will be just as unkind when she is in a position to judge their plays. The Epilogue ends on the opposite note: if they are complimentary, she will return the favour.

> If you her Wit, or Plot, or Fancy blame,
> When you Addresses make, She'll do the same;
> But if you Clap the Play, and Praise the Rhyme,
> She'll do as much for you another time.
>
> (21)

There is an underlying unease about the vulnerability of playwrights, be they male or female. The last line is particularly telling because it points to the importance of women in the fortunes of the theatre. Whether as patrons, audience, performers or writers, the post-Restoration theatre relied upon the money and the talent of British women. Ephelia's Prologue and Epilogue clearly points to her future activity as both writer and audience, though if Maureen Mulvihill's identification of her as Mary Stuart,

Countess of Lennox, is correct, her favour as a patron would be no small achievement for a male playwright.[6]

Anne Wharton's *Love's Martyr* comments incisively on the position of women in relation to absolute patriarchal rule and to the love poetry, which flourishes under such a regime. The play dramatises the apocryphal events leading up to the historically real incident of Ovid's banishment from the court of Augustus Caesar in 8 CE: a love affair between Ovid and Caesar's daughter, Julia. Wharton adds a sub-plot dealing with Delia's choice between the poet Tibulus and the patrician Tiberius. The play takes place within a strictly structured court, effectively comprising three estates: the patricians, Caesar, Marcellus, Tiberius, whose role is to govern (Caesar being foremost in power), the poets, Ovid, Tibulus, Cornelius, whose role is to celebrate their leaders and also love (Ovid being the primary poet) and the women, Julia and Delia, whose quests for agency are frustrated by the other two groups.

The male characters in the play are not particularly admirable. Caesar is presented as a self-centred and vacillating ruler, whose constant rhetorical device echoes the play's title; he claims to prize many things 'above Crowns', yet ultimately prizes those above all. Caesar appears centre-stage at the opening of the play, and he rhetorically claims centre-stage at the close, subsuming the deaths of Marcellus and Julia into his own tragedy. Marcellus adheres excessively to the notions of honour and propriety, providing the means whereby the villain Tiberius can destroy him. Tiberius's sentiments are quite out of keeping with Marcellus's sense of honour, or the poets' idealised notions of love:

> J love the Princes Julia but my Love
> is still by my allmighty Jntrest sway'd
> which makes me counterfeit an humble Passion
> for the fair Delia fair she is and chast
> as Cinthia was e're she Endimeon knew
> her innocence makes her believe J Love her
> and her ambition soon will make her yeild
> to me, but mine denyes my heart to her . . .
> What tho' she be unchast whch J but gues
> since greatness and not honour is my aym

---

6. The identity of Ephelia has not been established at the time of writing. Maureen Mulvihill argues that she is Mary Stuart (née Villiers), Duchess of Richmond and Lennox (1995: 309–11 and 1996). Warren Chernaik, however, suggests that Ephelia is a poetic fiction and that one author, or a group of authors, not necessarily female, could have written the poems (1995: 151–72).

and if my Interest should require it
I would againe restore her to his armes.
                    (1.1.390–6 and 404–8)

This libertine view is Julia's only alternative to being the object of Ovid's
desire, or subject to her father's will. Initially, the poets are presented sympathetically, but Cornelius soon becomes a creature of the court and turns
spy against Ovid. The close friends Ovid and Tibulus gradually dwindle
from rhetorical champions of love to figures of self-centred inertia in the
face of Caesar's anger. Ovid shows himself far less courageous than Julia;
Tibulus, having succeeded in his quest to gain Delia, does nothing to help
his friend out of danger.

The play's plots revolve around thoughts and actions of Julia and Delia,
who are drawn with greater depth than their lovers. For a short time both
women appear to assert some agency. Delia is offered the semblance of
choice between Tibulus and Tiberius and the progress of her calculations
is given considerable dramatic space. Her initial resolve 'wth pleasure I / a
Slave to God-like power would live and dye' (2.1.78–9) shifts to a recognition of the difference between person and position:

> J love not dull Tiberius but the Prince
> poor Poet I can only pity thee
> yet if your were as great J'd love you too.
>   (3.1.13–15)

Finally, she senses the dangers of associating with Tiberius, and realising
that her position as his beloved is tenuous, concludes the plot by favouring
Tibulus. The love affair between Julia and Ovid is played out in highly
rhetorical terms, which prove to be of little use to either in their dangerous
situation. The play underscores this by constantly looking forward to Julia's
death. For example, in the first scene, she anticipates what will ensue if she
crosses her father's will:

> Sr can you think I'd ask my life of you
> were it in danger, if J meant to shame it
> with dissobedience, no, J'd court my death
> rather then disobey and be immortall.
>   (1.1.193–6)

Furthermore, in 5.1, as Julia awaits the arrival of Ovid for their final
tryst, she is upbraided by the angry and unsympathetic ghost of her mother,
yet remains defiant. Ovid's poetic rhetoric, in which he claims they are
chosen by the gods to demonstrate that love knows no social boundaries,

is rendered null and void by the reappearance of this ghost, who confirms that Julia will die. All Julia has to look forward to is martyrdom, and from line 515 onward they merely wait for the inevitable discovery by Caesar and his retinue.

Ovid and Tibulus are strikingly undynamic when compared to ill-fated lovers, such as Pyramus, Romeo and Giovanni. Ovid barely seems worthy of the Roman princess who is prepared to die for him; his faith in poetry is sadly wanting as a *modus operandi*. He has boasted continually of the imperial supremacy of love:

> How dull a thing is Empire and how poor
> Kings are perplex'd but never pleas'd an hour
> Lovers can laugh at them and scorn their power.
>
> (2.3.342–4)

When Roman *realpolitik* exposes this as a rhetorical sham, Ovid makes no attempt to evade the consequences. Ultimately, he accepts his place as subject to the power of Caesar more readily than Julia and her death seems relatively immaterial to him. Instead he takes comfort from knowing that his soul will meet with hers in the afterlife. Tibulus seems a rather poor friend when compared with a Horatio or a Mercutio. Since 4.1 he has known that Ovid will endanger himself and Julia by going to her chamber. He also knows that Caesar is in a particularly unforgiving mood after the suicide of Marcellus, whose body Tibulus helped to carry offstage at the end of Act 4. Nevertheless, as he awaits Delia's declaration of love in 5.1, he is prompted to affirm what he cannot possibly believe to be true:

> J hate all Joyes but those whch Love can give
> for Love, and Love alone J wish to Live
> Empire I scorne as a low sordid thing
> The meanest Lover's greater then a King
> Ceasar him selfe to whome the world submitts
> Who sees soe many Monarchs at his feete
> would give his universall Diadem
> To be so blest as J tho' in a dream.
>
> (5.1.176–83)

Happy in their union, Tibulus and Delia disappear from the play, leaving the remaining characters to enact the tragic denouement which finally contradicts Tibulus's assertion: the meanest lover is not greater than a king, but merely the king's subject. Wharton's play thus demonstrates that the construction of feminine subjectivity, whether by the demands of a patriarchal government, which uses marriage as a hegemonic tool, or by the objectificatory discourse of male-authored love poetry, is partial and disempowering. Julia chooses to lose her life rather than her love, yet her death does not materially affect Ovid's ability to write poetry about her. The more fortunate Delia recognises the illusory nature of the marriage market as a means to better her position, yet Delia's choice of Tibulus could be seen as a dramatised confirmation of the 'original' Delia's position as a poetic creation of Albius Tibullus (c. 55–19 BCE).

Anne Finch's *Triumphs of Love and Innocence* also shows the way in which women's agency was ideologically circumscribed. Casting a queen and a transvestite woman as the play's most psychologically rounded protagonists exposes the conditional and ultimately fictive nature of the power conventionally invested in these theatrical types. The Queen of Cyprus expresses a complex interiority which, together with the fact that she is always called 'the Queen', stands in sharp contrast to her displaced position as a refugee in Rhodes, having been usurped and exiled from Cyprus. The structure of the play re-enacts her displacement, as she remains in her chambers, a site of sanctuary and incarceration, for virtually all the play. Only once does she venture out to the main rooms of the palace, unseen, to overhear a conversation among the male courtiers. In Act 1, she is the invisible object of negotiations among her servants, her protectors and her detractors, who all have an interest in her future. Her counsellor Riccio wants her to stay in Rhodes, as does the Grand Master Aubusson and his nephew, Blanfort, who is in love with her. Lauredan, General of Cyprus requests that she be given over into his care, apparently to virtual imprisonment; Aubusson's enemies, Rivalto, Linnian and Vilmarin support him.

Lauredan and the Queen are in love with each other, though each is initially unaware of the other's affections. The Queen's refusal to see Lauredan stems from fear that her own feelings will lead her to accompany him; loving him is dangerous. Lauredan, by contrast, has no such fear. The occasion of their falling in love is presented as simultaneously romantic, dangerous and disturbing. On the night of the coup in Cyprus, Lauredan invaded the Queen's chambers where she had taken refuge. The intrusion is repeated in Act 3, when Lauredan once again violates her sanctuary to profess his love. His real purpose in coming to Rhodes is not to take her prisoner, but to restore her to the throne of Cyprus. However, the terms upon which he will do so empty the position of all significance:

> Hear Madam! what your subjects have decreed,
> And what is too, confirm'd by the Venetians,
> Whose pow'rs expell'd and keep you from the throne,
> First, that Cornara, whom att last they find
> Too weak to hold itt, quitt the Sov'rain sway,

> And all my race, to wear itt by succession . . .
> You are their Queen, and mine.
> Again we will replace you on the throne,
> And bound the uttmost height of our ambition,
> To be the guard, still of your crown and Person.
>
> (3.2.111–16 and 127–30)

Her political right to the throne is erased and she is to receive it as a lover's gift, which has been offered by means of terror and violation. The violence continues as Blanfort arrives to confront Lauredan, who wounds him, seemingly fatally, and then sets sail from Cyprus. The Queen's future is thus jeopardised by the actions of an expressly unwanted and unlooked-for champion and it takes a near fatal accident at sea to reunite them.

Blanfort also compromises Marina, who is disguised as Aubusson's page Carino. She appears to be cast in the mould of the questing heroine, but unlike the empowered cross-dressers portrayed by Behn, Marina's disguise is the source of her danger. The villain, Rivalto, encouraged her to adopt the disguise and follow Blanfort to Rhodes, offering her protection, yet his real intention is to seduce her. Initially this threat is countered by the apparently comic nature of Marina's story, in which she always interrupts Blanfort as he tries to woo the Queen. Yet when the scene is set for the comic denouement, our expectations are destroyed. In a scene reminiscent of those between Orsino and Viola/Cesario, Marina and Blanfort exchange love stories. Marina retells the story of her first meeting with Blanfort, but appropriates his perspective. He becomes confused, looks closely at her and recognises her, but his old love is not revived. He leaves her with the assertion: 'know that Death, and nothing else shall part me / From the persuit of the fair Cypprian Queen' (2.3.152–3).

Without the expected sanctuary of Blanfort's rekindled love, Marina becomes a pawn in Rivalto's game to discredit Aubusson. Linnian and Vilmarin, Rivalto's accomplices, have discovered Marina's disguise simply by looking closely at her while in masculine dress. The very feasibility of cross-dressing is thereby undermined as a safe strategy for a woman to access masculine territory. They assume that Aubusson has been keeping her as his mistress, and plot with Rivalto to expose them both. Once Blanfort has disappointed Marina, she goes to her chamber and resumes her feminine attire. That night, Rivalto, Linnian and Vilmarin create a disturbance causing Aubusson to enter Marina's chamber, where they are discovered together. Marina is literally and figuratively exposed, as Linnian confirms her sex by pulling aside her shift and inviting the men to gaze upon her neck and breasts. In that instant, rather than reassuming her identity as the Duke of Mantua's daughter, Marina becomes nothing. 'Itt is Carino, butt it is a woman' (4.1.60), says Monthaleon, and Aubusson, despite his previous affection for her as Carino, rejects her: 'take her hence, remove her from my sight, / I care not who she is or how she came' (4.1.62–3).

The rumours about Aubusson's 'mistress' spread, discrediting Marina and obliging her to reject the love that Blanfort eventually declares for her. When Rivalto tries to rape her, she bravely asserts she would rather die, but this theatrically popular form of feminine heroism is presented realistically as a frightening and difficult option. As she hesitates, Rivalto tries to stab her. It is providence, not heroism, that saves Marina, as the drunken Capriccio emerges from the curtains of the bed and attacks Rivalto, while Marina flees to the Queen's chambers for refuge. At the play's conclusion, the Queen seems empowered, requesting 'That all may be examin'd in her presence' (5.3.71). However, once the characters are assembled there, Aubusson is the presiding power, not the Queen. The final scene can therefore be seen as a synecdoche for the whole play. Both the Queen and Marina are spectacles of imagined power and both are subject to masculine construction and appropriation. They occupy positions traditionally associated, in the public theatre, with female agency, yet the play rehearses the vulnerability of that agency in a fictional world constructed to reflect gender *realpolitik* rather than theatrical wish fulfilment.

If Wharton and Finch wanted to expose the extent to which women's agency is culturally circumscribed, performance of these plays in the public theatre, where the audience's 'correct' reading of the plays could not be guaranteed, was perhaps not the most appropriate means of dissemination. By restricting their plays to manuscript circulation among friends and relatives, Wharton and Finch retained a crucial authorial presence. The occasion of producing a play privately creates a dynamic in which the boundaries between performers, audience and author are blurred; the experience is collusive and inclusive, especially when the author is present as a locus of the text's ultimate meaning. Wharton's dedication suggests that while she might have misgivings about exposing her play to others, the play might have been previously available for reading and Mary Howe requested a copy: 'you dear selfe had not seen this senceless Play which deserves not the name of a Poem but that you commanded it' (Wharton 1997: 195). Finch hosted private readings, to which Alexander Pope miserably testifies: 'I was invited to dinner to my Lady Winchilsea, and after dinner to hear a play read, at both which I sat in great disorder with sickness at my head and stomach' (cited Reynolds 1903: lvi). Finch's Prologue to *Aristomenes* suggests the auspices for her play might be 'by a good winter's fire' (Finch 1903: 337) and expresses a simultaneous disdain for, yet acute awareness of, the power of the audience in the public theatre:

When first upon the Stage a Play appears,
'Tis not the multitude a poet fears,
Who from example, praise or damn by roate,
And give their censure, as some Members vote.

(337)

Finch may despise them, but acknowledges that they are the theatrical legislature where, as in the House of Commons, a woman has no chance of fair representation. With other spaces in which to realise their plays and with no financial need to sell them to the theatres, the benefits of doing so were not apparent, and the hazards of doing do were easily avoided.

For women who sought to earn money by playwriting, exposure upon the public stage was obligatory and in the 'crucial year' (Pearson 1988: 169) of 1695–6, seven new plays by women (including Behn's posthumous *The Younger Brother*) were premiered on the public stage, after which women playwrights became a significant force in the public theatre. On two occasions the playwright chose to retreat into total anonymity. The identity of Ariadne, author of *She Ventures and He Wins* (1695) and the 'Young Lady' who wrote *The Unnatural Mother* (1698) remain a mystery. *She Ventures and He Wins* was premiered at Lincoln's Inn Fields, in or before September 1695 (Van Lennep 1965: 452). The players, who included the cream of British theatrical talent, had just split from the Drury Lane Company and set up in competition for the finite London audience. It is possible that the choice of a new, female-authored play was a deliberate marketing ploy: this would be the first since the death of Behn.[7] The Prologue simultaneously creates and inserts 'Ariadne' into a tradition of British women playwrights:

Our Author hopes indeed,
You will not think, though charming Aphra's *dead,*
All wit with her, and with Orinda's *fled.*

(1695: A3r)

The Epilogue reworks the equation between playwrighting and prostitution that beleaguered Aphra Behn into a consensual and legitimate sexual relationship:

[The play] is her Maidenhead,
(that of her Brain I mean) and you that wed
Feel seldom easie Joys, till that is fled.

(A3v)

---

7. *The Rover, The Emperor of the Moon* and *Abdelazar* were revived and *The Forc'd Marriage* may have been revived (Van Lennep 374, 391, 402, 412, 443) between Behn's death and 1695.

Building on the Prologue's assertion of female tradition, the Epilogue looks forward to a future tradition and therefore argues for a special relationship between the female playwright and the women in the audience, who might be aspiring writers themselves:

> *Ladies, for your own sakes you must be kind;*
> *Lest, while we* [i.e. men] *scarce one writing Beauty find,*
> *Vain Men deny your Sex the Graces of the Mind.*
>
> (Ariadne 1695: A4r)

The play itself is cheerfully assertive of women's agency. The heiress Charlot Frankford is the desiring subject who drives and controls the action. She and her cousin Juliana open the play in male disguise, adopted for Charlot's quest to find a husband who will love her for herself not her fortune. Having found the ideal man, Lovewell, she marries him in Act 3 and jilts him before the marriage can be consummated. Leaving him with the impression that he has married a poor impostor, she puts him through various tests, which he passes and they are reunited in Act 5. The idealised nature of Charlot's story is thrown into relief by the more mundane sub-plot. Urania receives unwanted attention from Squire Wouldbe, a 'proud pragmatical coxcomb of poor extraction' (*dramatis personae*), kept in finery by his mother-in-law's pawnbroking business. Urania and her husband Freeman devise various plots to humiliate Wouldbe, firstly arranging for him to visit Urania while disguised as a woman. At the threat of discovery, Wouldbe adopts Falstaffian tactics by hiding in a water cistern and then in a feather tub, becoming increasingly ridiculous in appearance. When Wouldbe is not deterred, Freeman decides to expose his behaviour to Wouldbe's wife Dowdy and her mother. He lures the women to his inn, where the three couples from the main plot are at supper. The confused Dowdy and frustrated Wouldbe are paraded in front of the happy couples and given a dressing-down by Freeman and Urania. The denouement of the sub-plot therefore becomes the nuptial entertainment for the characters in the main plot, jarring with the comfort and happiness of Charlot and her companions.

The Unnatural Mother was premiered at Lincoln's Inn Fields probably no later than October 1697 (Van Lennep 1965: 486). It is a highly energetic piece, moving with rapidity from one evil deed to the next, with Callapia, the 'unnatural mother' of the title, driving most of the action. Rather than being paired with one virtuous opposite, a mode of casting identified by Howe (1992: 152–61), Callapia's single-minded evil is contrasted with two virtuous characters: her daughter Choufera and step-daughter Bebbemeah. Their friendship is the strongest relationship in the play, exceeding even the union between Bebbemeah and Munzuffer that ends the play. They both fall in love with Munzuffer, yet, as in Mary Wroth's *Love's Victory* (*see* Chapter 2), their friendship is not compromised. Choufera acts unselfishly in her friend's interest, whereas Callapia, who also desires Munzuffer, pursues him ruthlessly. She poisons her husband, then plots with her son Cemat to drug Bebbemeah and set her up in an amorous scene with a black slave in Act 3, which Munzuffer is invited to witness. The apparent objectification of the actress is counterbalanced by the fact that the scene is a fiction; in order to see her as an eroticised object the audience must concur with the obviously mistaken gaze of Munzuffer. He doubts her chastity and Bebbemeah flies to the countryside. Choufera, meanwhile, is the unhappy object of her brother Cemat's incestuous and rapacious lust. As in Behn's plays, the attempted rape is presented as an act of violence rather than desire. In Act 5, after a second attempt, Cemat stabs Choufera and she dies in Munzuffer's arms, revealing her love for him and instructing him to retrieve the wronged and innocent Bebbemeah. He finds her and threatens to kill himself if she will not come home with him; under such duress she agrees. Their nuptials are planned in the wake of several deaths, including that of Callapia, who has gone mad and committed suicide.

Pearson (1988: 120) has suggested that the author of *She Ventures and He Wins* and *The Unnatural Mother* are one and the same, and certain evidence suggests that this may be the case. The Prologue to *The Unnatural Mother* could refer to the earlier play when it says: '*A Woman now comes to reform the Stage, / Who once has stood the Brunt of this unthinking Age*' (1698: A2r). Each play demonstrates an acute awareness of the selling points of its genre. If the author(s) of *She Ventures and He Wins* and *The Unnatural Mother* were professional writers, and hoped to make money with their plays (the success or failure of either is not documented), perhaps the anonymity had a very practical function. The authors asserted, even capitalised on, the presence of the woman playwright in the public theatre, without compromising their literary careers, yet were still in a position to reap the benefits of the box office.[8]

Three more female playwrights, Catherine Trotter (1679–1749), Delariviere Manley (1672–1724) and Mary Pix (1666–1709), attempted to make themselves felt as a distinctive feminine presence. Their strategy was to foreground themselves as women playwrights, to embrace the necessary visibility of their gender and construct it as a positive feature. All three had

---

8. While even the veracity of the authorial claim to be female has been doubted (Greer *et al.* 1988: 24), Lyons and Morgan convincingly counter with the point that 'there is no evidence that any male author of the 1690s thought it worth his while to present himself as a female playwright' (Lyons and Morgan 1997: x).

their first plays produced within six months of each other and by writing mutually supportive Prefaces to each other's printed texts they created 'a discernable sorority' (Clark 1986: 199, 333). Comparing the Prefaces reveals a common pattern, as though the three playwrights and Lady Sara Piers (a close friend of Trotter) followed a party line from which to redefine the idea of 'a woman's play' and 'a woman playwright' on their own terms. As with Ariadne, reference to the legacy of Behn and Philips is the starting point for establishing a female dramatic heritage. Manley's Preface to *Agnes de Castro* (1696) defines Trotter as the next occupant of the throne left vacant by 'Orinda *and the Fair* Astrea' and in a Preface to *Fatal Friendship* (1696), Sara Piers vouches that Trotter has torn the prize from them as a more virtuous successor (Trotter 1698: A4v). Pix used the same figures to commend Manley: '*like Afra Eloquent, / Like Chast* Orinda, *sweetly Innocent*' (Manley 1696b: A3r). A second pattern common to all the Prefaces is an explicit attack on the male monopoly on drama, expressed using military imagery. For example, Manley says Trotter has '*disjoyned*' a male empire '*And snatcht a Lawrel which they thought their Prize*' (Trotter 1696: A2v), while Pix believes that in writing *The Royal Mischief*, Manley's '*infant strokes have such* Herculean *force*' that she conquers all enemies '*when you but begin to Fight*' (Manley 1696b: A3v). Finally, the Prefaces tell the public how the women drew inspiration from each other. In the published text of *Agnes de Castro*, the first play of the group to appear, Manley told Trotter:

> Fired by the bold Example, I would try
> To turn our Sexes weaker Destiny.
> O! How I long in the Poetick Race,
> To loose the Reins and give their Glory Chase;
> For thus Encourag'd, and thus led by you,
> Methinks we might more Crowns than theirs Subdue.
>
> (Trotter 1696: A2v)

Trotter's play has been the catalyst to unleash a rush of female creative energy, now gathering its own momentum. Chasing the glory of Behn and Philips, Manley looks forward to a female-authored dramatic corpus, which will allow the sister playwrights to dominate the canon. In the published text of *The Royal Mischief* (1696), Trotter returned the compliment by telling Manley '*You were our champion and the Glory ours. / Well you've maintained our equal right in Fame*' (Manley 1696b: A3r). The sense of sisterly solidarity was completed by Pix, who defined Manley as '*Pride of our Sex, and Glory of the Stage*' (A3v). The strength of the feminist front they presented in 1696 is clear from these Prefaces, which make frequent use of those vital pronouns 'we' and 'our' to destroy the image of the woman playwright as an isolated anomaly.

Catherine Trotter's *Agnes de Castro* premiered at Drury Lane in 1695 (Van Lennep 1965: 455) when she was only 16 years old. Its Epilogue, in which Mrs Verbruggen addressed the audience in the popular 'breeches' role, played on the absence of the author from the moment of production in order to distance the '*Virtuous*' and '*Fair*' poetess from the conventional sexual appeal of the actress. Straznicky has remarked that acting and writing were seen 'to be discrete activities, especially in the case of women professionals' (1997: 712) and Trotter exploits the distinction to present herself after the style of Philips, as intensely modest and moral. Her daring to '*check the Rage, / Of Reigning Vice, that has debauch'd the Stage*' was commended by Sara Piers as part of a much needed reform (Trotter 1698: A4). As she appears in the Epilogue though, Trotter is strangely out of place in the theatre, an anomalous woman who prioritises virtue as her crowning glory. The Epilogue teases spectators with promises of a glimpse of her beauty, but it spends more time lamenting the fact that the audience 'are not made for dull Platonick love' (Trotter 1696: A4). Trotter's interests in virtue and sublimated desire are seen in the triangular relationship between Prince Fernando, his wife Constantia and her companion Agnes, in which passion and restraint are finely balanced. The Prince's suppressed desire for Agnes is shown sympathetically (Trotter 1696: 6), while Constantia's intense love for both her rival and her husband raises her above the role of victim. She is a 'miracle of Virtue' (9), who tells her rival 'I my self, prefer her to my self / And love her too, as tenderly as he' (6). Since the play is set in Portugal, Trotter may be making another, retrospective comment on Catherine of Braganza's position as deserted queen (*see* Chapter 5). *Agnes de Castro* explores relationships between the female characters to offer a more positive response to male infidelity than Polwhele's *The Faithfull Virgins* and Boothby's *Marcelia* had done.

The opposite pairings of women in the play suggest that Trotter is commenting on the tradition of pairing 'vicious' and 'virtuous' female characters in tragedies, as pioneered by Rebecca Marshall and Elizabeth Boutell in 1665–70 and perpetuated in the 1690s by Barry and Bracegirdle at Lincoln's Inn Fields, and Knight and Rogers at Drury Lane (Howe 1992: 152–61). Trotter's play deviates from the pattern by presenting an idealised loving relationship between Constantia and Agnes (performed by Rogers), shadowed by the villainess Elvira (played by Knight) and her accomplice Bianca. Elvira, who was Fernando's mistress before his marriage, embodies the jealousy Agnes and Constantia ought to feel for each other as his wife and beloved. When Bianca argues that the Prince's infidelity must be punished or 't'would make all Men be Faithless' (2), she seems to have a point. The miraculous purity of Constantia, Agnes and Fernando's love makes such worldly judgements seem irrelevant, however. Elvira should empathise with Constantia, but she has been so indoctrinated with the idea of female rivalry that she cannot appreciate the loving relationship between the heroines. 'How stupidly she hugs the Poys'nous Serpent!' (15) is her scornful comment on Constantia. Elvira plays out the absent villainy of each of the heroines, dropping a letter to divide them, and then plotting to stab her rival Agnes (as a jealous Constantia would do), and accidentally stabbing the Princess (like an Agnes jealous of Constantia's nominal possession of Fernando). The self-destructive nature of female jealousy becomes clear when Elvira goes mad (34–5), her treachery finally revealed by Bianca.

Elvira's moral and emotional blindness is shared by the King, who cannot see the passion Agnes feels for Constantia, believing that she will be tempted by ambition to marry Alvaro (12). Agnes firmly reminds the King that 'A shining Prison, is a Prison still' (13). She challenges his authority by acknowledging him as a parent rather than a monarch and implicitly setting up an alternative proposal, to accept her relationship with Constantia:

> *King.*   So Haughty *Agnes*! sure you know me not.
> *Agnes.*   I know you, Sir, to be *Constantia's* Father,
>   A Princess, whom I love with all respect.
>
>   (13)

Whether Agnes is proposing a female coupling as a lesbian alternative is not made explicit in the play, although, for her, marriage to Alvaro would be going against 'those strong Bars which Nature's fix'd' (14). The passion the two women share certainly has a physical dimension:

> The Princess leaning on her Rivals Neck;
> They mingled Kisses with the tend-rest Words,
> As if their Rivalship had made 'em dear.
>
>   (20)

Constantia's death scene implies a sexual dimension to the relationship, as it does in the associations between death and orgasm in *Romeo and Juliet*. Once Agnes realises the Princess is dying, her heartfelt cry 'Was there no other way, / To make us friends, but parting us for ever?' (26) is followed by attempted suicide. She grabs the poinard 'Purple with her precious Blood' (26) and even though this attempt fails, vows to bury herself alive in Constantia's tomb since there is 'No Life without her' (30–1). Like the faithful virgins of Elizabeth Polwhele's play (*see* Chapter 5), she commits herself to a female soulmate in the afterlife:

> I shall meet my Princess where I go,
> And our unspotted Souls, in Bliss above,
> Will know each other, and again will love.
>
> (34)

The play briefly suggests the possibility of Agnes's attraction to Fernando, but what the audience witness is the passionate exchange of love between women. The female erotic subtext looks forward to women's tragedies of Queen Anne's reign, which, Kathryn Kendall has argued, were written in the context of the monarch's same-sex attachment to Sarah Jennings (1991). Even if the relationship between the heroines is not read in sexual terms, the play's depiction of female love as a primary bond challenges social norms.

In *The Fatal Friendship*, premiered at Lincoln's Inn Fields in summer 1698 (Van Lennep 1965: 494), Trotter shifts from the idealism of her first tragedy to consider female rivalry from a worldly perspective. The bigamous marriage of Gramont to Felicia, by whom he has a son, and to the wealthy heiress Lamira, is the result of paternal pressure. The two women respond very differently to their situations. Felicia collapses in grief when she discovers how she has been abandoned. Lamira is much more aggressive. As a single woman she enjoys the weight of managing her own business, telling Gramont:

> I had rather sustain that load for ever,
> Than seeking ease only to change my Burthen
> For a much worse, and Heavier.
>
> (Trotter 1698: 9)

When she does marry him and discovers she has a rival, she refuses to 'tamely bear my wrongs' (25) but vows vengeance: 'I'll haunt your Steps, and interrupt your Joys; / Fright you with Curses from your Minions arms' (26). Gramont seriously underestimates Lamira's intelligence by trying to flatter her. She is incensed when he tries to 'daub o'er my injuries with soothing words' (37). Her spiteful lies about a passionate wedding night with Gramont take a cruel revenge on her fellow victim Felicia.

Lamira then seems to have a change of heart, telling Felicia that they are both innocent 'tho both each others chief unhappiness' and that it is Gramont who is to blame: 'Him only should we hate, let us be Friends' (41). This seems a potentially empowering moment for the women, but the play shows that the price of female friendship is too high. Lamira, 'disgusted with the World' (41), plans to retire to a nunnery, leaving her dowry to her friend, but with absolute conditions: Felicia too must reject Gramont. It is here that the power dynamic between the women changes. Felicia, determined to remain faithful to her husband even in abject poverty, is presented as a tower of strength for rejecting Lamira's offer of economic and emotional independence. Her heroism is proved in a painful scene, where she is forced to choose between her husband and the life of their child (who has, rather improbably, been stolen by pirates). In the latter part of the play, Felicia's absolute wifely love is elevated over Lamira's absolute rejection of the patriarchal world order that is to blame for the tragedy.

In spite of this more conservative line, *The Fatal Friendship* does expose male matchmaking and a misplaced faith in the importance of homosocial bonds, as a brutally destructive force. Gramont's dilemma about the bigamous marriage (20–1) encapsulates the chaotic no-win situation in which all the characters are trapped. While the women are passionate, they do think practically about their situations, whereas the highly structured forms of behaviour recommended by the dominant order lead the men into a maze of disaster. As Rebecca Merrens rightly points out, *The Fatal Friendship* gives 'a crucial revision of the cultural assumptions concerning the gendering of chaos and order' (1996: 48). Its combination of passionate emotion and biting social critique was obviously effective since Trotter's early biographer, Birch, points out 'This tragedy met with great applause, and is still thought the more perfect of all her dramatic performances' (Birch 1751: 1, viii).

Delariviere Manley's *The Lost Lover* premiered in March 1696 at Drury Lane (Van Lennep 1965: 459), where it failed to make a third night. The Prologue tries to insist upon authorial presence in the performance: 'The Curtain's drawn now by a Lady's Hand' (Manley 1696a: A4r), and as in *She Ventures and He Wins*, the Epilogue likens her debut to the loss of virginity. More pessimistically, it predicts a lack of honesty in male responses, which will match their sexual duplicity: 'Tho' each in private wou'd be sworn her Lover, / Scarce one true Friend the Publick will discover' (A4v). Manley's fears that insistence upon her gender would prove counter-productive turned out to be right, and in tones reminiscent of Behn, Manley's Preface claims that 'the bare Name of it being a Woman's play damned it beyond its own want of Merit' (A3v). The style and content of *The Lost Lover* also suggest that Manley saw herself as the inheritor of Behn's legacy, yet, as Pearson notes, '[u]nlike Aphra Behn, she accepted that women writers had a "special role" as chroniclers of love' (1988: 190). While owing much to Behn, Manley departs significantly from her predecessor. She names her hero after Behn's most famous male character and uses a plot line similar to Behn's *The Younger Brother*, which premiered earlier in 1696. The sub-plot deals with Wildman's frustrated love for Olivia, who is married to an older man, the 'jealous husband' of the subtitle, a plot line that Behn had used frequently in her earlier plays. Yet Manley's play effectively 'reforms' the sexual licence enjoyed by many of Behn's heroes and heroines. Olivia does not respond to Wildman's advances; she frustrates his and the audience's expectations by instructing him to come to her chamber in disguise, only to reject him. This is not an easy decision and her words clearly indicate the extent to which she has internalised the social values of her day, which enforce a sublimation of her desire:

> Why do I tremble thus? I neither distrust my Vertue, nor his Care of it. Yet a secret Guilt condemns me, because I exceed in Form. If the Shadow of an Injury gives such Uneasiness, what do they suffer by Remorse who actually offend?
>
> (30)

Wildman has no choice but to accept her decision, and the Epilogue teases the audience with his and their frustrated expectations. However, the fact that Wilding immediately turns to pursue the affected poetess Orinda, suggests that Olivia has acted wisely, especially as this caricature seems a deliberate attempt to distance Manley from the 'cossetted' Philips role model.[9]

Manley shares with Behn the sympathetic treatment of the deceived and compromised woman. Belira is Wilmore's erstwhile mistress, who tries to prevent him marrying Marina by urging the two existing marriage arrangements. In Act 4 Wilmore and Belira have a protracted final showdown, in which she threatens to destroy his hopes of Marina and, crucially, her fortune. The scene ends with Belira resolved to wreak her revenge, although her plans are thwarted. The last we hear is that she has tried to stab Marina, was prevented by Wildman, and then left the house. Clark argues that 'the disproportionate emphasis on the heavy relationship between Belira and Wilmore created an imbalance in the otherwise slight comedy' (1986: 159). However, Manley also makes the more subtle point that the cast-mistress, with her thwarted hopes and abused feelings, is a serious subject, ill-suited to the comic genre. Indeed, Belira's last act is more appropriate to a tragic villainess. As Pearson has astutely observed, Belira is 'treated with much more sympathy and psychological inwardness than [other] analogous types' (1988: 197); indeed, the cast-mistress only works as a comic figure when forced into caricature. The analogy drawn by the Epilogue between the hypocritical male audience and deceitful lovers also suggests that in Belira, Manley has characterised herself. Doubly disadvantaged as a seduced and

---

9. *See* Mulvihill (1991).

fortuneless woman, she must make a living in a field where her gender renders her similarly vulnerable.

Female desires and frustrations were given full dramatic weight in Manley's tragedy *The Royal Mischief*, initially rehearsed at Drury Lane, but transferred to Lincoln's Inn Fields after a disagreement with the company. It premiered in April 1696 (Van Lennep 1965: 461) and ran for six nights, earning Manley two box office proceeds. While Manley identified her gender as causing the failure of *The Lost Lover*, in this case she identifies it as a fly in the ointment of *The Royal Mischief*'s success. Manley's Preface echoes Behn's grievance (expressed in her Preface to *The Luckey Chance*) that her subject matter is condemned as inappropriate to her sex and receives no such condemnation in similar works by men (1996b: A3r). Yet in *The Royal Mischief* Manley attempted something Behn had not: a truly woman-centred tragedy. Whether or not Manley was successful in her attempt is still a matter for debate. Howe is pessimistic:

> If there is a 'feminist' message in this play, it is one that can easily be ignored. Presumably male spectators just relished the erotic spectacle of Homais' promiscuity – she and her kind can easily be seen as no more than another variation on the actress as sex object.
>
> (Howe 1992: 51)

Rebecca Merrens, however, makes a more nuanced judgement:

> Manley reverses the analytic trajectory away from assuming, anatomizing, and 'proving' female corruption to provide a taxonomy of the flawed patrilineal culture that distorts Homais's desires and produces her 'heavy doom.' . . . Manley refuses to mitigate her critique of patrilineal violence by ascribing Homais's actions to an inherent 'tragic flaw' that, so the masculinist argument would go, destroys a corrupt woman.
>
> (Merrens 1996: 43–5)

In other words, wicked women are not born, they are made; in this sense the play rehearses the earlier arguments proposed by *The Tragedy of Mariam* (*see* Chapter 2), that women's duplicitous pursuit of sexual desires is made necessary and possible by a patriarchal regime.

Homais opens the play in conversation with her eunuch, Acmat, whose very presence uncomfortably signifies the excesses of the regime under which they live. They discuss Homais's previous lovers and her current desire for Levan Dadian, giving the impression that Homais herself is not particularly subject to excessive restriction. This is partly because of her unerring success in love, being possessed of 'Eyes [that] did never vainly shoot a Dart' (Manley 1696b: 2). The freedom of her spirit is brought into sharp relief with the material conditions of her existence, expressed when her husband, the Prince of Libardian, arrives home from war:

> it was unkind
> To give the Stile and Dignity of Regent
> The empty name of Honour without power,
> Whilst yon pamper'd Prelate bore the sway,
> Denied me leave to pass the Castle-Gates;
> And suffer'd none to have access, but just
> My Women, and my Slaves; hence 'twas I found
> My Servants were his Creatures, my Guards
> My Gaolers, and himself the Master Spy . . .
>   I'm a Woman, made
> Passionate by want of Liberty.
>
> (6 and 7)

The literal truth of the last line is demonstrated as we discover that Homais has evinced her desire for Levan Dadian by looking at his life-sized portrait during her incarcertion (17–18). Homais is successful in her pursuit, but her plot to rid herself of her husband is thwarted. In 5.1 'Homais *is discover'd Bound*' (37) and her husband invites her to poison herself, or to be strangled with a bow-string if she refuses. The image of female disempowerment could not be more acute, yet strikingly, Homais successfully negotiates her release. Her eventual death at her husband's hands is not the result of a ritualistic and legitimate execution, but a wound given in anger. Simultaneously incarcerated object and desiring subject, both cruelly oppressed and cruel oppressor, Homais is a complex tragic character. As Manley's Preface indicates:

> Mrs. Barry, who by all that saw her, is concluded to have exceeded that perfection which before she was justly thought to have arrived at; my Obligations to her were the greater, since against her own approbation she excell'd and made the part of an ill Woman, not only entertaining, but admirable.
>
> (A3r)

Elizabeth Barry's task was not inconsiderable. Homais stands alone and dominates the action, having over 420 lines. Anne Bracegirdle, who usually played the virtuous character opposite Barry's villainess, played Bassima (Osman's beloved), who is more appropriately paired with Elizabeth Bowman's vengeful Selima (Osman's wife). Homais uses Selima's jealousy to rid herself of Bassima, Levan Dadian's wife[10] and Osman, the dangerous

---

10. Although Bassima is Levan Dadian's wife, their mutual lack of love does not render her Homais's rival in the way that she herself is Selima's.

Vizier. She is therefore expressly not contrasted with the virtuous friendship of two women, but rather stands outside and above the conventional tragic pairing, operating as its arch-manipulator.

The very success of *The Royal Mischief*, doubly underpinned by the mutually supportive public assertions of female authorship by Manley, Trotter and Pix and material fact of their operating as professional team, unnerved the established theatre world. The resultant hostility is encapsulated in the satirical drama *The Female Wits*, written by W. M. and premiered at Drury Lane in 1696 (Van Lennep 1965: 467). The three playwrights are caricatured, and Marsilia (the Manley persona), argues 'Now here's the Female Triumvirate; methinks 'twou'd be but civil of the Men to lay down their Pens for one Year, and let us divert the Town; but if we shou'd, they'd certainly be asham'd ever to take 'em up again' (*Female Wits* 1704: 5). The active involvement of the author in the rehearsal process (Straznicky 1997: 708) is heavily satirised as Marsilia enters the theatre as a dominating director who, like Bottom, wants to play all the roles. She has no respect for the players' skills, resorting to the unforgivable sin of demonstrating to Mrs Cross (the Bracegirdle persona) how to perform an angry exit (32). When the actress understandably offers to exit from the production, the author threatens to 'do the Part my self' (38), subsequently showing the repentant Mrs Cross how to deliver her lines 'in a perfect whine' with the appropriate gestures (50).

However, the satire cruelly points out that Marsilia's presence is needed, 'to enlighten the understanding of the Audience' (44), because the play is such an incompetent piece of writing. Her presumption in claiming that her script is better than *Othello* (35) and in offering to rewrite Jonson's *Catiline* (1611) is mocked. Trotter's pretensions to learning, which rival those of the former laureate, are also ridiculed in the character of Calista. She tries to outdo Marsilia by claiming that she has already translated *Catiline* into Latin (9). As Rosenthal astutely observes, the play undermines the women's claims to high culture and shows how they 'violate gendered divisions of literary territory' (1996: 174). More importantly, the play creates divisions between them, collapsing the triumvirate as an effective bulwark against the vulnerable position of female dramatist. Calista and Wellfed find Marsilia's arrogant command of the rehearsal so tedious that they leave the theatre, abandoning her to the snide remarks of Mr Awdwell 'a Gentleman of Sense' (*dramatis personae*). The only figure who escapes relatively unscathed is Mrs Wellfed (Mary Pix). She arrives at the theatre on foot and is shown at ease among the actors, if a little eager to recruit them for her next play. Whereas Marsilia seems to regard theatre practitioners as an impediment to the clear transmission of her authorial voice, Wellfed enjoys performance. The numerous jokes about Wellfed's size point to her success as a writer; she is 'big enough to be the Mother of the Muses' (5). While the other two poets attempt to lay Jonson's 'Honour in the Dust' (10), Wellfed seems to be a female reincarnation of the popular myth of Jonson, 'a fat, Female Author, a good sociable, well-natur'd Companion' (*dramatis personae*). Unlike the other two playwrights, she has common sense enough to recognise the place of her script within the theatre; when Mrs Knight rushes off rather than hear Wellfed declaim one of her best scenes, she gives a much more balanced defence of authorship than either of her sister playwrights: 'I find Poets had need be a little conceited, for they meet with many a Bauk. However, scribling brings this Satisfaction, that like our Children, we are generally pleas'd with it our selves' (20). This reasonable balance between personal satisfaction and attention to the practicalities of the theatre is, the play suggests, the basis of a proper working relationship.

Of the three female playwrights, Mary Pix was the most prolific. The fact that she is also the least radical indicates something about the restrictions placed on women writing for the professional stage. Nancy Cotton Pearse comments 'she was not a vocal feminist' (1976: 12) and Jacqueline Pearson goes so far as to claim that her plays 'tend to repeat and endorse stereotypes of women's behaviour' (1988: 169). Pix certainly placed herself within a masculine dramatic tradition. Her plays *Ibrahim* (1696), *The Double Distress* (1701) and *The Conquest of Spain* (1705) drew on works by Beaumont and Fletcher, while in the Prologue to *Queen Catherine* (1698), Pix explicitly links her drama to Shakespeare's histories.[11] She registers the difficulties of participating in a male-dominated discourse, asking 'how shall Woman after him succeed, / And what excuse can her presumption plead?' Her answer to these questions appears to have been to appropriate existing dramatic forms for her own purposes. Pearson criticises Pix's work for 'assuming male viewpoints' but does not take adequate account of the subtlety of her technique (1988: 201). Pix works within apparently limiting conventional dramatic structures to promote alternative perspectives on female behaviour which are intrinsically feminist in nature.

Pix's clever manipulation of gendered stereotypes lies at the heart of her tragedies, in which she uses the conventions of romance to rewrite the genre and woman's roles within it. In *Ibrahim* (1696), the main dramatic action involves the overthrow and assassination of the Emperor, but matters of state are subordinated to personal tragedies of love. Rebellion against

---

11. Clark (1986: 193) identifies Fletcher's *Valentinian* (*c.* 1609–14) as a dramatic source for *Ibrahim* and argues that *The Double Distress* reuses the plot of Beaumont and Fletcher's *A King and No King* (1611). Pix's *The Conquest of Spain* (1705) draws on the same theme as Fletcher's *The Loyal Subject* (1618). Since all these plays were revived in the 1580s and 1590s, Pix could have seen them in performance.

Ibrahim is motivated primarily by his rape of Morena, fiancée to the hero Amurat. The rape is set up by Sheker Para, the Emperor's mistress, who is the victim of an unrequited passion for Amurat. Pix models her two female protagonists on the stereotypes of virgin and whore. Morena and Sheker Para seem to be poles apart. The former is a 'Saint above' (14) who has been carefully concealed in her father's house to live 'in the contented paths / Of virtue' (20). Sheker Para has been 'expose[d] to publick view' (2) to converse with men, a freedom which, she says, 'has undone me' (5), apparently transforming her into a devilish Fury determined to exact her will. The opposition could not be more direct, yet by focusing on the limitations of such prescriptive roles, and drawing implicit parallels between them, Pix undermines them, and with them, the whole system of categorisation as a means of controlling women. Morena's status as idealised 'Goddess' from 'an upper Orb of bliss' (7) is made to look unnatural when she first appears on stage to be betrothed to Amurat. His exclamation highlights the limits of his perception:

> Thou transporting Image that dances thus
> Before my dazled Eyes, art thou real?
>
> (8)

The image of angel or goddess is anything but a real representation of Morena; as an elevated object she cannot even declare her love for Amurat for shame of acknowledging her desires (8). Once she has been raped, she cannot fulfil the role so her entrapment within it is necessarily tragic.

In the rape, Pix explores a characteristic feature of romance fiction: women's often perverse attitudes towards male violence. Janice Radway has pointed out that, even though female fantasies of rape may be born out of anxiety, women readers of romance maintain a 'dual perspective' in which rape can be acceptable if it shows the hero finding the heroine irresistible (1991: 141–4). Rather than condoning rape as an expression of the heroine's attractiveness, romances can expose its violence. The rape plot in *Ibrahim* works in this way. When Morena is brought before Ibrahim who anticipates 'new unknown delight' in conquering her virtue, she graphically demonstrates the destructive nature of his passion by grabbing his scimitar and drawing it through her hands until she bleeds (24). Here, Pix rewrites the physical conflict between jealous rival women in Davenant's *The Siege of Rhodes* and Settle's *Ibrahim* (1677), where Roxalana attacks the pure Ianthe with a dagger (Howe 1992: 148–9). The dagger in Pix's scene is a masculine weapon and the striking visual spectacle of the phallic blade, the bloody hands, and Morena's white dress advertises the savagery of male desire in gory technicolor. Morena's willingness to mutilate herself is not an acceptance of her role as victim. With the words 'See Emperor, see, are these hands / Fit to clasp thee?' (24), she forces him to confront the brutality of his own behaviour. Sheker Para's role as self-seeking mistress is also limiting, for, in spite of her superficial claims for female equality, she internalises the dominant ideology of the Turkish court. Her courageous declaration of love for Amurat is refreshingly liberating in contrast to the modesty of Morena. She holds the progressive view that the 'Joys of Love are double, when our / Sex desires' (13), which moves away from the double consciousness of woman watching herself from the perspective of the male gaze. Instead, she recreates herself as an articulate, desiring subject. When Amurat rejects her love though, her inability to escape from conventional ideology becomes clear in the wonderfully apt lines 'Break all the flattering Mirrors! / Let me ne'er behold this rejected Face again' (13). Ironically, Sheker Para is just as much a victim as Morena. Revenge, the 'Wronged Womens darling Joy' (5), seems to offer a way to reconstitute herself as a subject, but the freedom it gives is illusory in that Sheker Para is still emotionally bound to the situation where she is helpless. Pix explores the tragic limitations of revenge again in *The False Friend* (1699).

At the end of *Ibrahim*, Sheker's malicious control has destroyed Amurat and Morena as well as starting a political revolution, so the play does register the power of female anger. Morena's actions are more confined, but the tragic finale offers an oblique angle on her role as victim. When she swallows poison as the only solution to her loss of virginity, Amurat says her 'Innocence' is still intact since 'thy Virgin mind was pure' (40). This radical re-evaluation of female chastity in mental terms accords woman an active role in the ownership of her sexuality and is a mark of Pix's feminist politics, as Ray notes (1996: 43). Morena's suicide also exerts a powerful influence on the hero and the future of the state, since Amurat decides to sacrifice his future as the new effective governor of Turkey in favour of romantic love:

> no Crowns, no Lawrels, not
> The greatest height Ambition raises
> Shou'd ever mount me above thy Slave.
> (41)

Morena thus ends the play with her chastity assured and the undying, sacrificial love of the most powerful man in the Turkish court, an ironic reversal of the situation that led to the tragedy.

Private passion is prioritised over matters of state again in *Queen Catherine; or the Ruines of Love* (1698), a historical tragedy based on the fate of Henry V's widow in the Wars of the Roses. Holinshed criticised Catherine's marriage to Owen Tudor as the impulsive act of an over-sexed widow, who

followed 'more hir owne wanton appetite than freendlie counsell, and regarding more private affection than princelike honour' (Holinshed 1965:
190). Pix's tragedy takes a completely contradictory viewpoint, placing greater
value on private affection than prince-like honour. The Prologue announces
a woman-centred history, specifically for female spectators:

> To please your martial men she must despair,
> And therefore Courts the favour of the fair:
> From buffing Hero's she hopes no relief,
> But trusts in Catherine's Love and Isabella's grief.
>
> (n.p)

Love is central to the plot dynamic of Pix's tragedy. All the protagonists
are motivated by private passions, the only exception being Richard of
Gloucester, whose villainy is equated with emotional isolation. Edward's
ambition for Catherine's crown is driven by spurned love rather than a
wish for government. Nancy Cotton says Pix 'reduces history to amorous
intrigue' (1980: 117), but the focus on an emotional dimension, an internal
history, is part of a valuable feminist project. Queen Catherine accords value
to the typically feminine realm of personal, emotional experience.

In Owen Tudor and the Duke of Clarence, Pix offers female spectators
two idealised romantic heroes who, like Amurat in *Ibrahim*, are willing to
sacrifice everything for love. Catherine celebrates Tudor's unrestrained
emotions as essentially feminine qualities:

> sure thy Mothers blessings,
> And her beauty, and her softness, hangs about thee,
> The rest of humane Race all seem rugged,
> Thou only art the Child of Love, the pattern
> Made for Poets to form their Hero's by.
>
> (21)

Owen and Clarence's emotional vulnerability works, as in the popular
romance, to appeal to female characters (and spectators), while simultaneously acknowledging their greater expertise in emotional matters. When
the Yorkists burst into Catherine's bedroom to murder Tudor, she shows a
shrewd ability to manipulate the emotional situation. She calculates that
by falling prostrate at Edward's feet she might be able to save Tudor, but
at the critical moment, Tudor's impatient intervention destroys the careful
policy of male ego-boosting she had begun. She turns on Tudor, angry that
he cannot play the political game of apparent submission to save their
love. Instead of prioritising public honour and reputation, *Queen Catherine*

promotes a different set of values. Owen wants to be recorded in history as a lover, not a military hero:

> Report me as a Man that *Catherine* smil'd on;
> Let some kind Pen transmit the glory to
> Posterity.
>
> (19)

Here Pix advertises her own valuable task as recording and presenting an alternative history.

Even more so than history or tragedy, comedy seems to offer Pix both liberty and confinement for the expression of feminist ideas. With a shrewd eye on audience tastes, she often relies on traditional comic structures and formulae. Within those boundaries, however, she is able to expose the difficulties of women's situations, especially in arranged marriages. As Ray observes, Pix 'present[s] a more liberal view of women and sexuality' than her male contemporaries or predecessors (1996: 39). Her understanding of female sexuality was amply displayed in her first comedy *The Spanish Wives* (1696). The plot (which resembles Behn's *The Luckey Chance* in its use of intrigue, comic disguises and deception), revolves round two arranged marriages between older men and the Spanish wives of the title. The Governor of Barcelona 'gives his Wife more Liberty than is usual in Spain' (*dramatis personae*). 'Tittup', played by the celebrated comic actress Susanna Verbruggen (Wilson 1958: 180), is allowed to entertain gentlemen who serenade her and dance and dine with them at her husband's table. He presides over all with a genuine good humour and generosity like the spirit of comedy itself. His deep affection for Tittup is returned, so their relationship appears touching. Opposite this, Pix sets up the tyrannical husband, the Marquess of Moncada, who has snatched the rich Elenora from Camillus, her previously contracted lord, out of love of her estate. His jealously possessive nature makes him keep Elenora imprisoned 'under eleven Locks' (1), while they are guests in the Governor's house, a measure which is 'barbarous to the Fair Sex' (11).

Elenora responds with spirit, complaining 'Am I not immur'd, buried alive?' (11) and warning her husband that too severe restraint makes female sexuality 'slip away and prove the fruitless labour vain' (35). This proves to be the case, as Elenora plots to escape with Camillus in scenes which provide much comedy at the Marquess's expense. Camillus's love for Elenora (which she returns) is combined with a rightful claim to her hand and a truly enlightened view of female sexuality. He declares 'I am in quest of Virgin-Beauty made mine by Holy Vows . . . Virgin did I call her? – By Heaven, I dare believe she is one, at least her Mind is such' (28). Like

Amurat in *Ibrahim*, this romantic hero sees chastity as a mental rather than a physical entity. His undaunted passion for the bride who has been another man's wife is a refreshing change. The issue of mental chastity is much more complex in the Tittup plot. The Governor's philosophy, while appearing to be liberal, is in fact remarkably oppressive. He triumphantly declares in song:

> *Give but a Woman her Freedom still,*
> *Then she'll never act what's ill:*
> *'Tis crossing her, makes her have the Will.*
> (2)

The Governor's kindly rule gives Tittup freedom to transgress, but robs her of the will to enact her desires. When an English colonel offers her the joys of 'vigorous Love' (9), she is unable to forget 'such a Husband, / So good, so honest, preventing every Wish' (4). Self-policing threatens to collapse when Tittup plans to meet the Colonel. With a surveillance technique worthy of a Big Brother figure, however, the Governor substitutes himself in the Colonel's place in order to induce a sense of guilt in Tittup which will regulate her behaviour all the more effectively. Although he threatens 'your Apartments must be your Prison' (40), such repressive measures will be unnecessary. Caught in the ideological trap of chastity, Tittup willingly resigns herself to a marriage in which her own desires remain unfulfilled: '*Good Humour shall supply the want of Youth / You shall be always kind, I full of Truth*' she pledges her husband (41). While the view of chastity as a mental condition is liberating for Elenora, Pix shows that, for Tittup, it is a form of interpellation no less restrictive than that of the Marquess's 11 locks.

Pix's later intrigue comedy *The Deceiver Deceived* (1698) explores the failure of masculine surveillance under the pressure of feminist conspiracy. Bondi, a possessive husband and father, pretends to be blind in order to oversee the activities of his young wife Olivia and his daughter Ariana, only to be horrified by what he discovers. Pix sets up Lady Temptyouth, 'the best of Women' (8) to help the ladies pursue their desires. While Bondi is supposedly incapacitated, Temptyouth busily oversees affairs in his household, arranging trysts between Olivia and Count Andrea, and helping Ariana to escape an arranged match to the foppish Count Insulls, so that she can marry the poor Fidelio. Count Insulls is re-matched to Temptyouth's impoverished protégée Lucinda, a happy outcome for all since Lucinda declares 'Oh a rich Fool was alwaies my desire, that I might show my discretion in managing him and his Estate' (33). Like her surrogate mother, Lucinda longs to control a supposedly male household. Attempts to restore Bondi's sight are thematically linked to removing his misguided attitudes towards women as possessions. In a symbolic dramatic climax, he is forced to trust in his wife's fidelity and accept his daughter's marriage to prevent losing all the material possessions in his household. When Olivia discovers that her husband was not truly blind she feels that her honour is irretrievably lost. Nevertheless, she outwits Bondi again by pretending she knew all along and flirted with Andrea only to provoke him to cast off the blindness out of jealousy. Levels of truth and deception become extremely complex in this final twist to the plot, as though Pix is deliberately trying to problematise perceptions of female behaviour.

In her two other early comedies *The Innocent Mistress* (1697) and *The Beau Defeated* (1700), Pix returns to romance conventions from the perspective of the female reader. *The Innocent Mistress* is, as Juliet McLaren cleverly suggests, a critical reaction to the misogynist stereotypes in 1690s comedies by men (1990: 90). Far from being lascivious or foolish, the heroine Bellinda (played by Barry) is addicted to reading chaste romances and has a platonic relationship with Sir Charles Beauclair, with whom she fell in love before knowing he was married. In *The Beau Defeated*, however, Lady Landsworth is an inspiring, resistant reader of romance who carves out her future according to her own desires. After the death of her first husband she declares 'I am resolv'd to indulge my Inclinations, and rather than not obtain the person I like, invert the Order of nature and persue, tho' he flies' (5). Like the witty heroines of other Restoration comedies, she uses disguise to test out Clerimont's attitudes to women before accepting him. Pix's reliance on the popular elements of Restoration theatre makes it unsurprising that she was so successful as a professional playwright. Within the tight structures of comedy and tragedy for commercial stage, however, she succeeded in modifying established attitudes so as to create what Patsy Fowler calls 'a more woman-friendly culture' (Fowler 1996: 49).

The Beau Defeated is the last play by the Pix–Trotter–Manley group to be covered by the scope of this book. Despite, or perhaps because of, the satire of *The Female Wits*, they all continued writing plays well into the eighteenth century. Trotter wrote *Love at a Loss* (1700), *The Unhappy Penitent* (1701) and *The Revolution of Sweden* (1706) and Pix wrote *The Double Distress* (1701), *The Czar of Muscovy* (1701), *The Different Widows* (1703), *The Conquest of Spain* (1705) and *The Adventures in Madrid* (1706). Delariviere Manley did not compose another play for ten years, namely *Almyna; or, The Arabian Vow* (1706), followed by *Lucius, First Christian King of Britain* (1717), but she continued to associate herself publicly with drama by writing from the position of Melpomen (Muse of Comedy) and Thalia (Muse of Tragedy), in *The Nine Muses* (1700), a volume of elegies upon the death of Dryden. Alongside the female triumvirate, another woman made her playwriting debut. In October 1700, Susanna Centlivre's *The Perjur'd Husband* premiered at

Drury Lane. Possibly encouraged by Pix (Clark 1986: 201), her dramatic output was to equal that of Aphra Behn. Joined by 15 more women playwrights in the first half of the eighteenth century (Cotton 1980: 19–23), Trotter, Pix, Manley and Centlivre established beyond question that women had a right to self-expression via dramatic production in the mainstream theatre, as well as in the alternative theatrical venues which their sister playwrights had used.

BIBLIOGRAPHY

Primary Sources

Ariadne (1695) *She Ventures and He Wins*, London.

Aughterson, Kate (1995) *Renaissance Woman: A Sourcebook*, London: Routledge.

Barwick, Grace (1659) *To All Present Rulers, Whether Parliament, or Whomsoever of England*, London.

Behn, Aphra (1996a) *The Works of Aphra Behn* (ed.) Todd, Janet, vol. 5 *The Plays 1671–77*, London: Pickering & Chatto.

Behn, Aphra (1996b) *The Works of Aphra Behn* (ed.) Todd, Janet, vol. 6 *The Plays 1678–82*, London: Pickering & Chatto.

Behn, Aphra (1996c) *The Works of Aphra Behn* (ed.) Todd, Janet, vol. 7 *The Plays 1682–96*, London: Pickering & Chatto.

Bell, Robin (ed.) (1992) *Bittersweet Within My Heart: The Collected Poems of Mary, Queen of Scots*, London: Pavilion Books Ltd.

Berkeley, Sir William (1987) *The Lost Lady* (ed.) Rowan, D., Oxford: Malone Society Reprints.

Birch, Thomas (1751) *The Works of Mrs Catherine Cockburn, Theological, Moral, Dramatic and Poetical, with an Account of the Life of the Author by Thomas Birch*, 2 vols, London: J. & P. Knapton.

Boothby, Frances (1670) *Marcelia; or, the Treacherous Friend*, London.

Brown, David (1652) *The Naked Woman*, London.

Cadbury, H. J. (ed.) (1948) 'Letters to William Dewsbury and others', in *Journal of Friends Historical Society*, Supplement 22, London.

Calendar of State Papers Domestic, 1657–8.

Cary, Elizabeth (1996) *The Tragedy of Mariam, The Fair Queen of Jewry* (1613) (ed.) Wright, Stephanie, J., Keele: Keele University Press.

Cavendish, Jane and Brackley, Elizabeth (*c.* 1645), 'Poems, songs a Pastorall and a Play', Bodleian Library: Rawlinson MS Poet 16.

Cavendish, Jane and Brackley, Elizabeth (1996) *The Concealed Fancies* in *Renaissance Drama by Women: Texts and Documents* (eds) Cerasano, S. P. and Wynne-Davies, Marion, London and New York: Routledge, pp. 127–54.

Cavendish, Margaret (1653) *Poems and Fancies*, London.

Cavendish, Margaret (1662) *Playes*, London.

Cavendish, Margaret (1664) *Sociable Letters*, London.

Cavendish, Margaret (1668) *Plays never before Printed*, London.

Cavendish, Margaret (1872) *The Life of William Cavendish, First Duke of Newcastle* (1667), and *A True Relation of my Birth, Breeding and Life* (1656) in *The Lives of William Cavendish, Duke of Newcastle and of his Wife Margaret Duchess of Newcastle* (ed.) Lower, Mark Anthony, London: John Russell Smith.

Cavendish, Margaret (1994) *The Blazing World and Other Writings* (ed.) Lilley, Kate, Harmondsworth: Penguin.

Centlivre, Susanna (1700) *The Perjur'd Husband*, London.

Cerasano, S. P. and Wynne-Davies, Marion (eds) (1996) *Renaissance Drama by Women: Texts and Documents*, London and New York: Routledge.

Child, Harold (ed.) (1909) *Iphigenia at Aulis Translated by Lady Lumley*, Oxford: Malone Society.

Danchin, Pierre (ed.) (1981) *The Prologues and Epilogues of the Restoration 1660–1700 Part One: 1660–1676*, Nancy: Presses Universitaires de Nancy.

Danchin, Pierre (ed.) (1984) *The Prologues and Epilogues of the Restoration 1660–1700 Part Two: 1677–1690*, Nancy: Presses Universitaires de Nancy.

Daniel, Samuel (1594) *The Tragedie of Cleopatra*, London.

Daniel, Samuel (1980) *The Vision of the Twelve Goddesses*, in *A Book of Masques in Honour of Allardyce Nicoll*, (ed.) Spencer, T. J. B. and Wells, Stanley, Cambridge: Cambridge University Press, pp. 19–42.

Daniel, Samuel (1995) *Tethys Festival*, in *Court Masques* (ed.) Lindley, David, Oxford: Oxford University Press, pp. 54–65.

Davenant, William (1634) *The Temple of Love*, London.

Davenant, William (1638) *Luminalia*, London.

Davenant, William (1656) *The Siege of Rhodes*, in *Dramatic Works* (ed.) Maidment, James and Logan, W. H., New York: Russell and Russell (1964), vol. 3, pp. 231–365.

Davenant, William (1657) *The First Day's Entertainment at Rutland-House*, in *Dramatic Works*, vol. 3, pp. 193–230.

Davenant, William (1663) *The Play House To Be Let*, in *Dramatic Works*, vol. 4, pp. 1–104.

Davenant, William (1995) *Salmacida Spolia*, in *Court Masques* (ed.) Lindley, David, Oxford: Oxford University Press, pp. 200–15.

Davies, Lady Eleanor (1995) *The Prophetic Writings of Lady Eleanor Davies* (ed.) Cope, Esther S., New York and Oxford: Oxford University Press.

Deacon, John (1657) *An Exact History of the Life of James Nayler*, London.

Delavel, Lady Elizabeth (1978) *The Meditations of Lady Elizabeth Delavel Written Between 1662 and 1671* (ed.) Greene, Douglas G., Surtees Society, Northumberland: Northumberland Press Limited.

Donne, John (1990) *John Donne* (ed.) Carey, John, Oxford and New York: Oxford University Press.

Edwards, Thomas (1977) *Gangraena*, Ilkley: The Rota and the University of Exeter.

Elizabeth I (1996) *Hercules Oetaeus*, in *Renaissance Drama by Women: Texts and Documents* (ed.) Cerasano, S. P. and Wynne-Davies, Marion, London and New York: Routledge, pp. 6–12.

Ellis, Humphrey (1650) *Pseudochristus*, London.

Ephelia (1679) *Female Poems on Several Occasions Written by Ephelia*, London.

Euripides IV (1958) (ed.) Grene, David and Lattimore, Richard, including *Iphigeneia at Aulis* (trans.) Walker, Charles R., Chicago: University of Chicago Press.

Euripides IV (1972) *Orestes and Other Plays* (trans.) and (ed.) Vellacott, Philip, Harmondsworth: Penguin.

Fane, Rachel (*c.* 1630) Untitled Dramatic Works, Sackville MSS U269 F38/3: Kent County Archives.

Fanshawe, Sir Richard (1964) *A Critical Edition of Sir Richard Fanshawe's 1647 Translation of Giovanni Battista Guarini's Il Pastor Fido* (ed.) Staton, Walter F., Jr and Simeone, William E., Oxford: Clarendon Press.

Farmer, Ralph (1657) *Sathan Inthron'd in His Chair of Pestilence*, London.

The Female Wits; or, The Triumvirate of Poets at Rehearsal by Mr W. M. (1704) London.

Finch, Anne, Countess of Winchilsea (1903) *The Poems of Anne, Countess of Winchilsea* (ed.) Reynolds, Myra, Chicago: University of Chicago Press.

Finch, Anne, Countess of Winchilsea (1998) *The Anne Finch Wellesley Manuscript Poems: A Critical Edition* (ed.) McGovern, Barbara and Hinnant, Charles H., Athens and London: University of Georgia Press.

Firth, C. H. and Rait, F. S. (1911) *Acts and Ordinances of the Interregnum, 1642–60*, vol. 1, London: HMSO.

Fitzmaurice, James; Roberts, Josephine A.; Barash, Carol L.; Cunnar, Eugene R. and Gutierrez, Nancy, A. (eds) (1997a) *Major Women Writers of Seventeenth-Century England*, Ann Arbor: University of Michigan Press.

Foxe, John (1851) *Foxe's Book of Martyrs* (ed.) Milner, Rev. J., London: William Tegg and Co.

Garnier, Robert (1975) *Two Tragedies: Hippolyte and Marc Antoine* (ed.) Hill, Christine M. and Morrison, Mary, G., London: Athlone Press.

Graham, Elspeth; Hinds, Hilary; Hobby, Elaine and Wilcox, Helen (eds) (1989) *Her Own Life: Autobiographical Writings by Seventeenth Century Englishwomen*, London: Routledge.

Greer, Germaine; Medoff, Jeslyn; Sansone, Melinda and Hastings, Susan (eds) (1988) *Kissing the Rod: An Anthology of Seventeenth Century Women's Verse*, London: Virago.

Historical Manuscripts Commission (1904) *Calender of the Manuscripts of the Marquess of Bath Preserved at Longleat, Wiltshire*, vol. 1, London: Her Majesty's Stationery Office.

Holinshed, Raphael (1965) *Holinshed's Chronicles of England, Scotland and Ireland*, New York: AMS Press.

Howell, James (1654) *The Nuptialls of Peleus and Thetis*, London.

Jayne, Sears and Johnson, Francis R. (1956) *The Lumley Library: The Catalogue of 1609*, London: the Trustees of the British Museum.

Jonson, Ben (1941, rpt. 1970) *The Masque of Beauty*, in *Works*, vol. VII (ed.) Percy, C. H. Herford and Simpson, Evelyn, Oxford: Clarendon Press, pp. 181–94.

Jonson, Ben (1995) *The Masque of Blackness*, in *Court Masques* (ed.) Lindley, David, Oxford: Oxford University Press, pp. 1–9.

Jonson, Ben (1995) *The Masque of Queens*, in *Court Masques* (ed.) Lindley, David, Oxford: Oxford University Press, pp. 35–53.

Jonson, Ben (1995) *Chloridia*, in *Court Masques* (ed.) Lindley, David, Oxford: Oxford University Press, pp. 147–54.

Jonson, Ben (1996) *Epicoene* (ed.) Holdsworth, R. V., London: A & C Black.

Killgrew, Anne (1686) *Poems*, London.

Klausner, D. (ed.) (1990) *Records of Early English Drama: Hereford and Worcester*, Toronto: University of Toronto Press.

Kyd, Thomas (1970) *The Spanish Tragedy* (ed.) Mulryne, J. R., *New Mermaids*, London: Ernest Benn.

Langbaine, Gerard (1691) *The Lives of the English Poets*, Oxford.

Lumley, Jane (*c*. 1554) *The Tragedie of Euripides Called Iphigeneia Translated out of Greake into Englisshe*, British Library: MS Royal 15.A.ix.

Lumley, Jane (1998) *The Tragedie of Iphigenia*, in *Three Tragedies by Renaissance Women* (ed.) Diane Purkiss, London: Penguin, pp. 1–35.

Lumley, John (1554) Folger MS L.b.499.

McGee, C. E. (ed.) (1991) ' "The Visit of the Nine Goddesses": A Masque at Sir John Crofts's House', *English Literary Renaissance*, 21 (3): 371–84.

Magalotti, Lorenzo (1980) *Lorenzo Magalotti at the Court of Charles II; His 'Relazione d'Inghilterra' of 1668* (trans.) and (ed.) Knowles Middleton, W. E., Waterloo: Wilfrid Laurier University Press.

Manley, Delariviere (1696a) *The Lost Lover*, London.

Manley, Delariviere (1696b) *The Royal Mischief*, London.

Marston, John (1969) *The Poems of John Marston* (ed.) Arnold Davenport, Liverpool: Liverpool University Press.

Milton, John (1968, rpt. 1988) *Comus and Other Poems* (ed.) Prince, F. T., Oxford: Oxford University Press.

Montagu, Walter (1997) *The Shepherd's Paradise* (ed.) Poynting, Sarah, Oxford: Malone Society Reprints.

Mush, Father (1877) *A True Relation of the Life of Mrs Margaret Clitherow 1586*, in *The Troubles of Our Catholic Forefathers Related by Themselves* (ed.) Morris, John, London: Burns and Oates.

Nichols, John (1788) *The Progresses and Public Processions of Queen Elizabeth*, 2 vols, London.

Osborne, Dorothy (1987) *Letters to William Temple* (ed.) Parker, Kenneth, Harmondsworth: Penguin.

Penney, Norman (ed.) (1907) *The First Publishers of Truth, being Early Records of the Introduction of Quakerism in the Countries of England and Wales*, London: Headley Brothers.

Pepys, Samuel (1970–83) *The Diary of Samuel Pepys*, 10 vols (eds) Lanier, Robert and Matthews William, London: Bell.

Philips, Katherine (1990) *The Collected Works of Katherine Philips, The Matchless Orinda* (ed.) Thomas, Patrick, vol. I, *The Poems*, Stump Cross: Stump Cross Books.

Philips, Katherine (1992) *The Collected Works of Katherine Philips, The Matchless Orinda* (ed.) Thomas, Patrick, vol. II, *The Letters*, Stump Cross: Stump Cross Books.

Philips, Katherine (1993) *The Collected Works of Katherine Philips, The Matchless Orinda* (ed.) Greer, Germaine, vol. III, *The Translations*, Stump Cross: Stump Cross Books.

Pix, Mary (1982) *The Plays of Mary Pix and Catherine Trotter*, vol. 1: Mary Pix (ed.) Steeves, Edna L., New York and London: Garland Publishing.

Polwhele, E. (*c.* 1670) *The Faithfull Virgins*, Bodleian Library MS. Rawl Poet. 195, pp. 49–78.

Polwhele, E. (1977) *The Frolicks* (ed.) Milhous, Judith and Hume, Robert D., Ithaca and London: Cornell University Press.

Poole, Elizabeth (1648) *A Vision: Wherein is Manifested the Disease and Cure of the Kingdome*, London.

Raymond, Joad (ed.) (1993) *Making the News: an Anthology of the Newsbooks of Revolutionary England 1641–60*, Moreton-in-Marsh: Windrush Press.

(1979–) *Records of Early English Drama*, Director Johnston, Alexandra F., Executive Director MacLean, Sally-Beth, Toronto, Buffalo, London: University of Toronto Press.

Roche-Guilhen, Madam Le (1677) *Rare En Tout: Comedie Meslée de Musique et de Balets, Represantée devant Sa Majesté Sur le Theatre Royal de Whitehall*, London.

Rogers, D. M. (ed.) (1979) *An Abstract of the Life and Martirdome of Mistres Margaret Clitherowe, English Recusant Literature*, vol. 393, Menstone: Scolar Press.

Rogers, Katharine M. (ed.) (1994) *The Meridian Anthology of Restoration and Eighteenth Century Plays by Women*, New York: Penguin.

Rowe, Elizabeth Singer (1696) *Poems on Several Occasions, Written by Philomela*, London.

Shakespeare, William (1997) *The Norton Shakespeare* (ed.) Cohen, Walter; Howard, Jean E. and Eisaman Maus, Katharine, with an essay on the Shakespearean stage by Gurr, Andrew, New York and London: W. W. Norton.

Sidney, Mary (1998a) *The Tragedie of Antonie*, in *Three Tragedies by Renaissance Women* (ed.) Diane Purkiss, Harmondsworth: Penguin, pp. 36–95.

Sidney, Mary (1998b) 'A Dialogue Between Two Shepherds: Thenot and Piers,' in *The Collected Works of Mary Sidney Herbert, Countess of Pembroke 1561–1621*, vol. 1, (ed.) Patterson Hannay, Margaret; Kinnamon, Noel J. and Brennan, Michael G., Oxford: Clarendon Press, pp. 100–1.

Sidney, Sir Philip (1973) *Miscellaneous Prose* (ed.) Duncan-Jones, K. and Van Dorsten, J., Oxford: Oxford University Press.

The Terrible, Horrible Monster of the West, London.

Time's Distractions (ed.) Welter Strommer, Diane, College Station, Texas: A & M University Press.

Townshend, Aurelian (1995) *Tempe Restored*, in *Court Masques* (ed.) Lindley, David, Oxford: Oxford University Press, pp. 155–65.

Trapnel, Anna (1654a) *The Cry of A Stone or A Relation of Something Spoken in Whitehall by Anna Trapnel, Being in the Visions of God*, London.

Trapnel, Anna (1654b) *Anna Trapnel's Report and Plea, or a Narrative of her Journey from London into Cornwall*, London.

Trapnel, Anna (1654c) *Strange and Wonderful Newes From White-hall*, London.

Travitsky, Betty (ed.) (1989) *The Paradise of Women: Writings by Englishwomen of the Renaissance*, New York and Oxford: Columbia University Press.

Trotter, Catherine (1696) *A Tragedy As it is Acted at the Theatre Royal, Written by a Young Lady* [*Agnes de Castro*], London.

Trotter, Catherine (1698) *Fatal Friendship: A Tragedy As it is Acted at the New Theatre*, London.

The Unnatural Mother (1698) London.

Van Lennep, William (ed.) (1965) *The London Stage 1660–1800. Part 1: 1660–1700*, Carbondale: Southern Illinois University Press.

Warren, Elizabeth (1645) *The Old and Good Way Vindicated*, London.

Wharton, Anne (1679/82) *Love's Martyr; or, Witt above Crowns*, British Library: Add. MS 28,693.

Wharton, Anne (1997) *The Surviving Works of Anne Wharton* (ed.) Greer, Germaine and Hastings, Susan, Stump Cross: Stump Cross Books.

White, Robert (1996) *Cupid's Banishment*, in *Renaissance Drama by Women: Texts and Documents* (ed.) Cerasano, S. P. and Wynne-Davies, Marion, London: Routledge, pp. 76–89.

Wight, Sarah (1647) *The Exceeding Riches of Grace Advanced by the Spirit of Grace*, London.

Wilson, Jean (ed.) (1980) *Entertainments for Elizabeth I*, Woodbridge: D. S. Brewer.

Wright, James (1699) *Historia Histrionica: An Historical Account of the English-Stage*, London.

Wroth, Mary (1621) *Urania*, London.

Wroth, Mary (1621?) *The Second Part of the Urania*, Newberry Library: MS FY1565 W95.

Wroth, Mary (1996) *Love's Victory*, in *Renaissance Drama by Women: Texts and Documents* (ed.) Cerasano, S. P. and Wynne-Davies, Marion, London and New York: Routledge, pp. 91–126.

Secondary Sources

Adam, Michel (1993) *Femmes Dramaturges et Actrices en Angleterre*, Rouen: Publications de l' Université de Rouen.

Arnold, Janet (1988) *Queen Elizabeth's Wardrobe Unlock'd*, Leeds: Maney.

Artaud, Antonin (1958) *The Theater and Its Double* (trans.) Richards, Mary Caroline, New York: Grove Press.

Barroll, Leeds (1991) 'The Court of the First Stuart Queen', in Levy Peck, Linda (ed.) *The Mental World of the Jacobean Court*, Cambridge: Cambridge University Press, pp. 191–208.

Barroll, Leeds (1996) 'Theatre as Text: The Case of Queen Anna and the Jacobean Court Masque', in Magnusson, A. L. and McGee, C. E. (eds) *The Elizabethan Theatre*, vol. XIV, Toronto: P. D. Meany, pp. 175–93.

Barroll, Leeds (1998) 'The Arts at the English Court of Anna of Denmark', in Cerasano, S. P. and Wynne-Davies, Marion (eds) *Readings in Renaissance Women's Drama: Criticism, History and Performance 1554–1998*, London: Routledge, pp. 47–59.

Battigelli, Anna (1998) *Margaret Cavendish and the Exiles of the Mind*, Lexington: University Press of Kentucky.

Baudrillard, Jean (1988) *Selected Writings* (ed.) Poster, Mark, Oxford: Polity Press in association with Basil Blackwell.

Bauman, R. F. (1983) *Let Your Words Be Few: Symbolism of Speaking and Silence Among Seventeenth-Century Quakers*, Cambridge: Cambridge University Press.

Bax, Clifford (1932) *Pretty Witty Nell: An Account of Nell Gwyn and her Environment*, London: Chapman and Hall.

Beilin, Elaine V. (1987) *Redeeming Eve: Women Writers of the English Renaissance*, Princeton: Princeton University Press.

Blackmore, David (1990) *Arms and Armour of the English Civil Wars*, London: Trustees of the Royal Armouries.

Bornstein, Diane (1985) 'The Style of the Countess of Pembroke's Translation of Philippe de Mornay's Discours de la vie et de la mort', in Margaret Patterson Hannay (ed.) *Silent But For the Word: Tudor Women as Patrons, Translators and Writers of Religious Works*, Kent, Ohio: Kent State University Press, pp. 126–48.

Boswell, Eleanore (1932) *The Restoration Court Stage 1660–1702*, London: George Allen and Unwin.

Brashear, Lucy (1979) 'The Forgotten Legacy of the "Matchless Orinda"', in *Anglo Welsh Review*, 65: 68–76.

Brennan, Michael G. (ed.) (1988) *Lady Mary Wroth's Love's Victorie: The Penshurst Manuscript*, London: Roxburghe Club.

Brooke, Nicholas (ed.) (1994) *Macbeth*, Oxford World Classics, Oxford: Oxford University Press.

Brown, Cedric (1994) 'Courtesies of Place and Arts of Diplomacy in Ben Jonson's Last Two Entertainments for Royalty', *The Seventeenth Century*, 9 (2): 147–71.

Bullough, Geoffrey (1966) *Narrative and Dramatic Sources of Shakespeare: Volume V*, London: Routledge and Kegan Paul.

Burling, William J. (1991) '"Their Empire Disjoyn'd": Serious Plays by Women on the London Stage, 1660–1737', in Schofield, Mary Anne and Macheski, Cecilia (eds) *Curtain Calls: British and American Woman and the Theater 1660–1820*, Athens: Ohio University Press, pp. 311–23.

Butler, Martin (1984) *Theatre and Crisis 1632–42*, Cambridge: Cambridge University Press.

Butler, Martin (1993) 'Reform or reverence? The politics of the Caroline masque', in Mulryne, J. R. and Shewring, Margaret (eds) *Theatre and Government Under the Early Stuarts*, Cambridge: Cambridge University Press, pp. 118–56.

Buxton, John (1964) *Sir Philip Sidney and the English Renaissance*, London: Macmillan, New York: St Martin's Press.

Cahill, Jane (1995) *Her Kind: Stories of Women from Greek Mythology*, Peterborough, Ontario: Broadview Press.

Campbell, Julie D. (1997) '*Love's Victory* and *La Mirtilla*, in the Canon of Renaissance Tragicomedy: an examination of the influence of salon and social debates', *Women's Writing*, (4) 1: 103–24.

Carlton, Charles (1992) *Going To The Wars: The Experience of the British Civil Wars 1638–51*, London and New York: Routledge.

Carroll, Kenneth L. (1972) 'Martha Simmonds: A Quaker Enigma', *Journal of the Friends Historical Society*, 53: 31–52.

Carroll, Kenneth L. (1978) 'Early Quakers and "Going Naked As a Sign"', *Journal of the Friends Historical Society*, 67: 69–87.

Carpenter, Sarah (1989) 'Early Scottish Drama', in Jack, R. D. S. (ed.) *The History of Scottish Literature*, vol. 1, Aberdeen: Aberdeen University Press, pp. 199–212.

Cerasano, S. P. and Wynne-Davies, Marion (eds) (1996) *Renaissance Drama by Women: Texts and Documents*, London and New York: Routledge.

Cerasano, S. P. and Wynne-Davies, Marion (eds) (1998) *Readings in Renaissance Women's Drama: Criticism, History, and Performance 1594–1998*, London: Routledge.

Chalmers, Hero (1997) 'Dismantling the myth of "Mad Madge": the cultural context of Margaret Cavendish's authorial self-presentation', *Women's Writing*, 4 (3): 323–39.

Chernaik, Warren (1995) 'Ephelia's Voice: The Authorship of Female Poems (1679)', *Phililogical Quarterly*, 74 (2): 151–72.

Cixous, Helene (1991) 'The Laugh of the Medusa', in Warhol, Robyn R. and Price Herndl, Diane (eds) *Feminisms: An Anthology of Literary Theory and Criticism*, New Brunswick: Rutgers University Press, pp. 334–48.

Clark, Constance (1986) *Three Augustan Women Playwrights*, American University Studies, New York: Peter Lang.

Cope, Esther S. (1992) *Handmaid of the Holy Spirit: Dame Eleanor Davies, Never Soe Mad a Ladie*, Ann Arbor: University of Michigan Press.

Cotton, Nancy (1980) *Women Playwrights in England 1363–1750*, Lewisburg: Bucknell University Press.

Crane, Frank D. (1944) 'Euripides, Erasmus and Lady Lumley', *Classical Journal*, 39: 223–8.

Creaser, John (1984) 'The Setting of *Comus*', in David Lindley (ed.) *The Court Masque*, Manchester: Manchester University Press, pp. 111–34.

de Lauretis, Teresa (1984) *Alice Doesn't: Feminism, Semiotics, Cinema*, Bloomington, Indiana: Indiana University Press.

de Lauretis, Teresa (1987) *Technologies of Gender: Essays on Theory, Film and Fiction*, Bloomington: Indiana University Press.

de Lauretis, Teresa (1990) 'Sexual Indifference and Lesbian Representation', in Case, Sue Ellen (ed.) *Performing Feminisms: Feminist Critical Theory and Theatre*, Baltimore and London: Johns Hopkins University Press, pp. 17–39.

Dent, John (1970: 2nd edition) *The Quest for Nonsuch*, Sutton, Surrey: London Borough of Sutton Libraries and Arts Services.

Devereux, E. J. (1983) *Renaissance English Translations of Erasmus: A Bibliography to 1700*, London and Buffalo, Toronto: University of Toronto Press.

Dillon, Janette (1998) *Language and Stage in Medieval and Renaissance England*, Cambridge, Cambridge University Press.

Diamond, Elin (1997) *Unmaking Mimesis: Essays on Feminism and Theater*, London: Routledge.

Diamond, Elin (1999) 'Gestus and Signature in *The Rover*', in Todd, Janet (ed.) *Aphra Behn*, London: Macmillan, pp. 32–56.

Duncan-Jones, Katherine (1991) *Sir Philip Sidney, Courtier Poet*, London: Hamish Hamilton.

Duffy, Maureen (1977) *The Passionate Shepherdess: Aphra Behn 1640–89*, London: Cape.

Eales, Jacqueline (1990) *Puritans and Roundheads: The Harleys of Brampton Bryan and the Outbreak of the English Civil War*, Cambridge: Cambridge University Press.

Elmer, Peter (1996) ' "Saints or Sorcerers": Quakerism, demonology and the decline of witchcraft in seventeenth-century England', in Barry, Jonathan; Hester, Marianne and Roberts, Gareth (eds) *Witchcraft in Early Modern Europe*, Past and Present Publications, Cambridge: Cambridge University Press, pp. 145–79.

Erler, Mary (1991) ' "Chaste sports, Juste Prayses, & All Softe Delights": Harefield 1602 and Ashby 1607, Two Female Entertainments', in Magnusson, A. L. and McGee, C. E. (eds) *The Elizabethan Theatre*, XIV, Toronto: P. D. Meany, pp. 1–25.

Esslin, Martin (1987) *The Field of Drama*, London: Methuen.

Ezell, Margaret J. M. (1987) *The Patriarch's Wife: Literary Evidence and the History of the Family*, Chapel Hill and London: University of North Carolina Press.

Ezell, Margaret J. M. (1993) *Writing Women's Literary History*, Baltimore and London: Johns Hopkins University Press.

Ezell, Margaret J. M. (1998) ' "To be your daughter in your Pen": the social functions of literature in the writings of Lady Elizabeth Brackley and Lady Jane Cavendish', in Cerasano, S. P. and Wynne-Davies, Marion (eds) *Readings in Renaissance Women's Drama: Text, Criticism, Performance 1550–1998*, London: Routledge, pp. 246–58.

Faulkener, P. A. (1985) *Bolsover Castle*, London: English Heritage.

Findlay, Alison (1998) ' "She gave you the civility of the house": household performance in *The Concealed Fancies*', in Cerasano, S. P. and Wynne-Davies, Marion (eds) *Readings in Renaissance Women's Drama: Text, Criticism, Performance 1550–1998*, London: Routledge, pp. 259–71.

Findlay, Alison (1999a) *A Feminist Perspective on Renaissance Drama*, Oxford: Blackwell.

Findlay, Alison (1999b) 'Playing the "Scene Self": Jane Cavendish and Elizabeth Brackley's *The Concealed Fancies*', in Comensoli, Viviana and Russell, Anne (eds) *Enacting Gender on the English Renaissance Stage*, Urbana and Chicago: University of Illinois Press, pp. 154–76.

Findlay, Alison; Hodgson-Wright, Stephanie and Williams, Gweno (1999a) ' "The Play is ready to be Acted": Women and Dramatic Production 1570–1670' *Women's Writing*, 6 (1): 129–48.

Findlay, Alison; Hodgson-Wright, Stephanie and Williams, Gweno (1999b) *Women Dramatists 1550–1670: Plays in Performance*, Lancaster: Lancaster University Television.

Fisken, Beth Wynne (1985) 'Mary Sidney's Psalmes: Education and Wisdom', in Margaret Patterson Hannay (ed.) *Silent but for the Word: Tudor Women as Patrons, Translators and Writers of Religious Works*, Kent, Ohio: Kent State University Press, pp. 166–83.

Fitzmaurice, James (1997b) 'Front Matter and the Physical Make-up of *Natures Pictures*', *Women's Writing*, 4 (3): 353–67.

Fowler, Patsy S. (1996) 'Rejecting the Status Quo: The Attempts of Mary Pix and Susanna Centilivre to Reform Society's Petrarchan Attitudes', *Restoration and Eighteenth Century Theatre Research*, 11 (2): 49–59.

Franceschina, John (1995) 'Shadow and Substance in Aphra Behn's *The Rover*: The Semiotics of Restoration Performance', *Restoration: Studies in English Literary Culture 1660–1700*, 19 (1): 29–42.

Fraser, Antonia (1969) *Mary, Queen of Scots*, London: Weidenfeld and Nicholson.

Freedman, Barbara (1996) 'Frame-Up: Feminism, Psychoanalysis, Theatre,' in Helene Keyssar (ed.) *Feminist Theatre and Theory*, Basingstoke: Macmillan, pp. 78–108.

Gallagher, Catherine (1999) 'Who was That Masked Woman? The Prostitute and the Playwright in the Comedies of Aphra Behn', in Todd, Janet (ed.) *Aphra Behn*, London: Macmillan, pp. 12–31.

Genest, John (1832) *Some Account of the English Stage from the Restoration in 1660–1830*, vol. 1, Bath: H. E. Carrington.

Gravett, Chris (1990) *Medieval Siege Warfare*, London: Osprey.

Greer, Germaine; Medoff, Jeslyn; Sansone, Melinda and Hastings, Susan (eds) (1988) *Kissing the Rod: An Anthology of Seventeenth Century Women's Verse*, London: Virago.

Greer, Germaine (1995) *Slip-shod Sybils: Recognition, Rejection and the Woman Poet*, London: Viking.

Greer, Germaine and Hastings, Susan (eds) (1997) *The Surviving Works of Anne Wharton*, Stump Cross: Stump Cross Books.

Goodman, Lizbeth (1996) 'Feminisms and theatres: canon fodder and cultural change', in Patrick Campbell (ed.) *Analysing Performance: A Critical Reader*, Manchester and New York: Manchester University Press, pp. 19–42.

Goreau, Angeline (1980) *Reconstructing Aphra*, New York: Dial.

Gosset, Suzanne (1988) ' "Man-maid begone: Women in Masques', in *English Literary Renaissance*, 18 (1): 96–113.

Hackett, Helen (1995) *Virgin Mother, Maiden Queen*, Basingstoke: Macmillan.

Halliwell, James O. (1860) *A Dictionary of Old English Plays*, London: John Russell Smith.

Hamilton, Elizabeth (1976) *Henrietta Maria*, London: Sutton.

Hannay, Margaret (ed.) (1985) *Silent but for the Word: Tudor Women as Patrons, Translators and Writers of Religious Works*, Kent, Ohio: Kent State University Press.

Hannay, Margaret P. (1990) *Philip's Phoenix: Mary Sidney, Countess of Pembroke*, New York: Oxford University Press.

Hannay, Margaret P.; Kinnamon, Noel J. and Brennan, Michael G. (1998) *The Collected Works of Mary Sidney Herbert 1561–1621*, vol. 1, Oxford: Clarendon Press.

Harbage, Alfred (1936) *Cavalier Drama*, London: Oxford University Press.

Harbage, Alfred (ed.) (1989) *Annals of English Drama*, revised by Schoenbaum, S., 3rd edn revised by Stoler Wagonheim, Sylvia, London: Routledge.

Hart, Lynda (1989) 'Introduction: Performing Feminism', in Lynda Hart (ed.) *Making a Spectacle: Feminist Essays on Contemporary Women's Theatre*, Ann Arbor: University of Michigan Press, pp. 1–21.

Harvey, Elizabeth D. (1992) *Ventriloquized Voices: Feminist Theory and English Renaissance Texts*, London: Routledge.

Hinds, Hilary (1996) *God's Englishwomen: Seventeenth-Century Radical Sectarian Writing and Feminist Criticism*, Manchester and New York: Manchester University Press.

Hobby, Elaine (1988) *Virtue of Necessity: English Women's Writing 1649–1688*, London: Virago.

Hodgson-Wright, Stephanie (1998) 'Jane Lumley's *Iphigenia at Aulis*: Multum in parvo, or less is more', in Cerasano, S. P. and Wynne-Davies, Marion (eds) *Readings in Renaissance Women's Drama: Criticism, History, and Performance 1594–1998*, London and New York: Routledge, pp. 129–41.

Holdsworth, R. V. (ed.) (1996) *Epicoene*, London: A & C Black.

Holland, Peter (1979) *The Ornament of Action: Text and Performance in Restoration Comedy*, Cambridge: Cambridge University Press.

Howard, Skiles (1998) *The Politics of Courtly Dancing in Early Modern England*, Amherst: University of Massachusetts Press.

Howe, Elizabeth (1992) *The First English Actresses: Women and Drama 1660–1700*, Cambridge: Cambridge University Press.

Hulse, Lynne (1994) 'Apollo's Whirligig: William Cavendish, Duke of Newcastle, and his Music Collection', *The Seventeenth Century*, 9 (2): 213–46.

Hulse, Lynne (1995) 'The King's Entertainment by the Duke of Newcastle', *Viator*, 26: 355–405.

Hulse, Lynne (ed.) (1996) *Dramatic Works by William Cavendish*, Oxford, Malone Society.

Hume, Robert D. (1976) *The Development of English Drama in the late Seventeenth Century*, Oxford: Oxford University Press.

Hutton, Ronald (1989) *Charles II: King of England, Scotland and Ireland*, Oxford: Clarendon Press.

Keeble, N. H. (1987) *The Literary Culture of Nonconformity in Later Seventeenth Century England*, Leicester: Leicester University Press.

Keeble, N. H. (ed.) (1994) *The Cultural Identity of Seventeenth Century Woman: A Reader*, London and New York: Routledge.

Kelliher, Hilton, (1993) 'Donne, Jonson, Richard Andrews and the Newcastle Manuscript', *English Manuscript Studies*, 4: 134–73.

Kendall, Kathryn M. (1991) 'Finding the Good Parts: Sexuality in Women's Tragedies in the Time of Queen Anne', in Schofield, Mary Anne and Macheski, Cecilia (eds) *Curtain Calls: British and American Women and the Theater, 1660–1820*, Athens: Ohio University Press, pp. 165–76.

Kewes, Paulina (1998) *Authorship and Appropriation*, Oxford: Clarendon Press.

Knowles, James D. (1988) 'Identifying the Speakers: "The Entertainment at Ashby" (1607)', in *Notes and Queries*, 35 (4): 489–90.

Knowles, James D. (1989) 'Marston, Skipwith and The Entertainment at Ashby', in *English Manuscript Studies, 1100–1700*, 3: 137–92.

Krontiris, Tina (1992) *Oppositional Voices: Women as Writers and Translators of Literature in the English Renaissance*, London: Routledge.

Kruger, Loren (1996) 'The Dis-Play's the Thing: Gender and Public Sphere in Contemporary British Theatre', in Keyssar, Helene (ed.) *Feminist Theatre and Theory*, New Casebooks, Basingstoke: Macmillan, pp. 49–77.

Lamb, Mary Ellen (1990) *Gender and Authorship in the Sidney Circle*, Madison, Wisconsin: University of Wisconsin Press.

Leslie, Michael (1998) ' "Something Nasty in the Wilderness": Entertaining Queen Elizabeth on Her Progresses', in Pitcher, John (ed.) *Medieval and Renaissance Drama in England*, vol. 10, London: Associated University Presses, pp. 47–73.

Levin, Carole (1998) ' "We Princes, I tell you, are set on stages": Elizabeth I and dramatic self-representation', in Cerasano, S. P. and Wynne-Davies, Marion (eds) *Readings in Renaissance Women's Drama: Criticism, History, and Performance 1594–1998*, London and New York: Routledge, pp. 113–24.

Lewalski, Barbara K. (1991) 'Mary Wroth's *Love's Victory* and Pastoral Tragicomedy', in Miller, Naomi and Waller, Gary (eds) *Reading Mary Wroth: Representing Alternatives in Early Modern England*, Knoxville: University of Tennessee Press, pp. 88–108.

Lewalski, Barbara K. (1993) *Writing Women in Jacobean England*, London: Harvard University Press.

Lewcock, Dawn (1996) 'More for seeing than hearing: Behn and the use of theatre', in Todd, Janet (ed.) *Aphra Behn Studies*, Cambridge: Cambridge University Press, pp. 66–83.

Lilley, K. (ed.) (1994) *The Blazing World and Other Writings*, Harmondsworth: Penguin.

Limon, Jerzy (1990) *The Masque of Stuart Culture*, London and Toronto: Associated University Presses.

Lindley, David (ed.) (1984) *The Court Masque*, Manchester: Manchester University Press.

Lindley, David (ed.) (1995) *Court Masques*, Oxford: Oxford University Press.

Lindley, Keith (1997) *Popular Politics and Religion in Civil War London*, Aldershot: Scolar Press.

Longley, Katharine (1970) 'The "Trial" of Margaret Clitherow', in *The Ampleforth Journal*, Autumn 1970, LXXV (III): 335–52.

Lynch, Michael (1990) 'Queen Mary's Triumph: the Baptismal Ceremonies at Stirling in December 1566', *Scottish Historical Review*, 69: 1–21.

Lyons, Paddy and Morgan, Fidelis (eds) (1991, rpt. 1997) *Female Playwrights of the Restoration: Five Comedies*, London: Everyman.

McEntee, Ann Marie (1992) ' "The [Un]Civill-Sisterhood of Oranges and Lemons": Female Petitioners and Demonstrators, 1642–53', in Holstun, James (ed.) *Pamphlet Wars: Prose in the English Revolution*, London: Frank Cass, pp. 92–111.

McGee, C. E. (1991) ' "The Visit of the Nine Goddesses": A Masque at Sir John Crofts's House', *English Literary Renaissance*, 21 (3): 371–84.

McGovern, Barbara (1992) *Anne Finch and Her Poetry: A Critical Biography*, Athens and London: University of Georgia Press.

Mack, Phyllis (1992) *Visionary Women: Ecstatic Prophecy in Seventeenth-Century England*, Berkeley: University of California Press.

McKeon, Michael (1987) 'Politics of Discourses and the Rise of the Aesthetic in Seventeenth-Century England', in Sharpe, Kevin and Zwicker, Steven N. (eds) *Politics of Discourse: The Literature and History of Seventeenth-Century England*, Berkeley: University of California Press, pp. 35–51.

McLaren, Juliet (1990) 'Presumptuous Poetess, Pen-Feathered Muse: The Comedies of Mary Pix', in Ann Messenger (ed.) *Gender at Work: Four Women Writers of the Eighteenth Century*, Detroit: Wayne State University Press, pp. 77–113.

Mambretti, Catherine Colne (1985) 'Orinda on the Restoration Stage', *Comparative Literature*, 37: 233–51.

Markley, Robert (1995) '"Be impudent, be saucy, forward, bold, touzing, and leud": The Politics of Masculine Sexuality and Feminine Desire in Behn's Tory Comedies', in Canfield, J. Douglas and Payne, Deborah C. (eds) *Cultural Readings of Restoration and Eighteenth-Century English Theater*, London: University of Georgia Press, pp. 114–40.

Marowitz, Charles (1972) 'Drama and happenings', in Hodgson, John (ed.) *The Uses of Drama: Acting as a Social and Educational Force*, London: Methuen, pp. 181–6.

Marsden, Jean I. (1991) 'Rewritten Women: Shakespearean Heroines in the Restoration', in Marsden, Jean I. (ed.) *The Appropriation of Shakespeare: Post Renaissance Reconstructions of the Works and the Myth*, Brighton: Harvester Wheatsheaf, pp. 43–56.

Marshall, Rosalind (1993) *Mary I*, London: HMSO.

Masten, Jeffrey (1997) *Textual Intercourse: Collaboration, Authorship and Sexualities in Renaissance Drama*, Cambridge: Cambridge University Press.

Maus, Katherine Eisaman (1979) 'Playhouse Flesh and Blood: Sexual Ideology and the Restoration Actress', *English Literary History*, 46: 595–617.

Mendelson, Sara Heller (1987) *The Mental World of Stuart Women: Three Studies*, Brighton: Harvester.

Mendelson, Sara Heller and Crawford, Patricia (1998) *Women in Early Modern England*, Oxford: Oxford University Press.

Merrens, Rebecca (1996) 'Unmanned with Thy Words: Regendering Tragedy in Manley and Trotter', in Quinsey, Katherine M. (ed.) *Broken Boundaries: Women and Feminism in Restoration Drama*, Lexington: University Press of Kentucky, pp. 31–53.

Mikalachki, Jodi (1998) *The Legacy of Boadicea: Gender and Nation in Early Modern England*, London and New York: Routledge.

Miller, John (1991) *Charles II*, London: Weidenfeld and Nicolson.

Miller, Naomi J. (1996) *Changing the Subject: Mary Wroth and Figurations of Gender in Early Modern England*, Lexington: University of Kentucky Press.

Morris, Brian (ed.) (1997) *The Taming of the Shrew*, Walton-on-Thames, Surrey: Thomas Nelson and Sons.

Mulvey, Laura (1975) 'Visual Pleasure and Narrative Cinema,' *Screen*, 16 (3): 6–18.

Mulvey, Laura (1988) 'Afterthoughts on "Visual Pleasure and Narrative Cinema" inspired by Duel in the Sun', in Constance Penley (ed.) *Feminism and Film Theory*, London: Routledge, pp. 69–79.

Mulvihill, Maureen E. (1991) 'A Feminist Link in the Old Boys' Network: The Cossetting of Katherine Philips', in Schofield, Mary Anne and Macheski, Cecilia (eds) *Curtain Calls: British and American Women and the Theatre 1660–1820*, Ohio, Athens: Ohio University Press, pp. 73–104.

Mulvihill, Maureen E. (1995) 'The New Candidate for Pseudonymous "Ephelia": Mary (Stuart née Villiers), Duchess of Richmond and Lennox (1622–1685)' *Women's Writing: The Elizabethan to Victorian Period*, 2 (3): 309–11.

Mulvihill, Maureen E. (1996) 'Thumbprints of "Ephelia": A Famous Case in English Pseudonyma', URL http://www.millersv.edu/~resound/submissions/ephelia/ephelia/html.

Nash, Julie (1994) ' "The sight on 't would beget a warm desire" ', *Restoration: Studies in English Literary Culture 1660–1700*, 18 (2): 77–87.

Orgel, Stephen (1996) *Impersonations: The Performance of Gender in Shakespeare's England*, Cambridge: Cambridge University Press.

Orrell, John (1977) 'The Paved Court Theatre at Somerset House', in *British Library Journal*, 3: 13–19.

Orrell, John (1979) 'Antimo Galli's Description of The Masque of Beauty', in *Huntington Library Quarterly* 43: 13–23.

Owen, Susan J. (1999) ' "Suspect my loyalty when I lose my virtue": Sexual Politics and Party in Aphra Behn's Plays of the Exclusion Crisis, 1678–83', in Todd, Janet (ed.) *Aphra Behn*, London: Macmillan, pp. 57–72.

Patterson, Annabel (1987) *Pastoral and Ideology: Virgil to Valéry*, Berkeley: University of California Press.

Payne, Deborah C. (1995) 'Reified Object or Emergent Professional? Retheorizing the Restoration Actress', in Canfield, J. Douglas and Payne, Deborah C. (eds) *Cultural Readings of Restoration and Eighteenth-Century English Theater*, London: University of Georgia Press, pp. 13–38.

Pearse, Nancy Cotton (1976) 'Mary Pix, Restoration Playwright', *Restoration and Eighteenth Century Theatre Research*, 15: 12–23.

Pearson, Jacqueline (1985) ' "Women may discourse . . . as well as men": speaking and silent women in the plays of Margaret Cavendish, Duchess of Newcastle', *Tulsa Studies in Women's Literature*, 4: 33–45.

Pearson, Jacqueline (1988) *The Prostituted Muse: Images of Women and Women Dramatists 1642–1737*, New York: Harvester Wheatsheaf.

Pepys, Samuel (1970–1983) *The Diary of Samuel Pepys*, 10 vols (eds) Lanier, Robert and Matthews, William, London: Bell.

Perry, Henry ten Eyck (1918) *The First Duchess of Newcastle and her Husband as Figures in Literary History*, Boston: Ginn.

Potter, Lois (1989) *Secret Rites and Secret Writing: Royalist Literature 1641–1660*, Cambridge: Cambridge University Press.

Price, Curtis (1979) 'The Songs of Katherine Philips' *Pompey* (1663)', *Theatre Notebook*, 33: 61–6.

Purkiss, Diane (1992) 'Producing the voice, consuming the body: women prophets of the seventeenth century', in Grundy, Isobel and Wiseman, Susan (eds) *Women, Writing, History 1640–1740*, London: B. T. Batsford, pp. 139–58.

Purkiss, Diane (ed.) (1998) *Three Tragedies by Renaissance Women*, Harmondsworth: Penguin.

Radway, Janice (1991) *Reading the Romance*, Chapel Hill and London: University of Carolina Press.

Randall, Dale B. J. (1995) *Winter Fruit: English Drama 1642–1660*, Lexington: University Press of Kentucky.

Ray, J. Karen (1996) '"The Yielding Moment": A Woman's View of Amorous Females and Fallen Women', *Restoration and Eighteenth Century Theatre Research*, 11 (2): 39–48.

Reynolds, Myra (ed.) (1903) *The Poems of Anne, Countess of Winchilsea*, Chicago: University of Chicago Press.

Richards, Judith (1997) 'Mary Tudor as "Sole Quene"?: Gendering Tudor Monarchy', *Historical Journal*, 40 (4): 895–924.

Roberts, Jeanne (1997) 'Convents, Conventions and Contraventions: *Loves Labor's Lost* and *The Convent of Pleasure*', in Collins, M. J. (ed.) *Shakespeare's Sweet Thunder; Essays on the Early Comedies*, Newark: University of Delaware Press, pp. 140–64.

Roberts, Josephine (1983) 'The Huntington Manuscript of Lady Mary Wroth's Play, *Love's Victorie*', *Huntington Library Quarterly*, 46: 156–74.

Rosenthal, Laura J. (1996) *Playwrights and Plagiarists in Early Modern England: Gender, Authorship and Literary Property*, Ithaca and London: Cornell University Press.

Rowe, Nick (1994) '"My Best Patron": William Cavendish and Jonson's Caroline Drama', *The Seventeenth Century*, 9 (2): 197–212.

Sanders, Julie (1998) '"A Woman write a Play?": Jonsonian strategies and the dramatic writings of Margaret Cavendish; or did the duchess feel the anxiety of influence?', in Cerasano, S. P. and Wynne-Davies, Marion (eds) *Renaissance Women's Drama: Text, Criticism, Performance 1550–1998*, London: Routledge, pp. 293–305.

Sharpe, J. A. (1990) *Judicial Punishment in England*, London: Faber and Faber.

Shepherd, Simon and Womack, Peter (1996) *English Drama: A Cultural History*, Oxford: Basil Blackwell.

Shifflet, Andrew (1997) '"How Many Virtues Must I Hate?": Katherine Philips and the Politics of Clemency', in *Studies in Philology*, 94: 103–35.

Skretkowicz, Victor (1999) 'Mary Sidney Herbert's *Antonius*, English Philhellenism and the Protestant Cause', *Women's Writing*, 6 (1): 7–26.

Spencer, T. J. B. and Wells, Stanley (eds) (1967, rpt. 1980) *A Book of Masques in Honour of Allardyce Nicoll*, Cambridge: Cambridge University Press.

Starr, Nathan Comfort (1931) 'The Concealed Fansyes: A Play by Lady Jane Cavendish and Lady Elizabeth Brackley', *PMLA* 46: 802–38.

Straznicky, Marta (1995) 'Reading the Stage: Margaret Cavendish and Commonwealth closet drama', *Criticism*, 37: 355–90.

Straznicky, Marta (1997) 'Restoration Women Playwrights and the Limits of Professionalism', *English Literary History*, 64: 703–26.

Summers, Montague (1935) *The Playhouse of Pepys*, London: Kegan Paul, Trench, Trubner and Co Ltd.

Suzuki, Mihoko (1997) 'Margaret Cavendish and the Female Satirist', *Studies in English Literature 1500–1900*, 37 (3): 483–500.

Swift, Carolyn Ruth (1989) 'Feminine Self-Definition in Lady Mary Wroth's *Love's Victorie, c. 1621*', *English Literary Renaissance*, 19 (2): 171–88.

Tennenhouse, Leonard (1986) *Power on Display: the Politics of Shakespeare's Genres*, New York and London: Methuen.

Thompson, Peggy (1996) 'Closure and Subversion in Behn's Comedies', in Quinsey, Katherine M. (ed.) *Broken Boundaries: Women and Feminism in Restoration Drama*, Lexington: University Press of Kentucky, pp. 71–88.

Todd, Janet (ed.) (1996) *Aphra Behn Studies*, Cambridge: Cambridge University Press.

Todd, Janet (1999) 'A Spectacular Death: History and Story in *The Widow Ranter*', in Todd, Janet (ed.) *Aphra Behn*, London: Macmillan, pp. 73–84.

Tomlinson, Sophie (1992a) 'She that plays the King: Henrietta Maria and the threat of the actress in Caroline Culture', in McMullan, Gordon and Hope, Jonathan (eds) *The Politics of Tragicomedy*, London: Routledge, pp. 189–207.

Tomlinson, Sophie (1992b) '"My Brain the Stage": Margaret Cavendish and the fantasy of female performance', in Brant, Clare and Purkiss, Diane (eds) *Women, Texts and Histories 1575–1760*, London: Routledge, pp. 134–63.

Trease, Geoffrey (1979) *Portrait of a Cavalier: William Cavendish, First Duke of Newcastle*, London, Macmillan.

Trubowitz, Rachel (1992) 'Female Preachers and Male Wives: Gender and Authority in Civil War England', in Holston, James (ed.) *Pamphlet Wars: Prose in the English Revolution*, London: Frank Cass, pp. 112–33.

Veevers, Erica (1989) *Images of Love and Religion: Queen Henrietta Maria and Court Entertainments*, Cambridge: Cambridge University Press.

Waller, Gary (1991) 'Mother/Son, Father/Daughter, Brother/Sister, Cousins: The Sidney Family Romance', *Modern Philology*, 88 (4): 401–14.

Waller, Gary (1993) *The Sidney Family Romance: Mary Wroth, William Herbert and the Early Modern Construction of Gender*, Detroit: Wayne State University Press.

Walton, Michael J. (1984) *The Greek Sense of Theatre*, London and New York: Methuen.

Warnicke, Retha (1983) *Women of the English Renaissance and Reformation*, Westport, Connecticut: Greenwood Press.

Wenham, Peter (1970) *The Great and Close Siege of York 1644*, Kineton: Roundwood Press.

Wheatley, Christopher J. (1992) '"Our Fetter'd Muse": The Reception of Katherine Philips' *Pompey*,' *Restoration and Eighteenth Century Theatre Research*, 7 (2): 18–28.

Wilders, John (ed.) (1995) *Antony and Cleopatra*, London: Routledge.

Williams, Gweno (1998) 'Why may not a Lady write a Good Play: plays by early modern women reassessed as performance texts', in Cerasano, S. P. and Wynne-Davies, Marion (eds) *Readings in Renaissance Women's Drama: Text, Criticism, Performance 1550–1998*, London: Routledge, pp. 95–107.

Wilson, John Harold (1958) *All The King's Ladies: Actresses of the Restoration*, Chicago: University of Chicago Press.

Wiseman, Susan J. (1998) *Drama and Politics in the English Civil War*, Cambridge: Cambridge University Press.

Woolf, Virginia (1977, rpt. 1987) *A Room of One's Own*, London: Grafton.

Wynne-Davies, Marion (1998) '"My Seeled Chamber and Dark Parlour Room": the English country house and Renaissance women dramatists', in Cerasano, S. P. and Wynne-Davies, Marion (eds) *Readings in Renaissance Women's Drama: Criticism, History, and Performance 1594–1998*, London and New York: Routledge, pp. 60–8.

INDEX